Long Haul Through Africa

JANE MATTHEWS

Copyright © 2021 Jane Matthews
All rights reserved.
ISBN: 9798832503172

The right of Jane Matthews to be identified as the author of this work has been asserted by her in accordance with the Copyright, Designs and Patents Act 1988.

Published by:
Small books
MK14 5AP

DEDICATION

For Amy and Paul whose journey also started in Africa

AUTHOR'S NOTE

Before we begin I need to make it clear that the events in this book happened almost 40 years ago. More than half my lifetime, and certainly long enough for my memory to have blurred some of the details.

I have done my best to be accurate and have gone back to the journals I kept at the time. I've also checked some of my memories with a few of those who were there - which mostly proved to us all that there are as many different stories about the same events as there are people telling those stories.

A word about the people who appear in my account: in my diaries and my memories we did not all, always, behave well – and I include myself in that. As I look back now I feel nothing but affection for all of those who were part of the journey. So I want to ask for their understanding if I have sometimes portrayed them a little unsympathetically – not as they now are but as a very different version of me saw them at the time.

Inevitably I am writing with the benefit of hindsight: I hope you'll forgive me for sometimes writing from the perspective of the years that have passed rather than wholly as the young woman I was when I set out for Africa in 1984.

As I write it is 2020 and we are in the middle of a pandemic. The other day my daughter Amy asked if, since we're locked down together, there'd be time for her to find out a little more about my life.

Living through the fear and uncertainty of these strange times I guess many of us have drawn closer to those we love; and knowing each other better has become somehow more urgent. I understand why she might now what want to know more about the events that, by the end of the 1980s, led to her arrival on this planet. And why I, aware I have fewer years in front of me than behind me, might finally want to set down the details of a journey that shaped me.

The best and most significant journeys always happen on the inside as well as the outside and so it was for me. The five months I spent travelling through Africa changed the trajectory of my life. They opened my eyes, my mind and my soul: after which life would never be quite the same.

During this period of lockdown we cannot travel much beyond our front gates, and yet in my memory the vast inky skies of the Sahara, Lake Victoria shimmering silver at dusk, the feeling of peace and homecoming when we reached the edge of the Great Rift Valley, are almost as vivid now as they were at the time.

Many times over the last four decades I've reflected on how fortunate we were. Not only did we survive a three-week ordeal in the Chad Desert, we were able to see places and peoples that have since become closed-off to travellers. Few these days would venture into the parts of Algeria we visited, any more than they'd experience the exuberance of what was then Zaire, or the friendliness of Rwanda's people, unaware of the dark times that were coming.

My story is a personal story of growing-up but it is also a window on a part of the world that has changed almost beyond recognition, since the mid 1980s.

This book is for my children but also, in deep gratitude, for those who I journeyed with and are therefore a part of me becoming who I am.

INTRODUCTION

We were going to die. There wasn't a shred of doubt in my mind.

No-one knew where we were. *We* didn't know where we were.

Not only were we marooned in the desert, water running out, vehicles broken and bodies too, we were also being stalked by gun-toting bandits.

In every direction the gravelly sand stretched, as unrelenting as the heat scorching us where we sat, helpless and hopeless.

Our biggest mistake had been trusting the expedition leader's hunch that, with Nigeria's borders closed to land traffic, we could avoid a massive and expensive detour into West Africa by attempting a crossing of the Chad desert. It would cut a significant corner and bring us via Cameroon, back to the route he'd originally planned.

Our second big mistake was our ignorance, both political and geographical. Chad had only just opened its borders after a bitter and bloody civil war. Though war was supposed to be over, factions continued to operate in remote areas away from the country's capital. The so-called desert route was actually across what had once been Lake Chad, now drastically shrunken by drought and over-exploitation and abandoned by the local population.

No overland company in recent times had attempted to make the journey we were on.

Which meant there was no information to guide us. From the moment we crossed the Niger border into Chad we were on our own.

Well, not quite alone. In a scene borrowed from some corny Wild West movie, we'd just learned that a small group of armed bandits were planning a raid on our beleaguered camp. They'd kill to get their hands on our trucks.

I raised an objection: they couldn't kill 50 of us.

They wouldn't need to, my companions pointed out. Killing two or three of us would be enough to persuade the rest to relinquish our vehicles without a fight.

Which would leave us with no shelter, water, food or means of escaping this endless desert.

There was no-one coming to save us because our expedition leader hadn't bothered to tell anyone where we were going.

Nor could we expect help from the few, desperate communities we'd passed through. They barely had enough for themselves: in a land of abandoned villages and dry wells our numbers and impact on their resources made us the unwelcome.

***

Cut off from the world, we'd no idea that back in Britain the eyes of our loved ones were now fixed on the desperate plight of people across the Sahel region of Africa, wasted by drought, famine and politics. This was the Christmas of 1984 and Band Aid and we too were under 'that burning sun…where no rain or rivers flow'.

Our limited perspective only allowed us to understand that right now our lives were on the line. Even if we managed to evade the bandits we were about to run out of water. The containers we carried under each truck were less than one third full.

That meant there was scarcely enough to keep 50 of us going another day in this relentless heat: the kind of smothering heat that drains every ounce of energy and fries your brain so you can no longer think.

Only our two mechanics had some purpose, taking turns to slide under one of the trucks where they were painstakingly repairing a fuel pump using metal cannibalised from the wheel jack.

On board, some of our group battled with serious illness: malaria and glandular fever, chronic asthma, hepatitis, broken bones. It seemed like weeks since a *Médecins Sans Frontieres* Landrover had happened on us at the start of this endless desert, and handed us antibiotics with instructions to get our sick to hospital urgently.

But there was no urgent. How could there be when every day since they'd left us we'd either been shoving the two massive ex-army trucks through deep sand, one short sand mat at a time? Or we'd been languishing in the dust, waiting for an endless list of repairs that would restore enough power to the trucks to assist us in getting them moving onto the sandmats. Without help from the engine even our combined strength was not enough to power the trucks forward so much as a millimeter.

This latest setback with the fuel pump meant we were once again stuck. We had been since the engine ground to a halt the previous night. I recalled the expression on our guide's face: fear, the first time he had shown any. He had urged that we did whatever it took to move the trucks to a hiding place and cover our tracks in case the bandits returned.

I took refuge in a tattered copy of *Lorna Doone* that someone had brought along. Strangely, its' descriptions of Exmoor had a calming effect, transporting me to a hidden valley where clear waters bubbled between rocks and spongey moor.

And with those pictures in my mind came a kind of peace.

I looked up from the book at the desolate scene around. Of course we would die here. And there was nothing I could do about it.

All the anxiety about being shot or dying of heatstroke, thirst or sickness, shifted. I really was not afraid to die if it could feel as peaceful as this moment adrift in the desert.

There was only one thing that still bothered me: the thought that when news of our disappearance reached my family they would imagine the worst, unable to shake from their minds the thought of me terrified, desperate, alone in the days leading up my death.

What if this was their enduring legacy…and they never got to find out that the time I'd already spent in Africa had been the richest and best of my life?

I wanted them to know I'd found peace with the idea of death. I didn't want them to grieve.

There was no need. We were dying – and yet I had never, ever, felt more alive.

CHAPTER 1

My 'G truck' companions for the trip across Africa, posing at the Equator

So much for the romance of travel. I swear that when I looked at the seductive photo albums from previous Africa overland trips, none of them featured people spending their first night on the floor of the arrivals hall at Dunkerque.

Nor had any of the photos had quite so many people in them. I hadn't actually done a headcount. But there was no corner of this echoey building that wasn't covered in crumpled sleeping bags.

Five weeks earlier, when I met the owner of Long Haul Expeditions, one of the few questions I'd asked was how many people I'd be travelling with. I distinctly remember his mumbled answer: twelve to fifteen.

It was now almost midnight and the motley crew shuffling about in a vain attempt to get comfortable looked more like a Glastonbury campsite than an 'expedition'. Every so often sighs and ugly little snorts interrupted my attempts to relax. I felt envy for those who were able to escape to the sanctuary of sleep. My mind was far too busy.

The surprises were coming thick and fast – and not in a good way. So far nothing about this trip was what I expected or had been led to believe.

But let me start at the beginning and tell you how it was that at midnight on a wet November night, I came to be unfurling my sleeping bag onto the floor at the French border.

***

Up until the previous week I'd been living in a messy flat share in Greenwich, commuting into Westminster each day to work as journal editor for a small academic institute.

I was also a year or so into dating a man who wasn't as committed to me as I pretended to myself I was to him.

Life was ok, but somehow 'ok' never seemed to be enough for me. In the past ten years I'd abandoned a teacher training course, left careers in journalism, then PR, tried my luck working for a year in Germany, landed my current job, and moved house nine times.

There was a restlessness in me that wouldn't let me settle and I spent a lot of time justifying the latest changes in my life to bemused friends and my anxious family.

Then I spotted a small ad in one of those free travel magazines that spill out of metal bins at London's mainline stations. I suppose if I hadn't been looking for my next fix of change I wouldn't have noticed the magazine. As it was, the moment I read the ad I knew this was what I would do next:

Long Haul Expeditions: *Five months across Africa – London to Nairobi, via the Sahara, West Africa's sunshine coast, the jungles of Central Africa to East Africa's safari parks. £895. Departing November 5th 1984.*

I believe we all have these moments of 'knowing' in our lives, when a single conversation, a few words, a picture, prompts an unignorable 'yes' inside us.

Those few words in a magazine were my lightbulb moment: *this* would shake up my life again. This would show my uncommitted boyfriend that I needed him even less than he needed me - said a rather spiteful voice inside my head.

Here was an acceptable escape route from a life that had become, well, ordinary.

***

Looking back now I suspect there was probably something at work in my subconscious too: a distant memory of being seven years old, and placed by my teachers into 'Livingstone house' when our class moved up to the junior school.

I was always a bit of a swot so I got a copy of the *Ladybird book of David Livingstone* from the school library and devoured every word, lingering over pictures of this fantastical continent where lakes are bigger than seas and wild animals own the forests.

I've no idea if my fascination with Livingstone impressed my teachers but perhaps in some ways it impressed itself on me. Deep inside, a seed was sown, to softly germinate two decades later when the time was right for me to step into the book's pages in real life.

A few days after seeing Long Haul's advert I trekked out to Barnet, ostensibly to find out more, though in reality I'd already made up my mind I was doing this trip. What I really wanted from the organisers was more information with which to regale anyone who'd listen to my plans. The whole thing sounded to me like some sort of great *Girl's Own* adventure.

My *London A-Z* led me to the door of an unprepossessing post-war semi on a street where every other house looked the same. I fished in my bag to check I'd got the right address, unsure how this dull location could have anything to do with a company organising overland expeditions. But the man who opened the door seemed to be expecting me. He was older than I'd imagined, wispy grey hair swept back across his balding head. Beneath the hair though, his face was tanned and healthy, and his eyes bright.

"Terry," the man thrust out a hand then nodded towards the dark interior of his home. "Come. In here." I followed him down a short hallway which led to a nondescript kitchen. Off to one side was a pine table with benches either side. Terry apparently ran Long Haul from this kitchen table: it was smothered in albums, files and handwritten notes with names and phone numbers on.

"It's all in here." He fished out a couple of albums, swept the rest of the paperwork to one side to make a small space in front of me, then turned his back.

"Tea? Coffee?" asked the back, which I now noticed was stooped, as though these suburban surroundings were too cramped and he had to make himself smaller in order to fit. He would have been tall had it not been for this slight hunchback. There was no surplus flesh on his bones: his dark teeshirt and faded jeans hung loose from his bent frame.

He levered himself down in front of me: "Any questions let me know."

What do I remember about the photos? The bright colours certainly, and how many shots showed smiling faces sitting around campfires against a towering wall of forest.

There were desert shots too: endless dunes, blonde as straw, and figures no bigger than dots scattered across their smooth summits.

There was ocean, huge waves rolling in from the Atlantic onto the golden beaches of West Africa.

And there were scenes that took me straight back to that Ladybird book, with all its strangeness, mystery and promise.

Sold: to the 28-year-old with an aversion to settling down. I was on my way.

***

Well, not quite, as it turned out.

D-day, departure day, was set for the auspicious November 5th – my personal equivalent of setting a rocket under my life.

By the previous weekend the few bits of furniture I owned were sold, my room in the flat share was re-let, we'd had farewell drinks at work, and, despite my disappointment in him, my boyfriend had graciously allowed me to camp out in his room with nothing but the contents of the two bags I'd be taking through Africa.

A word about those bags. Terry's instructions were crystal clear on this point: for our five month trip we were allowed one canvas bag no bigger than 24" by 18" plus a daypack whose maximum size was 18" by 12". The only way around this measly allowance was to sneak in as much extra clothing as possible by wearing it to our departure point. Which probably explains why my first meeting with my fellow travellers at Kings Cross revealed I'd be sharing the next five months with an army of Wombles.

One day before we were due to leave a letter arrived from Long Haul. It was short on detail – some issue with getting visas for Niger and Rwanda – but the upshot was that our departure was being delayed for three days until 8th.

No fireworks to send us on our way then. Just my sister Shushie, accompanying me to Kings Cross station where a coach was waiting to take us to Ramsgate, and onto France where we'd meet with the overland truck.

It was a generous-sized coach, a 60-seater.

"How many people did you say are going?" Shushie looked doubtful.

"Twelve; no more than fifteen."

"Okaaaaaaay. Maybe most of these people are here to say goodbye then." We both surveyed suspiciously the large and growing jostle of people handing their bags to the coach driver.

Sure enough, after Shushie and I exchanged our tearful farewells and I climbed on board I could see that just about every seat on the coach was full. Despite Terry's assurances on numbers, we were less a football team than a football crowd.

And now we were in Dunkerque and our journey was apparently delayed again because Terry was still in Paris sorting paperwork. Even if he hadn't been, customs had shut for the night. We camped down where we stood.

Alongside me someone spluttered in their sleep. The floor tiles were freezing through the thin fabric of my sleeping bag. I couldn't imagine getting any sleep tonight.

Yet young bodies are resilient things. Slowly, like a battery running down, the sounds in the hall softened and merged to a single soothing note. The voices around me became the murmur of the ocean, waiting to greet us in 20 weeks' time.

I slept.

CHAPTER 2

It was only a few months since I'd been in France. Shushie and I had decided on a consolation getaway after her wedding to a handsome American serviceman was called off. He'd met someone else – but delayed telling her until their big white wedding was a mere eight weeks away.

Those circumstances made it a bitter-sweet holiday of course, but it's pertinent here because it took our Cosmos coach less than 24 hours to reach Perpignan's beaches.

By way of comparison, riding in Terry's *two* lumbering ex-army trucks, it was to take us a full nine days to reach Europe's southern borders.

The first problem was that the trucks, which arrived to greet us in Dunkerque the next morning, were built for battlefields, where strength outranks speed. For all I know they might have been festering in some forgotten corner of Dunkerque since the Second World War: they had that look about them.

On the very best European roads, in good conditions, their top speed was a pedestrian 30mph. The last time I'd travelled at that speed had been as a seven-year-old in the back of dad's Hillman Imp on the way to Blackpool, a trip that took the best part of a day.

Suffice to say that when we finally cleared customs and hit France's motorways our slow crawl in convoy did not endear us to all the other drivers on the road.

Meanwhile, sitting aloft in the back of one of the trucks, unable to see anything out of its spray-splattered plastic windows, I was wondering just how long it would take us to drive across Africa if 30mph was all we could manage on decent roads?

***

'G' and 'Q' trucks took their names from the first letter of their registration plates. Their conversion to passenger-carrying overland vehicles had been minimalist. In place of khaki canopies the trucks had blue plastic covers stretched over their frames.

Inside, there were two lines of what looked like old bus seats, separated by the narrowest of footwells. The bus seats lifted to reveal little lockers underneath. We were told we'd be sharing five to a locker, intended for stowing our day-to-day things.

The only other additions to these spartan headquarters were a small safe behind the driver's cab and a cassette player attached to the roof.

On board I got my first chance to do a proper headcount. There were 25 of us rammed into the back of each vehicle, with Terry, his two driver/mechanics and two 'couriers', up in the cabs bringing our total numbers to 55. In case you imagine for one moment that life on board a decommissioned army truck is a reasonably comfortable way to travel, let me tell you that we were sitting so close to each other I could count my companion's ribs.

It wasn't only that there was no wiggle room on the seats; almost from day one the footwell down the middle had to double as an overflow luggage store.

Both trucks towed a trailer but by the time these were loaded with a couple of Calor Gas cannisters for cooking, drums of diesel, dried food supplies, plus all those 24"x18" bags, everything else had to be squeezed in where our feet should have rested.

That included all the day-packs, jackets, and once the gas ran out, heaps of wood for the cooking fire. This meant we travelled with our legs perched awkwardly on top of all the clutter, knees almost by our ears.

Only our sleeping bags enjoyed luxury quarters: they had their own accommodation inside a blue plastic sack lashed to the truck's roof like a giant blister.

Terry travelled in the ever so slightly more modern 'Q' truck and insisted on leading the two-truck convoy. I was allocated to 'G' whose driver was a fresh-faced young Kiwi called Wayne. As we climbed aboard for the very first time he stood straddling the trailer coupling, handing us up over the tailgate with a cheery 'Gday mate'.

On our truck the blonde-haired courier called Heather sat up in the cab with Wayne. I'm using the term 'courier' a little loosely here because beyond the rather ridiculous instruction to be 'discreet' when 50 of us bedded down in Dunkerque's arrivals hall, we'd not heard from Terry or his team about the drive ahead.

Long Haul's owner shared his cab with a second driver – a young Aussie called Mike, and the other courier, Alison, whose pressed clothes and neat hairstyle suggested she was more at home shepherding mystery tours around England's stately homes than trucks through Africa.

But we were underway and that was something.

***

Luckily, given the long hours we were expecting to drive from one end of Europe to its southern tip, we at least had the distraction of those slightly desperate get-to-know-you conversations. They followed a predictable pattern: where are you from and why have you come?

As I did the rounds, choosing to sit next to someone new after each loo stop, I learned that about half the group were British, like me; the other half were Aussies and Kiwis 'doing' Africa as part of their walkabout year overseas – seeing the world being a rite of passage for any antipodean before hunkering down to a career.

The Brits I spoke to during that first day's travelling were more equivocal about what had brought them to Long Haul: family bereavements or family troubles, relationship break-ups, ill-health, redundancy and at least one early midlife crisis. Our number also included one birdwatcher (his name was Steve but inevitably he became known as 'Birdman') plus several people carrying expensive-looking camera kit who said they'd come to photograph Africa.

Towards dusk, after a short stop at a motorway service area, I returned to the truck to find the seat next to me claimed by a guy in a brown corduroy bomber jacket.

He had sandy hair, a day's growth on his chin and a lived-in face that lit up as soon as he started talking.

"Name's Will. How are you?" my new neighbour extended a formal hand. His accent was a surprise: pure BBC belying the crumpled appearance of someone who spent his life on the road.

"Fancy a drink to warm us?" Without waiting for my reply Will struggled to free his right arm from the lock we were all in and reached inside his jacket, producing a hip flask containing brandy.

I didn't much like spirits; neat spirits even less. But usual rules did not apply in these strange new surroundings so I took the bottle with a smile and allowed the brandy's fire to warm me and soften the edges of our surroundings. Will was easy company and as we shared our why-we'd-come stories, passing the bottle backwards and forwards, the world seemed to shrink to what was inside the plastic walls of the truck.

Dimly I was aware of other people opening more bottles and someone turned up the volume on the cassette player. Already a kind of separation was taking place, dividing us from everything that was Out There.

Encouraged by this strange mood of intimacy, and, no doubt, the brandy, I told Will a little about the errant boyfriend, about supporting my sister through her heartbreak, and the ongoing pain of coping with mum's mental health breakdown – she'd been diagnosed with paranoid schizophrenia - which had now lasted more than a decade.

I told him I was on this trip partly because I'd grown exhausted trying to care for and take responsibility for my family.

Casually, Will slipped an arm around my shoulders and told me that his mum had committed suicide by putting her head in a gas oven.

As we shared our stories word passed down the line that because of the visa delays Terry had decided we'd drive through the night rather than stop and camp. I dropped my head onto Will's shoulder, breathing in the pubby scent of his jacket, dozing rather than sleeping – my mind was still too busy for real rest.

Without anything being said Will and I had made our pact of understanding and established a claim on each other.

***

In a way that would soon become depressingly familiar, Terry's plan to make up for our delayed departure with 24-hour drives was shattered the very next day by a loud explosion under G truck's bonnet.

The water pump had blown, firing off the fan like a missile to gouge a plate-sized hole in the radiator. And since Terry hadn't packed any spares, and it was a bank holiday weekend in France, we had no option but to wait out the weekend.

The other truck went ahead to dump its trailer and passengers then returned to tow us to the nearest service area where we pitched tents on the grass verges behind the fuel pumps.

We ended up staying there for three days.

That stop in a service station car park outside Bordeaux gave me the opportunity to wake up to my naivety in imagining Terry's itinerary had any more substance than the average fairy story. We'd been travelling for less than two days and, by the time the breakdown was fixed, we'd be running more than a week behind schedule.

Moreover, far from being a part of a small group, I was beginning to understand that I'd have to get used to living cheek by jowl alongside a whole army of other Long Haulers.

However, we put the waiting time to good use, organising ourselves and adjusting to camp life.

Terry called a meeting, which is a grand way of saying he got us to gather around so he could lay out some ground rules. As I huddled at the back of Q truck with all the others I was surprised that the passion he'd shown talking about the trip back in Barnet had vanished so totally. He seemed physically older than the man I'd met then, shrunken somehow, and his voice was weary, resentful that the vagaries of travel were already thwarting him.

As he spoke Terry never looked at any of us but kept his eyes fixed on the ground, as if he might find the answers to his frustration there.

"First thing, since we've got to stop here, you need to find tent partners; two to a tent. And then you'll need partners for the cooking and guarding rota too."

He grimaced as if he'd just remembered something unpleasant. "Probably best if you find cooking partners of the opposite sex. We want the food to be edible. Each pair gets £10 from the kitty to do dinner and breakfast the next day. When you're cooking, you get to sleep on the truck, over the lockers. Saves putting a tent up and it keeps all our stuff safe if we have people sleeping on it at night.

Next to me Will nudged my arm. I had my partner it seemed.

Terry droned on: "We need a volunteer to do a cooking rota once you've got your partners. And a guard rota too."

"What do you mean guarding?" I couldn't see who was asking.

"What do you think I mean?" Terry sounded impatient. "Staying with the vehicles at all times when we're stopped somewhere. We lost half our bags on the last trip because people were so careless. Be careless with your own stuff if you want but don't dare lose mine, or the equipment.

"Next thing is we need someone on each truck to manage the kitty. We've got odd numbers on the trucks so kitty volunteers are excused from the cooking and guarding rota."

At the front, closest to Terry, an arm shot up. I knew from the Barbour jacket that it belonged to a good-looking guy I'd been talking to earlier that day. He'd introduced himself as Chris and I reecalled him saying he worked in finance and lived, as I did, in London.

At first I'd enjoyed our chat; I was a little dazzled by Chris' confidence and no doubt his dark hair and rather brooding expression. Only when it became apparent that he was also a little dazzled by himself, did I begin to tune out of the conversation.

"G truck people: you can hand over your hundred quids now then it's done," Kitty Chris instructed. Terry's joining instructions had specified we'd need to contribute to a communal food and fees kitty, and suggested we bring £100 for this and a further £3-400 spending money for the rest of the trip and entrance fees. I was relieved it was relatively little since the speed of my decision-making meant I'd had only a month to save up.

All around me people started chatting, negotiating with each other for tent and cooking partners. In the hubbub we almost missed the fact that Terry hadn't quite finished.

 "One more thing, we may have to change the route and miss out Togo and Benin."

Suddenly there was silence. A heavy disbelieving silence.

Remember me saying how taken I was with photos of West Africa's beaches? According to the itinerary we were supposed to reach them in time for Christmas. Which in my book came close to making up for the fact I'd be apart from my family during the festive season for the first time ever.

Who wouldn't choose to swap grey London streets, deep in slush, for the wide open beaches of the Atlantic's Gold Coast?

"What the fuck?" A man from our truck was the first to come back at Terry. I hadn't spoken to Tim yet but, on board, he was impossible to ignore: one of life's big characters, and a natural leader.

You know how sometimes, even though the law says you are a grown up, it seems that other people are more adult. Tim was like that. There was an air about him of knowing more and being more than the rest of us.

All I really knew about him was that he claimed to be well-travelled and to prove it wore faded teeshirts on which I could just make out the names of far-flung destinations. He wore a soft leather waistcoat over the top of these ancient shirts, which gave him a certain style, and a flat leather cap.

"Don't blame me," Terry sounded petulant. "Nigeria's shut its borders and if we can't travel there it'll cost us far too much time to go around Upper Volta to get into Togo and Benin, and then have to loop back the same way. We're keeping an eye on it but if the border stays shut we'll probably have to find a way through Chad."

Without waiting for Tim's reply Terry climbed awkwardly down from the back of the truck and stalked off towards the service station, presumably to drown the difficulties of overland travel in whisky shots: this was mainland Europe remember, where you are trusted to buy booze while travelling.

For a while after he'd gone the news we might have to miss a chunk of the route took over from any discussion of partnering up.

I was probably among those less bothered by what, in retrospect, was a fairly major change to the route. At this point the names Togo and Benin meant very little to me - though the loss of Christmas on a beach, any beach, was certainly a blow.

But I could sympathise with those of my companions who remained at the back of the truck, angrily complaining to each other that they'd chosen Terry's company over all its competitors precisely *because* it included time in West Africa as well as the north, centre and east.

The thing was, Nigeria's land borders had actually been closed since April that year. This wasn't new information, so it was unlikely our route was ever going to be the one Terry advertised. Nor did it escape Tim's notice that cutting out such a major section was going to save Terry a lot of time but also hundreds of dollars in fuel. That evening there was talk of little else as we swallowed down a lukewarm supper of rice and canned meat: it was obvious the calor gas cookers were barely up to the challenge of the catering-size pots we needed them to heat to feed 55 people.

***

My companions weren't the only ones unhappy with Terry's leadership either. It took less than 24 hours for our ramshackle camp to outstay the initial welcome from the service station's management. Perhaps they'd expected we'd join Terry in keeping the bar busy. Instead of which we used the garage's toilets as bathroom and laundry, then criss-crossed washing lines from tree to tree in an attempt to dry our underwear. A stone's throw from the fuel pumps we spurned the bar in favour of cheap wine a few enterprising souls had hitched to Bordeaux to buy for us.

By the second day the garage staff decided to lock the washrooms and our camp took on an even more vagabond air as pink flags of toilet paper dotted the grass.

It pains me now to think how ignorant we were: careless of how our behaviour affected people and places en route. Worse was to come but even at this early stage I felt embarrassed by our lack of care. I wished I could distance myself from Long Haul so people wouldn't think me as mannerless as some of my companions.

I slept fitfully that first night in the service area, conscious my thin ground mat really did very little to protect me from the cold seeping up from the ground beneath the tent. I was conscious of Will beside me too; both of us trying – and failing in the cramped inner tent – to keep a respectful distance from each other.

Still, he proved himself the perfect tent partner by getting up early the next morning to have a cigarette and fetch me a mug of tea. I stretched out gratefully, relishing the warmth of the spot where he'd been on my stiff bones, breathing in the comforting smell of tobacco mingled with damp autumn air coming through the fabric.

The tea was barely warm: apparently the Calor Gas cannister was already coughing and spitting as if it was running dry. Still, it was the thought that counted.

"Wayne's not a happy man, old girl," Will said, plonking himself down in the tent's open flap while I gratefully sipped. "He's out there now chucking stuff all over the place."

"How come?"

"He reckons half the spares never got packed. Told me he'd checked over the trucks back in the UK and given Terry a list of stuff to get. There was supposed to be a spare radiator but no sign of that. And a heck of a lot of other things missing."

Will paused to light the roll-up he'd been making as he spoke. The smell reminded me of home. He was smoking the same brand as my grandfather used to.

"Well that's a worry I suppose", I said.

"Too rightey," Will took a long drag. "It's the same story with the gas Wayne says. Apparently the bottles never got filled after the last trip." That explained the lukewarm tea then.

"So what else does Wayne say?" I wasn't sure I really wanted to know.

Will shrugged. "I asked if he thought we'd make it to Kenya. He said better not to ask."

***

Eventually France returned to work and Wayne was able to organise a replacement radiator for G, repairing the fan and a few tubes which had also taken a battering when everything exploded under the bonnet.

Sometimes we kept him company while he was working, sitting on the side-lines, asking him about his home and credentials for being here with Long Haul.

Wayne told us he came from a farm in a remote part of New Zealand, one of a family of 10 children. Or was it 12, I forget, as apparently did his parents one day when they drove up country for a picnic and were almost home when a headcount revealed they'd left one of their sons behind.

He'd grown up in a family which by and large solved its own problems and fixed its own machinery. They were a resourceful lot, unused to relying on outsiders for anything they needed – the perfect background for a job with an outfit like Long Haul. As was Wayne's nature, which was relaxed and accommodating to the point of sometimes seeming to be a pushover. In the short time I'd known him I'd not seen our driver without a smile on his tanned and freckled face.

His reaction to any setback was a shrug, even when, a few hours after resuming our journey south, the alternator broke.

The other driver/mechanic, Mike, was less sanguine as he laboured alongside, mumbling 'heap of junk' in his broad Australian accent. Still, he was probably glad to be useful. Behind the scenes there'd been another setback when it emerged that despite being taken on as a driver, Aussie Mike didn't actually have an HGV licence: our expedition leader would have to take the wheel of Q truck himself.

Eventually we were moving again, never stopping for more than a 10 or 20 minute comfort break at Terry's insistence that we had to make up for lost time.

Inside the truck there was only motorway to see through the plastic windows of our canopy so we turned within and pooled the two or three books each of us had bought into an onboard library.

The first flurry of conversations were spent. We read and ate and dozed a lot of the time.

Down through the Pyrenees, where the first snow had fallen like a layer of dust on the landscape; we slept stacked up like tumbling dominos, needing each other's warmth.

At Madrid we drove into a hypermarket car park and were ordered by Terry to steal two trolleys to use as cooking grills. I warned you that our behaviour was ignorant.

Then south again, to the sunshine coast where pinched hotels awaited a new season. And on to Algaceraz and the ferry linking Europe with Africa.

Its port gave Algaceraz a year-round purpose, in stark contrast to its slumbering neighbours. As we drove into the market square early on a Saturday morning the town was already bursting with life.

As Wayne cut the engine Will and I jumped down to wander through stalls piled high with bowls of live snails and fish in ice, mounds of shining fruit and fat vegetables. Every stall was surrounded by a knot of jostling people dressed in the navy and blue serge of those working the land. On street corners African traders from across the Straits of Gibraltar hawked handbags and watches, spread out on vibrant African cottons. It was a half-caste of a place: not yet Africa, but too brash, too exuberant and excitable to belong wholly to Europe.

We reprovisioned, repacked the lockers and the trailers, and drove on to the port. The town's narrow streets rumbled under the trucks' tyres. Traders squeezed by with baskets of fresh bread on their heads. The rich smell of roasting coffee hung in the air and beneath, just detectable, the salty promise of the Mediterranean.

CHAPTER 3

Morocco may now be a popular tourist destination, luring those in search of something a bit different to its lush riads and larger-than-life markets. But out of season the place held no warmth or welcome. As the big blue trucks rumbled through Martil's narrow main street the faces looking up at us were closed, even hostile; as we inched a way forward, almost scraping rough stone walls, some of the crowd picked up sticks and stones. They clattered against the vehicles' sides.

Perhaps the hostility I sensed was in part a product of my own imagination, the missiles merely a reaction to the disruption we were causing to local people who wanted to get on with their marketing. Right up to the point of departure I hadn't felt any fear about the trip: just adrenaline carrying me through the need to organise everything from yellow fever, typhoid and hepatitis injections to circulating post restante addresses. I really hadn't had time to think too much about potential dangers that might lie ahead - even when I was scouring charity shops for high boots to wear in places where there might be snakes and scorpions (essential kit according to the joining instructions).

Nine days limping through Europe had given me plenty of time to start worrying, as it dawned that Terry and his vehicles were not necessarily to be trusted. Now there was this strangeness too: in place of my familiar London life as a young professional, with camp life on the move, crowds of strangers, and the knowledge most of what was happening was outside my control.

Instead of the excitement I'd hoped to feel, the first tendrils of doubt and fear were winding themselves around my mind.

I'd become scared of getting ill - and with good reason. Already most of us were suffering on and off from bad cases of the squits. It was hard to stay clean when opportunities for handwashing were few and far between, and we were very careless about sharing germs with each other as we passed wine or water bottles around in the back of the truck.

I continued to worry about what might be happening at home, without me on hand to take care of my grieving sister and sick mother.

And now I'd experienced life on the trucks, I was scared it would be too much, too claustrophobic, this living alongside 54 other people day and night for five months.

But my biggest and growing fear was something deeper and nameless to do with my own safety: the strange otherness of Morocco brought it right to the surface.

At 28 I was still the product of a sheltered middle-class upbringing: for all my restlessness I was a rule-follower rather than a rule-breaker. It scared me that the moment we disembarked from the ferry the couriers ushered us into the backroom of a garage to change money on the black market – then warned us to hide the notes in our clothes and personal belongings until we'd cleared Moroccan customs. I couldn't quite suppress a vision of being thrown in a dirty jail – *Midnight Express* style.

As for Long Haul's shortcomings, if I needed any more proof it was right around the corner: as the trucks groaned uphill from the port Q truck's trailer sheered off its coupling, zig-zagging back the way we'd just laboured, coming within a whisker of flattening an unfortunate cyclist, before up-ending in a ditch.

By the time Wayne brought our truck safely into the verge most of Q truck's passengers were out of the back, snapping pictures.

Let me say that, for all his many faults, I did have some sympathy with Terry's frustration that everything that went wrong was first and foremost a photo opportunity. All *he* wanted was for his mechanics, Wayne and Mike, to sort the problem quickly so we could be on our way before the terrified cyclist had a chance to summon the authorities. I guess he had seen it all before and understood, in a way we didn't yet, that the road ahead would be pitted with such setbacks and we needn't make a drama of them.

But at least on this occasion it was only another mechanical problem. Among Terry's seemingly bottomless store of African Horror Stories was one he'd shared around the campfire about the time his group stumbled on a dead body.

"We were in Upper Volta. A wood stop. Some of the women started screaming. They'd found this young girl, just a teenager, with both legs hacked off at the knee. Bled to death I suppose. The ground was brown around her."

For once, because 55 people can make a lot of noise, you could hear a pine needle drop.

"What did you do?"

"I tell you what the bastards did," Terry spluttered. "Ran to the truck and got their cameras."

"Did you ever find out what happened?" I asked. I could so easily imagine our leader deciding not to get involved and driving on by.

"She said we had to report it," he nodded crossly in the direction of his courier Heather. "Waste of time of course. When we got to a village and found someone who could speak French he said they knew the girl was there. She was one of theirs."

***

We spent that first night on African soil locked behind the high walls of a campsite while the people of Martil shopped, argued, laughed and shouted by the light of a thousand flames burning bright on market stalls and street corners. Smells of roasting meat drifted over the wall where we were once again heating cans of beans carried from home. And the cacophony of car horns, traders' calls and barking dogs gave the impression that something celebratory was happening just out of our sight.

In contrast, the atmosphere on our side of the high stone wall was subdued. Here we were, finally on African soil, and instead of being a part of the vibrant street life we were caged, the campsite gates locked against us by its owners. I suspect the reason was less for our protection than to ensure any money changing hands did so in the campsite shop where the only things on offer were flat coke and stale biscuits left over from the summer season.

It was a relief to emerge from behind the wall the next morning to a world transformed by sunlight, journeying away from the town through hills purpled with pine, plunging to valley floors where streams ran clear as mirrors.

The air tasted of forest and damp soil and for the first time we wound up the truck's plastic window flaps and breathed it all in.

We reached our next town, Chefchaouen, at midday, a stone-walled fortress, perched on the side of a hill.

Since our visit in 1984, the town's tourist industry has burgeoned, with more than 200 hotels now catering for mainly Spanish tourists wanting to photograph its distinctive blue-rinsed buildings. Forty years ago we were simply an oddity.

"Looks like we've been spotted." I was sitting next to a woman called Annie whose no-nonsense approach to everything made her the perfect foil for my nerves. Annie was about my age but had already done a lot of solo travelling, including walking 192 miles Coast to Coast across northern England that summer. Everything about her, from her tight plaits to her loose clothing, was practical.

I looked to where Annie was pointing, towards a gaggle of small children tumbling down the hill towards us like little boulders. There was no question of our trucks outpacing them. Away from European motorways the engines struggled to reach 5-10 miles an hour.

A moment later the children besieged our vehicles, delirious with excitement, diving onto the trailers, hanging from the canopy lashings, dangling from the wing mirrors.

"Can you hear scuffling? They must be on the roof too," I said.

Annie craned her neck out of the side. "The little buggers are on the bonnet. Bet Terry's not happy about that…"

"Cadeau, cadeaux?" A small hand tugged the sleeve of my jacket through the open flap, its owner clinging to the ropes used to lash the canopy to the frame. Annie, was a schoolteacher and no more willing to take nonsense from these children than her classes back home: she shushed the boy away impatiently.

The rest of us were slower on the uptake: it took time for it to dawn that this was not so much a sweet welcoming committee as a raiding party.

All those little hands poking through the flaps were already fishing about in bags left carelessly open on the seats; while the ropes lashing tarpaulins over the trailers were dangling in the road as other hands closed in on the luggage beneath. Our trucks were like two dumb animals, under attack from a swarm of mosquitoes who could smell a good meal

Annie reached forward and thumped her fist on the window at the back of Wayne's cab. "Go faster. They're robbing us." Wayne responded immediately, crashing his foot to the floor so the truck lurched forward, but our little visitors were persistent and even more exhilarated by the burst of speed.

At the back of our truck a couple of the men grabbed the firewood we'd collected in the hills and launched themselves onto the trailer, waving the branches wildly and screaming like banshees.

The shock of this counter-attack succeeded where speed hadn't; one by one, the children dropped back to the ground to form a rag taggle escort, accompanying the trucks to the town walls.

It was only a brief reprieve.

Unlike their children, the people of the town were not so easily shaken off – and had no intention of letting us leave without stripping us of as much of our wealth as they could. And why shouldn't they when it might be another six months before the next tourists hit town? As we climbed down from the trucks they moved in, insisting we buy whatever it was they had to sell, jostling each other out of the way, grabbing our arms and thrusting things under our noses.

This was not the indifferent hostility of Martil but a greedy, exhausting obsession with our presence in their town. They seemed resentful of our arrival, resentful of our wealth and resentful of their own need to milk it. So long as we remained in or around the city walls we were pursued, hassled and intimidated.

"Hashish. You want some?" Behind us, another voice, "Come with me. I show you good time. Excellent hashish. Best price. Sssh!"

Annie was not the sort to be cowed. She had a way of fixing her eyes on whatever it was she was interested in, appearing not to notice the people crowding around us. I gratefully attached myself to her to explore this strange town.

As we passed through a pair of imposing gates into the medina we noticed a wooden table. Behind it, in the shadow of the ancient stone walls, sat an equally ancient Moroccan carving Oxo-sized cubes from a large block of cannabis. The skin of his face and hands was the same dark mahogany colour as the hashish, his eyes black with concentration.

I wondered why others had sidled up to us, pretending secrecy, when weed was so openly available on the street. Indeed its sharp-sweet odour overlay every other smell in Chefchaeouen; it hung over the cobbled streets, and settled on the skin of the town's inhabitants. Possibly you could get high by simply breathing the air here.

Inside the medina the streets were quieter. It was a maze of narrow alleys leading off each other in a way that had no pattern we could discern.

The houses merged into each other, once white but in this November gloom they looked dour and shabby, their doors and windows like toothless mouths.

Soon there was no-one in the streets but Annie and I and after the melee of our arrival the silence felt almost suffocating, as though the stone walls of the buildings were slowly closing in on us. Still I had the sense that through small holes in the stone or between the slats of shutters we were being watched.

Then, from nowhere, a teenage boy appeared, tapping my shoulder. "Miss, look here miss. Postcards. You buy? Cheap. Ten dirham, look." He was about 15, the same height as me, and conscious of our guest status, and his speaking English to me, I turned politely and took a handful of cards from him.

Recalling this incident now I realise how this need to appear polite has several times almost been my undoing when I'm travelling: a need not to offend and to be seen to be respectful of local people, even when my gut is telling me something different.

It was warning me now, as I looked at the collection of stained postcards, oily from where they had passed through many other hands. But I knew our next stop, Fez, was also our first poste restante and I could send word of my travels back home. A little dirt didn't matter, so, from the clutch of cards, I fished out two of the least dog-eared and handed the boy a 20 dirham note from my money belt.

"Non. Non. Forty dirham I say. Too little. Too little." The boy shoved my outstretched hand away roughly.

His previously blank expression suddenly became moodily mobile as he thrust an arm at my money belt and shook it hard. "You give me 40 I say."

If it hadn't been for Annie's stern presence I might have relented and given the boy the money. As it was I was marginally more intimidated by wanting her good opinion than I was by this boy's cheek. So I shook my head, slipped the two cards into the pack, and offered them back to him.

His face turned to fury as he hit my hand away again, sending the cards spilling on the floor. "Why you no buy? Stupid tourist. Fuck you! Fuck you stupid tourist. Fuck off! You buy my cards."

Annie grabbed my arm and yanked me on. "Come on. Let's get out of here. Little prick." She hurried me away from the postcard seller, deeper into the medina's oppressively narrow streets. Her confidence reassured me and yet, behind us, the boy still followed on, shouting.

"I kill you, fucking tourist. Here in the medina. I have knife. Watch out tourist. My friends and I, we find you and kill you."

I couldn't understand how Annie remained so calm. As I watched nervously over my shoulder, waiting for the lynch mob's appearance, she casually strode ahead, snapping away on her camera, pointing out to me the beautiful curved shapes of shuttered windows, capturing the clutter of buildings piled on top of each other.

Only when she'd finally had enough and we returned to the safety of the trucks did I take a deep breath, relieved to again be a part of a large group into which I could vanish and remain anonymous should the postcard seller try to make good on his threat to take revenge.

***

Exhausted by Chefchaeoun's people, we chose to drive a few miles out of town to camp, under a small stand of pine trees.

Now we were in Africa, away from formal campsites – and motorway laybys – we had a new daily routine: a pre-dawn wake-up call to ensure, at Terry's behest, we lost no daylight travelling time. We quickly learned how to take down and pack away tents in the pitch darkness.

Breakfast was almost always porridge taken from the dwindling dry supplies brought from home. Followed by a full day's driving with occasional stops for roadside fruit and veg sellers, photos, to duck behind bushes, or gather firewood for the evening meal.

Finally, as it became dark, the relief of pulling into a secluded forest or field edge and at last hearing something other than the incessant roar of G truck's engine and grinding gears. You could almost cut the silence as we stumbled, stiff from another 15-hour drive, onto firm ground.

The silence lasted only a few minutes before the activity began: putting up tents, getting sleeping bags down from the roof, digging fire, rubbish and toilet pits, journaling in diaries, then assisting the day's cooks in chopping and preparing vegetables for yet another veggie stew.

This was a time before quite so many people had chosen a veggie or vegan lifestyle but on a cooking budget of £10 a day meat would have been out of the question anyway.

***

That night, after supper, that night we heated water for coffee and huddled around the fire's warmth. We might have left behind the snow of Spain's high places but the North African nights were still bitterly cold. Will appeared beside me with his guitar and began picking out a few notes, pausing, then starting on another melody which faded out almost as quickly as the one before. Abruptly, he stood, dropped the guitar on the ground, and headed off into the blackness.

Will puzzled me so much. At the start, back in France, we'd stayed awake late into the night talking about our families and jobs and dreams for when we got back from Africa. Now I was usually asleep hours before he crawled back to our tent, talking and swearing to himself as he fought with the zip and then his sleeping bag. Vaguely I would clock the smell of whisky hanging over our tent like a flysheet, before subsiding back into my own night world of dreams.

To begin with it had occurred to me Will might be boyfriend material now I considered myself free. Not only free, but getting to the stage in my life where a part of me thought I wanted to find a partner and do some of the settling down I'd so far avoided. That coule be its' own adventure.

Yet I'd quickly realised Will was not the partner I was looking for and if I allowed friendship to become something more I would simply be swapping my caring responsibilities at home for a new set with him. There was a neediness in him and I could tell he was struggling with something he wasn't willing to talk to me about.

Often when we stopped he'd vanish, reappearing only when Wayne tooted the horn to let us know we were moving on.

He still brought me a mug of tea in the mornings but didn't linger to talk, heading off somewhere by himself and not returning until breakfast was done and he could help with the packing up.

Noiselessly a lad called Dave slipped into Will's place, picking up the guitar and strumming out the haunting notes of Pink Floyd's *Wish you were here.*

It was the perfect music for such a gift of a night: the tongues of red flame, faces burning in their glow while the trees cast shadows over us and the rich scent of pine mingled with the earth and wood and damp. Above our heads, like the ceiling of a palace, pinpoints of starlight formed a sparkling canopy: more stars than I had ever seen or imagined were possible, billions of miles away.

As I looked around at my companions, burnished by firelight, breathing in the comforting smell of woodsmoke, listening to Dave's music, I was overcome by a sense of deep, deep peace, settling on me, telling me all was well in my world, at least in this moment. In the midst of the group there was no longer fear; only the rich scent of all the possibilities that lay ahead.

To this day woodsmoke has the power to transport me back to that moment and those feelings of peace and freedom.

Back at our tent I found Will sprawled across both sleeping bags, snoring heavily with his mouth open. Even my clumsiness as I tried to take out my contact lenses by torchlight and reclaim my sleeping bag didn't disturb his stupor.

CHAPTER 4

Dyepits in Fes

"How do you slam a tent door?" Kathy's yelling rudely shook Will and I from sleep. If I needed any more persuading that now was not the time to get embroiled in a relationship with my tent partner I simply had to look at what living cheek by jowl was doing to Kathy and her boyfriend Keith.

They had come together but had scarcely stopped arguing. Being in company on board the truck seemed to make no difference; they bickered noisily and relentlessly.

But it was cooking duties that brought their ire to boiling point. Kathy might be Scottish and Keith a Kiwi, but he also laid claim to Scottish ancestry – which meant both KNEW how porridge should be made: except what they knew was different.

Their abrupt wake-up felt especially cruel as for once I'd been deeply asleep. Most nights I struggled to get to sleep, and struggled to *stay* asleep: the temperature sank so low at night that even an all-weather sleeping bag couldn't keep out the chill. I no longer undressed for bed but crept into the cold bag fully dressed, with the blue quilted ski jacket I'd borrowed from Shushie wrapped around my head and ears.

Still, there were plenty of opportunities to catch up on sleep during the day. We were mostly driving from sun-up to sun-down, along empty Moroccan roads winding as lazily through bleached countryside as a drunk on his way home.

The only other vehicles we saw had four legs: mules carrying weather-beaten old men with nut-brown skin, their legs perched over panniers bursting with produce from the market.

Every so often we'd stop beside the road where someone was selling carrots, tomatoes and bread from the back of a beaten-up old jeep, a chance for the day's cooks to get supplies and the rest of us to grab ingredients for a sandwich lunch.

Throughout our time in Africa we became impervious to the weevils which had been cooked into the loaves.

Eventually we began to leave the hills behind, descending to a plain where just occasionally there was evidence of farming. Which meant there were fewer opportunities to gather wood. As one particular day drew on and we still had nothing for that night's fire Terry pulled Q truck into the side of the road anyway.

"You'll have to do a search for something to burn," he ordered from his cab window, without bothering to climb down. "We're just about out of gas."

People headed off in twos and threes, returning empty-handed. It seemed there was nothing to be had.

Until we heard a shout for help: a group from Q truck emerged in the distance dragging several large wooden stakes. As they got closer I could see they were actually fence posts, trailing wire along the ground.

"What the fuck?" Annie spluttered beside me, her normally pale complexion turning pink with rage. "They belong to a farmer. That's just vandalism," she yelled as they approached the trucks.

"Hurry up. Get it on board. We need to get going." Terry ignored her, while the vandals smirked, clearly pleased with themselves.

I didn't speak up, but once we were moving again I could feel the anger boiling up in me at our arrogance in just helping ourselves to whatever we needed. I worried about the farmer finding his fence missing, and what that would mean for him.

That night, when everyone gathered around the fencepost fire I didn't want to be with the rest of the group. I wandered out of the camp to get some peace and watch the sun set. The landscape was flat and featureless and yet it was the perfect stage for a North African sunset: as the sun sank beneath the horizon there was a moment when its light reached the scrubby fields like a fanfare, bathing them in jewelled colours - topaz, ruby, amethyst, sapphire.

Here, by myself, I could get lost in the beauty of the world and forget about Terry and the others for a while.

***

Another small consolation to me was that some of the local people had their own tried and tested methods of getting what they wanted from *us*, at least in Fes.

Fes is sometimes known as Morrocco's cultural capital and is a UNESCO world heritage site, primarily because it boasts the country's oldest and largest medina – as we were to discover.

More importantly, it was our very first chance to stop for more than an hour. Terry had granted us 24 hours in the city which meant there was time to collect letters at the trip's first post restante, to handwash clothes, shop for the next week's food - and be proper tourists.

It appeared that the locals wanted us to do the last of those things first. As we drove into Fes' campsite the sight of not one but two trucks packed with potential prey drew every hawker from within a five mile radius. We were instantly besieged.

"English? Francais? Deutsch?" A cascade of voices, frantic to get a bit of the action.

"Want guide? I show you medina. Come with me."

"I'm cheap guide. No go with him."

"These men lose you and steal your money. I'm good guide."

Each of them waved testimonials in the air, knocking each other's arms aside, scrabbling to get as close to the trucks as they could.

It was impossible to take time to choose between them. The most important thing was to throw in our lot with whoever was standing closest and escape the raucous melee.

I joined a small group being shoved into a taxi by one particularly aggressive guide. Only once the doors slammed shut and we were moving did I see that I was joining our driver Wayne, Dave the guitarist, and a chap from Essex whose flat vowels – and the need to distinguish between him and 'Birdman' Steve - had earned him the nickname Cockney Steve. Our guide craned his head back from where he was sitting alongside the taxi driver, nodding and assuring us over and over that we'd made a good choice and he'd give us the best time. He introduced himself as 'Ahmed'.

I suspect Ahmed dressed to reassure European visitors: he wore brown trousers with some of the biggest flares I'd seen since the 70s, and over them a shouty floral shirt finished with a wide blue tie. His clothes were tight-fitting, considering the heat, and he was barely taller than me.

Only the ubiquitous red and white chequered scarf Ahmed wore around his neck, over the knot of the tie, and his bare feet, dusty in a pair of open leather sandals, spoke of his true heritage.

His black hair was thick and stuck wetly to his scalp from a mixture of strong-smelling oil - and the sweaty effort required to secure our business from the clamouring competition back at the campsite.

As a guide Ahmed knew his business, nosing a speedy route through Fes' maze of alleys and shops, mosques and homes.

The whole walled town seemed to be on three or four levels, connected by cobbled streets and rough stairways. It would be so easy to get lost here, distracted by black holes in the ground from which smoke drifted, and mysterious voices demanded after us "tourists?" "look, buy here".

There were donkeys and mules tethered outside some of the homes, hay strewn over the cobbles; water from cooking and washing turning sour in the streets. But we had no time to stop as Ahmed charged ahead, urging us to keep up, before suddenly ducking through an arch which opened into the town's tannery.

The whole of the area behind its high walls was laid out in a grid, rows and rows of stone pits, each a different shade of red or yellow. Men with their tunics gathered up, the skin of their legs long since dyed pink, trod leather skins into the water. Above them the leather skins that had already been treated and dyed flapped from rope lines stretched along the top of the wall.

It was the kind of technicolour scene that demands a double-page spread in magazines. Yet I could focus on nothing but the stench of the place. It clung to everything, including us, the rotten smell of drying skin and decaying flesh. How did people work in it? I could barely bring myself to breathe. The air stuck in the back of my throat, acrid and sour. I desperately wanted Cockney Steve to finish taking all his photos so we could escape back into the streets but even when he'd done so we had to wait for Wayne, who'd wandered over to talk to the men sunk to their thighs in the dye pits. His expression was one of fascination, head nodding gently as if he could spend the whole day listening.

"We go on," an impatient Ahmed shouted down to him, pulling at my arm to indicate we were leaving through a different arch. Under the arch an old man sat in the shade on a low stool, wrinkled arm held out to block our way.

"You must pay the guardian." We did so, and were not the least surprised to see Ahmed double back to fetch his cut from the man's outstretched hand.

***

Our next stop couldn't have been more different: a carpet factory housed in a tall building, its façade beautifully decorated with inset marble in an array of colours. Inside, we entered an airy courtyard, overlooked on every side by ornate balconies and stained glass windows, colouring the light. Hot and dusty, my attention was drawn to an intricate fountain in the centre, trickling lazily to rainbow-coloured marble tiles below.

We followed Ahmed through the courtyard into a room whose ceiling was from carved wood. Every other surface, walls and floor, was draped in carpets: thick, highly decorated rugs whose patterns mesmerised the eyes like visual puzzles. The effect was to muffle every sound so that even though there were other groups in the room the hush was as profound as in a cathedral. It made you want to speak only in whispers.

A tall man approached and indicated that we should sit down on the rugs, then he hailed a boy to bring us glasses of cool mint tea served in glasses the colour of rubies.

Once we were seated the man signalled to another boy who helped him bring a roll of carpet to us. Silently, they unfurled it onto the floor, like a red and blue tide lapping at our feet.

The carpet seller had a hypnotic voice, the sort to assure us there was absolutely no rush; no-one need hurry; we were in the safe and certain hands of someone who knew what he was doing and could be trusted. Even Ahmed seemed a little awed, deferring to this tall expert in his immaculate beige djellaba.

Seductively our new friend explained how carpets are made, inviting us to admire the craftsmanship, the depth of its pile, its vibrant colours and patterns which had been handed down over centuries. "When you make love on such a carpet you forget its price," he promised, with a wink at my male companions.

It was clear from his assured tone, his deference to us as people of taste and resources, that we would want to buy these carpets, no question. Lovers of art and luxury that we were, we scarcely even needed to know the price, though he would share it with us if we insisted, and could be sure it would be a special rate.

I've always been a sucker for a good salesman. Once I nearly forked out £1,000 for a vacuum cleaner. So, true to form, the longer I listened to this salesman's silky voice, the more vividly I began to imagine being back in the comforts of home, a roaring fire in the grate, wine shining in a crystal glass, and beneath me this deeply luxurious carpet.

"Thanks but no thanks mate. Nowhere to store it." Cockney Steve's voice, a touch regretful, cut through my fantasy, saving me from myself. Of course there was no way we could fit a quality carpet on board trucks which already looked and felt like a travelling jumble sale.

The mood changed in a moment. Seeing his commission vanishing like a puff of smoke Ahmed seemed to wake up and become agitated. "Why you no buy? What is wrong with you?"

The salesman merely shrugged with a regretful half-smile, but Ahmed's anger was obvious. As we followed him back into the heat and press of the medina he recoubled his efforts to earn the commission we'd just robbed him of, hurrying us from store to store, insisting we should buy the plates, or spices, or meats or glassware each of his many 'relatives' had for sale.

I knew it had become a battle of wills and there was no chance of Ahmed returning us to the relative peace of the campsite until he'd parted us from at least a little money. Our tour became more and more bad-tempered as we continued to shake our heads and muttered curses under his breath. In the end, to save us all from the need to meet one more of Ahmed's second-cousins-once-removed, I agreed to buy a cheap scarf that I thought might keep my neck warm at night.

***

Not every guide was quite so unlucky as Ahmed. Back at the campsite we found Tim sitting on the dusty ground, muttering and cursing himself and the locals.

His head sank so low into his leather waistcoat that I almost felt sorry for him.

Will told me the story later: their guide had taken them to a small antiques shop, and fed them the line that, just like antique furniture, the older the rug the greater its value. He assured them their group was lucky to have found a guide who wouldn't hoodwink them into going to the carpet co-operative and buying worthless new carpets which would take years to gain any value.

Tim, it seemed, was an entrepreneur as well as a world traveller and could see a way of making this trip pay for itself by buying a few rugs to sell on - particularly when he was able to beat the antiques shopkeeper down from his asking price to less than half the amount.

Only after the rugs were bought for $1,000 did it occur to Tim that he couldn't bring such valuable antiques on board. At the post office, where he tried to negotiate sending them home, a kindly official assured him they weren't worth the cost of a stamp.

We found him sitting in the sand, his rugs spread around him, urging anyone who passed to use them as groundsheets. "That's all they're fit for", he spluttered.

As Will and I hunkered down into our sleeping bags I thought about the Moroccan farmer whose fence we'd stolen. Perhaps somewhere in the greater scheme of things the law of karma was at work.

CHAPTER 5

Life on board the truck was always cramped, especially after each day's wood

Borders have always been a source of stress to me: how long will the queue be? Will the e-gate recognise my passport? Or will I be hauled up for some heinous offence I don't even know I've committed.

In Africa border crossings take stress to a whole new level. Inevitably, when you and your companions look like an army of hobos, the vehicles will need to be searched. Which means everything you own will be thrown into the dust - some of it hauled out on display, either to get a cheap laugh – tampons as ear plugs anyone? – or to elicit a backhander to smooth the way.

We quickly learned to stow our cameras deep in the lockers after one of the group had his expensive kit confiscated – along with his passport – at a police check in Algeria. The only Israeli in our group, a girl called Jacquie, who perhaps should have known better than to pack the uniform she'd worn during a period of military conscription, had most of her luggage confiscated item by item as we passed through successive borders and police checkpoints.

Then of course our papers – including those for the vehicles – had to be painstakingly checked, which is no small feat when the group numbers 55. The border officials could take as long as they liked. In these lonely and what often seem like arbitrary locations, there is no-one to appeal to; no embassy to call on; no-one other than the uniformed men in front of you setting the rules of engagement.

We were on our own and learned that the best way to cope was by sitting quietly in the sand with a book as an hour merged into four, and sometimes to a whole day's wait or more. Our main source of anxietywas not that we would be held up forever – even in the remotest places the novelty of seeing how many 'gifts' could be acquired from such a large, captive audience was tempered by the unpleasantness of having us camping, cooking, arguing and shitting on the doorstep – but by the certainty that Terry would punish us for this latest delay by insisting on another all-night drive to make up time.

Actually, heading from Morocco into Algeria via its border town of Oudja only cost us a day's hanging around - the extra time needed because on top of all the other border rituals we had to complete money declaration forms. At that time Algeria operated a very strict policy requiring all tourists to change £160 at the bank into the local dinars – beautifully shaped coins whose designs resembled intricate carpets.

It doesn't seem unreasonable that governments might want to get their hands on US dollars and sterling, and certainly not that they might want to prevent visitors exchanging too much of this valuable currency on the black market – as we had in Morocco and would do many times again (justifying to ourselves that by exchanging our hard currency in dark rooms and cupboards at more than triple the going rate we were supporting local people to build their personal escape funds).

Just the same, this was 1984 when £160 was worth what would today be around £400 and represented half of the entire budget Terry had suggested we'd need to see us through the five months. In driver Wayne's case, it was every penny he'd brought with him!

The only way to avoid changing this sum was with a student card. I'd been lucky enough to acquire an NUS card from one of my London flatmates, who was not only a legitimate student herself but was studying art and forged a Camberwell College card as a farewell gift to me.

Apart from me, there were just three other carriers of student cards on the two trucks, leaving everyone else with a dinar dilemma.

They had to change up their money but knew they were unlikely to be able to spend that much in the two weeks we'd be in Algeria, mostly in the Sahara away from anything resembling a shop.

From the border we drove to the town of Ghardia where there was a bank. I offered to guard while everyone else queued to change money. But my peace was short-lived as a couple of my more enterprising companions raced each other back to G truck to try and do a currency deal.

"Hey Jane, you've got a student card, want to buy some money?" Kitty Chris was first back, breathless from running down Ghardia's main street. "I'll give you a fair rate. You know you want to do your bit, help us out."

He gave me what he must have thought was a winning smile, but Tim was right behind him.

"Whatever that bastard offers I'll beat it," he said. "Just sold a bottle of whisky to a shopkeeper for 300 dinars (the official rate was 6 dinars to the £1). I've got more bloody Algerian money than I know what to do with now."

I bought a little money from them both and vowed if I needed more I'd exchange with others on board who had been less pushy.

The irony was that in trying to spend their dinars, everyone soon realised they were not wealthy at all. Dave's plastic football cost him the equivalent of £35, and Will paid £40 for a thin blanket which I hoped he planned to share during the bitterly cold nights. Almost everyone else bought sheshes – the cotton headscarves local people wound around their heads and faces to protect their lungs and skin from the scouring effects of dust and sand in this sub-Saharan landscape. They paid more for the cheap cotton than they'd have done for a Gucci scarf.

Algeria had a very different feel to Morocco. In place of cluttered and ancient medinas, narrow streets and relentless attention from local people, over the Algerian border it felt as if the landscape was opening up. The air smelt of dryness and dust – even more so whenever we were moving and the trucks' tyres sent sand spinning in clouds into the back of the vehicles.

It was this swirling dust I think – and the sharp extremes of temperature – that were to blame for the fact that most of us now had heavy catarrhal colds and thick choking coughs that persisted day and night.

We hacked and spluttered and our eyes ran sore and red. Every day on board G truck began with a battle about whether the truck's back flap should be up – so we could see the scenery – or down, to preserve the lungs of those who'd been slow to board and were forced to sit closest to the back tyres.

Four weeks in, many of our soft edges – and most of our illusions about the glamour of an expedition - had been worn down by the day to day realities of overland travel.

Firstly, we'd learned it was impossible to stay clean and dust-free.

Even if a camp site had a working shower, five minutes' on board the truck undid any benefit. Truck life was intensely physical, hauling things on and off the trailer and roof, digging pits, dragging wood, building fires and erecting tents. There was grime under our fingernails and in every pore.

My hair felt like a Brillo Pad, buffeted by air moving through the back of the truck, and was crusted in sand. My skin was rough and torn by the truck's edges when I clambered up and down.

At one border I was amused to see a hairdryer thud onto the ground when the border guards emptied Kathy's bag. Where did she expect to get electricity from?

But I had my own embarrassing secret: a Ladyshave tucked into the bottom of the locker I shared. In these conditions, hairy legs were the least of my problems.

Why either of us imagined vanity would have any place on board is a mystery to me now, but the only camping I'd done before was with a boyfriend in the relative comfort of western Europe where the showers ran hot, the loos flushed, and there were mirrors on the walls.

Our wild camping, even the campsites themselves, were more basic than anything I could have imagined when I was preparing for the trip, blithely assuming there'd at least be a portaloo on board.

That was another 'no': mostly we just squatted beside the road, dovetailing left or right of the truck depending on whether we were male or female.

Even that amount of comfort wasn't guaranteed. If Terry or Wayne failed to respond to an urgent knock on the cab roof, and whoever needed the stop had a particularly awful case of the squits, those unfortunate people sitting at the back flap were forced to become handrails, gripping onto the arms of whoever was suffering while they hung their bottoms out over the back and poured their misery onto the road.

This, then, was life on the trucks. Grimy, uncomfortable, and very very public.

But there were so many compensations. Each sunset since we'd crossed over into Africa was an incredible spectacle of changing light and colour; so were the starry nights. Once or twice I had out-of-body experiences, walking alone from the camp to lie on my back, feeling myself pulled up into the vastness, billions of miles from the earth, adrift in space, no more than another pin prick lost in the black night canopy.

To this day I can still clearly recall how, on one of these precious nights, I suddenly found myself understanding how totally insignificant my own life was. I wasn't even a grain of sand compared to all of the mysteries that were out there. As for the troubles I'd thought I was leaving behind, they too seemed tiny in relation to this much greater scheme of things. It was strangely reassuring, this new perspective that the universe would go on, with or without me.

My reverie was interrupted by the sound of boots crunching on the gravel. Through the dark I could just make out the figure of one of the many Australians on board.

Tom was probably the last person I had spoken to during the initial flurry of introductory conversations. He seemed to me very self-contained and held himself apart from most of the chatter and complaining on board.

Behind a pair of thick glasses – the type that send you a little dizzy when you try and meet the eyes behind them – his expression was earnest. He had dark hair which lay flat against his scalp with a side parting. His clothing was neat and still bore evidence of having been pressed at some point. If Annie was head girl, then Tom seemed to me the school swot.

Yet on the few occasions we talked I recognised something of a kindred spirit, at least as far as my left-leaning politics went. Tom was thoughtful and well-informed, particularly when it came to the horrors imposed on the aboriginal population of his homeland. He spoke slowly and carefully, which I really valued compared to some of the noisy egos on board.

As he approached I spoke quietly, afraid to shatter the magic of this starry night. "Have you ever seen anything like this?"

"Yeah." His Australian accent was hardly noticeable. "Not at home in Perth. But when I'm out of the city. Sometimes I walk at night so I can see the sky." He hovered some distance from me, as if needing permission to be here. "I had this job up north, miles from anywhere, living alone in a caravan. Friends thought I must be hating it, no facilities or anything. But I loved it."

"Good practice for this trip I guess."

"Well the living rough I suppose. Not the being alone. I wasn't expecting this kind of crowd."

Tom continued to hover and I began to feel awkward. Without the others around us, sharing this moment of honesty felt uncomfortably intimate. When the silence between us became too heavy I pushed myself back up onto my feet and told him I was heading back to the camp.

But as we emerged back into the campsite I was surprised to find it ablaze with light, the air ringing with the shouts of new arrivals.

It was long past my usual bedtime but the novelty of other travellers who'd crossed the Sahara - the first other overlanders we'd come across - was irresistible. We needed to exchange information on both sides about what lay ahead and behind, to learn from them what we should expect and might want to avoid as we drove deeper into the desert.

Their vehicle looked like nothing so much as an outsized white fridge on wheels, giving a new meaning to the word 'basic'.

The interior was lit by a single dim fluorescent light but there was little inside to see: a few chairs, a couple of bags, the rest empty space.

Outside there was paint missing, great jags and dents in the bodywork, and a layer of sand over windows and tyres.

A man jumped down from the cab. He was tall with weeks of growth on his chin and dust ingrained on his face. The jeans he wore had large holes in both knees and above them it was impossible to tell what colour his t-shirt might be: it was the same desert colour as his face.

"You lot British?" he asked.

"British, Aussie, Kiwi," Tim strolled over from the campfire to join Tom and I gawping at the truck. "You? Where have you come from?"

"Yeah, on our way back to the UK. We've had a few problems, but the end's in sight."

"Problems?"

"The usual. Breakdowns, borders, mud, sickness and then the bloody Sahara. Sand got into everything. Didn't think we'd make it but," he sighed," Here we are…"

"How many of you?"

"Five. Now. There were 19 when we set out."

"When was that?" Tim asked

"Twelve bloody months ago."

Even Tim was lost for words for a minute. "A year? It's taken you a year?"

"Yeah, and that's not the worst. We planned on six months which means all the paperwork is shot. Visas, vehicle insurance, international driving licence. We're in a lot of trouble if we get stopped." He rubbed a grubby arm across his eyes, blinking in the harsh light.

"Don't get me started on the bloody currency forms. Hardly got a cent between us, never mind a hundred and sixty quid each. C'est la vie. What will be will be."

"Don't suppose you have a beer to spare do you," beneath the grime his face lit up with hope for a moment.

"Sure," Tim said. "Wait on. I'll be back."

It seemed a good moment to leave the new arrivals to it. I didn't want to get drawn into this truck's dramas, especially as its driver seemed to have a lot more faith than me that things would somehow work out.

He'd said how much they were all looking forward to being home in time for Christmas. Yet it would take the most extraordinary luck for their penniless paperless overland trip not to run into the buffers at the first Algerian police point. All we could do was tell them where we'd encountered police checks in case they could somehow avoid them.

Terry was insisting we make another pre-dawn start so Tom and I left the giant fridge group putting up tents and praying for miracles. By the time they woke we'd be finding out for ourselves whether the Sahara was as tough as they warned.

What we couldn't know was that by Christmas our own plight would look every bit as hopeless as theirs.

CHAPTER 6

I imagine it's almost impossible to read of the Sahara without bringing to mind scenes from old Hollywood movies: rolling sand dunes like golden mountains piercing a bold blue sky.

I hate to disabuse you but in eight days driving across Algeria's world-famous desert we saw that *Lawrence of Arabia* landscape just once.

The reality was neither as romantic nor, thankfully - given the shape of Terry's vehicles - as tough. Our route was actually called the trans-Saharan highway, though it mostly involved indistinct tracks across a barren gravel bed; the earth was the same dusty brown colour as the Saharan sky. I gather this is the same route the Paris-Dakar rally used to take.

We were not alone. All day long, huge road trains carried their bounty through the Sahara, the majority heading north, carrying goods from Central Africa to ports serving Europe and the West. As they thundered past us they blasted their horns, a moment's solidarity in the vast emptiness.

Occasionally this vital supply artery boasted a few miles of tarmac. Perhaps there had been more once, an actual road slicing through the Sahara desert. Now, the little that remained was a liability, its edges suddenly crumbling to nothing so the trucks tyres gripped only fresh air before plunging back into the potholed gravel bed.

In other places the relentless weight of lorry convoys had serrated the surface so the tyres whined tunes on the grooves, rattling us about like seeds in a maraca. We grew to dread these corrugations in the track: the way they jangled every bone and sinew, shaking even the teeth in our heads.

On either side of the 'highway' were the empty shells of cars and lorries that hadn't made it, their paint scoured away by sand storms, interiors bleached by endless sun. They were a salutary reminder of the importance of sticking as best we could to the route, even when it was no more than a faint indentation in the surface. If we were to break down we would need to be found.

The important thing was to keep moving to schedule. Terry warned that our desert crossing would take a week and we couldn't be certain of finding water. The eight large water containers each truck carried in a frame underneath the chassis were only to be used for drinking water. The cooks had to come up with 'no-water' meals - no pasta, rice or anything that absorbed water - and there was definitely no water to spare for washing; not even for our hands which were filthy from contact with everything on board. There was no surface that wasn't coated in dust, sand and grit.

Terry's resolve was quickly tested when we juddered to a halt seemingly in the middle of nowhere. I was relieved to have a break from being shaken and stirred so immediately joined the scramble to climb out of the back of the truck and see why we'd stopped.

On the side of the track was an old bus, a piece of wartime England almost, with its high windows and rounded roof. Its passengers, though, swathed in long robes, dark faces muffled against the heat and glare, were unmistakably of the desert.

Between us we managed enough French to gather they'd broken down earlier that day. Their bus driver had hitched a lift with a passing truck but it could be evening, or even a day or more, before he returned with help.

They needed some of our water.

Our supplies came from the last well we'd passed, four hours earlier. The water was a dirty brown, tainted by minerals in the soil and it tasted bitter and salty: an unattractive prospect except in an emergency. Still, when Heather relayed the bus passengers' appeal to Terry his response was a flat 'no': we had no water to spare.

Heather looked embarrassed at this blatant breach of the desert code, but our leader was in no mood to change his mind and simply wound up the truck window when his courier tried arguing with him.

Disgusted, she turned on her heels, fetched her own water bottle from G truck, and offered to pour it into the travellers' flasks and containers. Most of us on G truck followed suit – though whether from altruism or to make a small protest against Terry I'm not sure.

He sent back a message that those of us who'd emptied our bottles could NOT refill them from the group's supply – an instruction we happily ignored. What could he do about it, holed up in the Q truck cab to avoid his stroppy paying customers?

***

On another day we finally drove into dunes. From a distance they looked no different from those that fringe many British beaches. Only when we jumped from the trucks, whooping like excited schoolkids, did we begin to appreciate their scale.

I tried to climb one of those closest to the beached trucks, watching the shifting sands reclaim each hollow where my feet had stood. Each time I stepped forward the sand subsided so I slipped back almost as far as I'd climbed.

Somehow, the longer I climbed, the further away the summit seemed to be, a trick of the light and space in such an otherworldly landscape. I realised I would never reach the top. The sands would swallow me up long before I reached the dune's crest – which probably changed every day anyway.

These dunes were mountainous, curling endlessly away in waves and peaks and soft hollows, sculpted and then re-sculpted each day by the desert winds.

It was disorienting in a way the flatness hadn't been. At least on the dirt track we had the trail of vehicle skeletons and faint tyre tracks showing we were not out here alone. By contrast, in this ever-shifting sand world it was easy to believe we could disappear and no-one would ever know where or why.

We returned to the trucks, chastened somehow, and grateful for their shelter.

***

We camped rough every night, though Terry and Wayne made sure they motored a fair distance from the 'road' before we pitched tents. Its tenuousness made us fear other trucks losing their way after dark and mistakenly thundering over our little camp. We needed to make sure we weren't flattened under their tyres.

But after several days in the wilderness there was the promise of a water supply and proper campsite again, part of a little desert oasis called In Salah.

Oases have perhaps been as romanticised as deserts: in our imaginations they are places of life and colour. Heather told us In Salah had irrigation ditches where previous trips had enjoyed the closest thing to a bath since setting out.

Yet the settlement we drove into was a mean, grubby place, clawed from the desert by people who seemed almost insubstantial, as if they and their tumbledown homes might vanish at any moment. They hardly seemed to notice us, gliding past our camp like white spectres.

Probably they were in a hurry to escape the sickly smell of death that hung over In Salah's camping ground: heavy and cloying like rotten fruit festering in the heat.

Actually it was worse than rotting food. Holding a t-shirt over my nose I walked to the edge of the campsite and found a pile of moulding animal pelts, alongside them mounds of spilled guts, black with flies. Close by, bleached bones lay scattered across the ground, one the long-jawed skull of a camel.

It must have been the oasis' slaughter grounds, where they brought animals for butchering, away from buildings that people actually lived in.

The irrigation ditches were as disappointing as the campsite. Those who went in search of them, soap and towels clutched in grimy hands, reported finding only a network of shallow scummy channels, stagnant water fermenting in the bottom. The palm trees, which are of course an essential part of any oasis, were stunted or broken, their fronds hanging limply off the stem like the broken spokes of an umbrella.

So far, so very far removed from what we had imagined.

But beggars – and overlanders – can't be choosers, and we made the best of the few facilities we did have: a standpipe to refill the water containers, and one small store where we were able to buy weevil-infested loaves, stale biscuits, and tins of sardines stamped 'gift of the people of Norway'- famine relief food which had perhaps been hijacked on its way further east to the drought-stricken parts of Africa.

We shouldn't have bought it. Black markets only thrive when they find customers. But, as I have already said, between the naivety of the best of us and ignorance of the rest, we didn't give it a second thought.

The other thing this oasis did provide was an opportunity to regroup now we understood the realities and demands of overland travel. Most of the men on Q and G trucks lined up near the standpipe to shave each other's heads – a sensible way of coping with the ever-present sand and dust.

Women, too, decided short hair was easier to handle and lined up with them.

Others brought piles of clothing stiff with desert debris to rinse under the standpipe. We couldn't get it clean, but at least we could wash out some of the grit which turned clothes to sandpaper against our skin.

After I'd rinsed my own clothes, I took a book into our tent to be alone. I knew Will wouldn't be there: he was still wandering off by himself every time we stopped. And any chance to escape the press of people was welcome.

I was learning who to sit next to for the endless drives on board G truck. Apart from Annie and Tom, both of whom were comfortable with silence, I enjoyed chatting to Gai and Sue. Gai was another Aussie, dark-haired and around my age, but she couldn't be less like me. There was nothing she couldn't turn into a joke, though she saved her most cutting humour for the men on board. It appeared none of them had so far measured up to her idea of what a man should be.

Sue was from Reading and responsible for bringing the three books from feminist publishers now sitting in the on-board library. With feminism and politics in common, we were never short of things to talk about when the mood for conversation struck either of us.

But it wasn't always possible to keep distant from the sprawling, noisy rows which had become a regular feature of on-board life: we argued about the cooking rota and about the way we slung each other's stuff around when fishing in the lockers for our own; we rowed about whether the £10 daily budget was enough to feed 25 people on, about who had been spotted taking more than their share of supper or water, who'd stolen whose toilet paper, who wasn't pulling their weight.

These were all trivial things but I can see how, in our suffocating shrunken world, the rows acted as a safety valve, allowing us to direct exhaustion and frustration into the small stuff of daily life. And vent we did: often the whole of G truck waded in with opinions and abuse, the volume rising almost to a point where we drowned the truck's engine.

Something similar happened on Q truck where a silly argument about which music cassette to play had resulted in someone ripping the cassette player from its housing and throwing it overboard. That was one way to solve an argument.

In In Salah Scottish Kathy triggered one of these free-for-alls by refusing to take her turn cooking.

"I'm no doing it without more money. I canna feed you all on ten bloody pounds. That's that."

"But there's nothing to buy here even if we give you more money," Annie reasoned.

"Which I'm not, by the way," Kitty Chris interrupted before Annie had finished speaking. I noticed he'd begun to talk about our joint kitty funds as though they were his personal property.

"I didna ask you. I didna ask any of you fuckers. I'm tellin youse, I'm not cooking."

Unwisely Chris came back at her. "What are you making such a fuss about? Jane and Will cooked tuna and veg for you last night and hardly touched the budget. There's still food in the stores."

"Fuck off, bastard. No-one asked you."

Jacquie, our ex-Israeli Army conscript waded in: "If we give you more money everyone'll want more money and the kitty'll run out before we reach Nairobi."

"That's rich from you," Chris turned his attention to Jacquie. "Thought you'd be the first to vote for more money for food. Never seen anyone move so fast to stuff their face when supper's served."

"Haven't noticed you holding back Chris," I said, though quite why I thought Jacquie needed defending I don't know. Chris was right: she was always first in the queue for food and first back for seconds, even thirds on occasion. But then so was Chris.

"Jane?"

"Yep?"

"Shove it up your arse."

It was all stupid petty unimportant stuff. And I'm only telling you about it to show you how far removed from my initial vision of overland travel our everyday experience sometimes was.

The youngest on board G truck was an ex-Marine called Paul, invalided out with glandular fever. Slight and short, his shaved head made him look even younger than his years. He had only just turned 19 and therefore earned the ironic label of 'leader'. At the other end of the scale there were a handful of people in their early to mid 30s. But if you'd judged our age by our brawling behaviour you'd have assumed we were a travelling kindergarten.

CHAPTER 7

South of the oasis the desert scenery altered again. For days there had been only flatness but now vast rock sculptures rose from the sand: giants, ghouls, fantastical creatures all formed from boulders tumbled on top of one another.

The further south we travelled, the more this stone gallery gave way to actual peaks, like crone's fingers pointing skywards. These were the foothills of the Hoggar Mountains, a towering former volcanic fortress surrounding our next stop – the desert town of Tamanrasset.

We reached Tam at dusk, just as the setting sun coated each razer peak in gold, melting to rose pink and finally a deep red, as though a heartbeat pulsed within. I almost envied the people of this desert outpost their magnificent backdrop: imagine watching the earth catch fire like this every night.

Like Fes, Tam was a little more used to receiving tourists. The main difference was that for the first time since arriving in Africa we were made to feel welcome in shops and the town's market. Not because people wanted to sell to us, as they had in Fes; but for the joy of making conversation with strangers. Almost everyone we encountered tried to speak English to us, asking how we were, where we had come from (I was lucky to be able to answer 'London' since that was the only place in the UK anyone had heard of).

The campsite had a large, clean – and above all operational – shower block, flushing toilets, and pitches marked out in lines of neat white stones. We, however, were directed to a paddock at the back of the site, already occupied by an old horse. I assume this was down to how much Terry was willing to pay for the privilege of camping, but it was short-sighted of him for the dear old horse had done so much pacing that the earth in his field was rock solid. It was just about impossible to hammer tent pegs into the ground: that first night, when the wind came blowing down into the town from the mountains, half of our tents were flattened. The only consolation was that Terry's tent also bit the dust.

Still, there was an air of celebration as we sat around the campfire that night, breathing in the smell of woodsmoke, and beneath it a hint of the diesel we sometimes used to get the cooking fire going.

For the first time we actually had a *scheduled* two day stop: two days with no 5.30am wake-up calls, no water rationing, and no 15 hour days jogging along in the back of a truck trying to catch up on the schedule.

I sat on my sleeping mat with Will's blanket around me. Tam was more than 4,000 feet higher than the surrounding Saharan plain so the air felt chillier. Once again the dancing flames were hypnotic, catching our silhouettes as shadows which they cast on the side of the horse's stable.

As I huddled in the darkness, it struck me how how different this was from my life just five weeks earlier. At home so many of my days were lived on automatic, not noticing the small details, the smells or the tastes of daily life. It was always about getting on to the next thing and rarely taking the time to notice how big the night sky was, how different people's faces looked in firelight, or to watch a sunrise gratefully.

As soon as the next day day broke Annie, Gai and I shot off into the town to find the post office and, hopefully, letters from home. I could hardly contain my excitement when the clerk, flicking slowly through both the Js and the Ms – because how should anyone here know which was my family name – handed me nine letters.

Clutching our post like a promise we found a street café – a street café! – and devoured the news from home as we sipped hot coffee. The liquid was stiff with grounds and sweet as honey, but as welcome as an old friend after five weeks of the instant dishwater we served in camp.

I had family letters, full of inconsequential details about getting ready for Christmas, and letters from friends, bringing bulletins about the miners' strike and hoping I was enjoying my adventure.

There was also a letter from the ex – at least I now considered him so. He wrote that time and distance had caused him to reflect and he now understood what I'd said about us needing to either move our relationship forward or end it. When I returned we should give it another go, he wrote.

I set his letter aside, uncertain how I might reply. My growing closeness to my companions on the road made me view what I'd once have jumped at with a curious detachment.

Right now, finally having some fun as a proper tourist, I couldn't actually imagine what kind of life I might have when I returned to London, much less who I might share it with – if I chose to share it with anyone.

After coffee we went exploring. It was strange to see houses with lush gardens planted for pleasure, rather than homes whose doors opened directly onto the streets. Many of the buildings were made from the same rust-coloured stone as the rock sculptures we'd passed in the Sahara: their colour gave an impression of warmth in contrast to the stark whiteness of desert buildings.

The same warmth emanated from the local people: deeper into Tamanrasset's centre we came to more street cafes where people sat drinking coffee and coke, shaded by leafy trees.

Traders called out to us, merely smiling when we shook our heads and passed on. Others raised a single hand in greeting. We might almost have been in a European city, but for the presence of the Tuaregs, the desert 'blue men', named for their navy robes and skin tinged by a lifetime wearing dyed cloth.

It wasn't only their clothes that marked the Tuareg out from Tam's other residents. They were taller, with finer features, and an otherness which might have been disdain or simply difference.

Even as they moved noiselessly along the streets they seemed to be apart from it; more strange even than we were.

***

The following day Terry gave us the option of joining an excursion up into the Hoggars in search of the hermitage of Charles de Foucauld. De Foucauld was a French cavalry officer turned explorer turned Catholic priest. Eventually he settled in the Sahara hoping to form a congregation, and became something of an expert on Tuareg culture. His life at a remote hermitage ended abruptly with his assassination by another tribe in 1916. The church made him a saint.

No doubt his story helped put Tamanrasset on the map for a whole new breed of religious pilgrims because Terry was easily able to secure the services of a guide to lead us through a strange mountain moonscape, negotiating hairpins and rockfalls, precipices and impossible corners. For six hours we ground our way uphill until, finally, the track ended at a small lodging house.

Outside the air was noticeably thinner, like drinking iced water, which helped shake off the soporific effects of the long drive. A certain alertness was useful because the hermitage teetered on a ridge above a steep drop down into an endless landscape of rock.

At this height the wind was as wild as a banshee, buffeting us, the walls of a lodging house for visitors, and swirling along the ridge to the lonely shape of de Foucauld's outpost.

Battling our way towards it, the only sounds the howl of the wind, our boots crunching on gravel and our breath coming heavily, it was easy to understand why he had chosen this place to retreat from the world.

The hermitage was no more than a stone shed divided into two tiny rooms: a cot for sleeping in, a desk where de Foucauld worked, and the chapel where he meditated on the meaning of his life and the world he'd rejected.

From the open chapel window the desolate splendour of this mountain wilderness must have been a daily reminder of his own insignificance – much like my own experience under a North African sky. At so many points along our route it was the sheer scale of this continent that both scared and inspired me.

Here was not a place to think small thoughts or get involved in arguments about cooking. It was a place to reimagine the world. Layer upon layer of rocky outcrops, rough-edged like sea foam turned to stone, softening away into the hazy distance.

There was nothing familiar here - even the wind wailed a different song.

More than anything I wanted to experience this hermitage away from the clamour of my companions' voices. Behind me I could hear someone say: "what a God-forsaken place this is!"

So I wandered on, along the ridge, tuning into the wind's lonely sounds until the group's noise fell far behind. What I felt was precisely the opposite. This was not God-forsaken but rather a place where the Gods might have lived. Whether you worshipped Jehovah or Jupiter, this was a place for believing in something outside yourself, for truly confronting life and the choices it offers to us.

Sunday school and RE lessons were a fact of my childhood years, but once I left home I abandoned faith as I abandoned much that my parents stood for.

It would be many years before I would once again describe myself as a spiritual person. Yet standing alone on the ridge beyond the hermitage, looking out over the rock-sea, I felt that unless you had faith, unless you came here believing in something greater than your own little life, you would go mad.

To be reminded sometimes of your insignificance in the greater scheme of things can be liberating. But to live with it each and every moment of the day, as de Foucauld did, must surely lead in the end to feeling life itself has no meaning.

***

We returned to the trucks in silence, each of us lost in our own thoughts about how we'd experienced the mountain top.

For some, a quick glimpse had been enough. They were feeling stale and stuffy from the six hour drive up to the hermitage and decided to begin the walk down the mountains ahead of the trucks in order to stretch their legs.

The only snag was that no-one had thought to make a note of who had gone. Nor to check if anyone had been left behind on the mountain top. We'd bumped and slid back down the mountain track for half an hour when we caught up with the walkers and it dawned on Terry he might not have all his passengers. No-one had counted how many of us joined this expedition and this was long before the era of mobile phones.

So Terry ordered our truck to head back the way we'd come just in case we'd left someone behind; it was the first and only occasion I saw him show any sense of responsibility for his passengers.

Wayne dutifully turned our truck around, giving those who couldn't face an extra hour's bumping on a dirt track the chance to decamp to Q.

Of course when we reached the top again there was no-one left at the hermitage; no sign of any life up there at all. But set free for the very first time from the need to shadow Terry, Wayne headed downhill with abandon, pushing the truck to speeds we'd only dreamed of as we lumbered across two continents.

By the time we screeched back into the campsite he'd closed the gap on his boss to just a few minutes.

Supper, which as usual comprised vegetables in some kind of sauce made from the powdered tomato soup we'd carried from home, was still hot as we flopped to the ground around the campfire – ears still hurting from the roaring of G's motor.

There was to be no peaceful conclusion to this long day though. Just before he disappeared to his tent Terry said he had some news.

"The couriers have checked while we've been here. Nigeria is still closed to overland traffic and that's not going to change. We'll be going through Chad as I said. Thought you should know now it's certain."

"Wait," Tim was not going to let Terry slope off. "While we're talking about the route, some of us think we shouldn't always be driving in convoy. It's bloody hopeless. We stop somewhere and we swamp the place. Fifty of us trying to get food and a drink. It makes no sense mate.

"I signed up to see Africa, not spend my every day with this crowd."

Those of us who'd stuck with Wayne on G truck during our detour greed. We'd seen today that Wayne was the better driver, our truck the faster and more powerful, we could imagine being set free, uncoupling from Terry, getting to places before him and being able to spend more time exploring rather than sitting shoulder to shoulder on the truck.

But Terry was having none of it. "Out of the question. You've got most of the spares. If we break down and you're hours ahead of us then we're stuck."

"You could always go first mate." It was the first time I'd heard Wayne challenge Terry.

"You're paid to drive not think, Terry said rudely."

"OK." Wayne shrugged.

"Anyway, we've always done this on other trips. No-one's complained."

"Maybe other trips weren't travelling with 50 other people," I said.

Terry shot me an angry look. "What do you mean?"

Tim interrupted: "Aw come on mate. You know what Jane means. There's some here thought there'd only be twelve of us. Not a whole fucking army.

"And another thing while we're talking about your itinerary," Tim had obviously been building to this showdown. His tone was aggressive, his finger jabbing in Terry's direction. "It's pure bloody fiction. You told me when I came to your place that we'd get a say in running things. If we want to go slower or change the route or anything we could decide. If the group agreed we'd do it.

"So we're saying we don't want to drive in convoy. We all agree. What do you say to that?"

Terry had had enough. He almost spat the words: "I'm fed up with you lot moaning. It wasn't like this on other trips. If you don't like it then sod off. No-one's forcing you to stay. I AM NOT splitting the trucks up."

And with that he was gone. Argument over. But his words had the effect of lighting blue touch paper under Tim.

Long after I climbed into my sleeping bag I could hear whispered voices around the campfire: Tim, Will, and a small group of others, discussing when and where might be the time to strike out from Long Haul. It had only taken five weeks for Terry's grandly entitled 'expedition' to begin to fall apart.

CHAPTER 8

South from Tamanrasset the desert asserted itself again: a limitless pale landscape, as though the sun had bleached it of colour. It stretched south towards the Niger border and what I mentally thought of as Black Africa.

For the next two days we stuttered across this wilderness, bogging frequently in sand that had turned silty and soft. Very quickly we learned to recognise the tell-tale signs of the trucks sinking: a crunch of gears, a throaty grumble from the engine, then a high-pitched whirring as tyres spun futilely, digging themselves deeper into the sand.

The trucks carried only two sand mats each: these were heavy metal grids about four feet long that had to be rammed under the front tyres to provide some traction when Wayne fired the engine. Those who weren't matting found a handhold on the truck's sides and shoved to help G get moving forward onto the metal.

One of the challenges we all faced was that the trucks had apparently been lengthened to fit in more passengers, which, together with the trailers we towed, dramatically increased the drag.

The additional weight at the back acted like an anchor, literally tugging the truck down into the ground.

Sometimes even twenty-five people pushing and shoving wasn't enough to shift our ex-army home. Whenever this happened, G and Q trucks teamed up and we used all four mats under the tyres of one truck, before running a relay with them back to the other vehicle.

It was a painfully slow stop-start operation but perversely we rather enjoyed having something to do rather than sit idly on the trucks. These were the difficulties Terry's photo albums had promised and we rose willingly to the challenge.

Well, most of us did. Sickness was becoming an increasing problem on board. On top of persistent diarrhea, the catarrhal colds seemed impossible to shake off. The loo rolls we'd brought from home were hard-pressed to meet the demands from both ends and a battered copy of *War and Peace* had now been moved from the library to the back of the truck to serve as emergency toilet paper.

Will seemed to me the worst affected of anyone. The first time his wheezing and hacking woke me in the night I assumed he'd caught the same cold bug as the rest of us.

But there was a waxiness to his skin, his forehead permanently damp and feverish, that troubled me. Despite his new blanket, and my warmth pressed up against him, there were spells when he shivered so violently I thought he might knock the main tent pole down.

The shaking never woke him though: that was another strange thing.

***

Algeria's parting gift to us was a frustratingly long delay to cross the border. Thinking about Heathrow's grubbiness and Dover's dismal customs shed I realise it's unfair to complain about another country's entry and departure points. Is there a place anywhere that shows its best face to arrivals and departees?

Still, In Guezzam would make most border points look like paradise. Here was yet another town that chose to put its killing pit alongside its visitors, and to delay them sometimes for days on end without providing so much as a rubbish bin, never mind a toilet or two.

To make matters worse, the arrival of two monstrous trucks may have been the most exciting thing to happen in a while: no sooner did the engines' notes die than we were surrounded by a crowd of people, pressing in on us, jostling each other to peer into the back of the truck where our sick lay groaning in the heat.

In time we would grow to expect and not mind these watchful crowds. But at this point we hadn't yet understood that Africans do not, like us, get hung up on showing interest in other people's lives, nor recognise our strange notions of personal space. We *were* strange and our routines – washing, cooking, talking, reading – were as fascinating to them as episodes of *Big Brother* used to be to us. And why shouldn't they stare when it was we, not they, who were the outsiders?

I struggled with the flies as much as I did these observers, pressing in on us. Naturally insects have no notion of personal space and they collected in their dozens at the corners of our eyes, on our lips, crawling up into our nostrils and ears. The only way to remove them was to swat them where they fed on us, merely clearing the way for 30 or 40 more to settle in their place.

I sought escape under G truck, hollowing a shallow space in the sand where I could sit with my current read: Dervla Murphy's *A Place Apart* – a very personal journey into the complexities of Northern Ireland. Like most people back in Britain my understanding of the so-called 'Troubles' was limited to horror and fear at the IRA's bombing campaigns. Just before I left for Africa they'd bombed Brighton's Grand Hotel where Tory grandees, including the Prime Minister, were staying.

 I was no fan of Margaret Thatcher, nor politicians' record in Ireland, but I could never accept killing people was the answer to any political problem.

The deeper into the book I read, the more convinced I was becoming that there are almost never black and white answers. Rather, I was beginning to feel that there are an infinite number of shades of grey. It's just that as a species we're not very good at complexity.

This was a message that deeply appealed to me. Each night around the campfire we'd argue about politics, about women's rights, worker's rights, and sometimes even whether we were right to be travelling as we were, without sensitivity to the communities we passed through.

I realised there was a large element of posturing in all of this, not hearing each other but using the opportunity to dig ourselves deeper into our own opinions. Like most people with my safe suburban upbringing, I'd been taught there is only ever right and wrong, good and bad. Yet now this book challenged me to consider whether there was something limiting about all this certainty.

***

When we finally cleared Algeria's border and rolled across No Man's Land to the Niger side it was clear we had entered a whole new world. As day follows night the contained-ness of North Africa melted into a bright land of colour and song. Beneath their long, grey overcoats the Niger border guards wore shirts of vibrant colour, big bold florals, and flared trousers in clashing shades. Their mouths broke into wild toothy smiles at the prospect of searching us and from their hut came the loud beat of reggae played at full volume.

Checks passed, and hands shaken all round, the guards waved us on our way to Niger's first major town, Arlit. There was a palpable lifting of energy in the back of the trucks as we skimmed along a proper road after the weeks of sand and grit.

Just outside Arlit is a mine where Niger's largest reserves of Uranium are being yanked from the soil, primarily to fuel France's nuclear industry. Since the turn of the 21st century charities such as Greenpeace and Oxfam have been raising awareness of the exploitation of Niger's people, not only because their land is being turned to desert by the industry's greed for water, but because what water they do have is dangerously contaminated by mining.

At the time though we were as always ignorant of any of the politics of this small community. It mattered only that after North Africa's starkness, Arlit was exuberant with life and noise. There were women on the street, and in the bars, dressed in all the colours of the rainbow. And the children who gathered around the trucks no longer threw sticks and stones but giggled as they practised their few words of school English.

Naturally it was my turn to guard again - it always seemed to be when we reached somewhere interesting.

By now I had a different cooking and guarding partner. There had been too many disasters rendering the evening meal inedible because someone had accidentally splashed diesel into the stew or chopped garlic into the fruit salad. Those of us who *could* cook – including Will and I – were now required to switch to partner up with those who were clueless.

As a result I was now paired with Cockney Steve.

Steve was one of a small group of lads on G truck, including Leader, who dealt with their boredom on board by entertaining the rest of us. They were rarely still, whether the entertainment took the form of using the truck's frame as monkey bars and swinging from one end to the other, or mimicking Terry's loping walk and miserable expression.

Steve told me he had a long-term girlfriend at home and I guessed she did most of the cooking because Steve would have struggled with peeling an egg. He was, however, good at was taking orders from me, and great fun when we were 'on duty'.

Not this time though. Steve had come to Africa mainly to take photos and it must have been torture to be guarding with me while everyone else was out there exploring this bold, bright new world. Further up the street we could see women nursing babies, cooking snacks in sizzling frying pans, and sitting cross legged behind wonderful cloths on which fruits were spread. There were also children to talk to and the sound of Michael Jackson belting out *Thriller* from one of the bars.

It was rather like that moment when Dorothy emerges from the black and white Kansas plains to wake up in the technicolour land of Oz: thrilling and almost surreal.

Aussie Tom appeared with two glasses of cold beer, frothy heads oozing down the sides of the glasses, to make up for the fact that everyone else was, apparently, sitting in a sunny pub garden. I decided I liked him even more.

***

Our next port of call, Agadez, proved even more exuberant, if that's possible. We threw up the tents as quickly as we could and charged into the centre where Heather said we'd find a huge market.

This time her hyperbole lived up to the reality. In stark contrast to the meagre offerings we'd seen in North Africa, Agadez's stalls were brimming with choice and abundance: cuts of meat were laid on wooden tables, bloodied from the years; alongside them tables where fruits and vegetables were arranged in glorious patterns, like coloured crystals shining in the sunshine - bananas, lemons, lime, mango and papaya.

There were nut sellers and rice sellers but above all there were those selling spices: piles of red, yellow, orange and deep gold, like the barrels of coloured sand they sell at Alum Bay on the Isle of Wight. Behind these spice mountains sat men with red and yellow hands, grinding more to add to the piles.

Annie and I stopped at one of the many kiosks selling refreshments: thick, muddy tea made from water poured directly from a thermos, then laden with spoons of sugar until we pleaded with them to stop.

We joined other customers dipping balls of fried dough into the warm liquid, presumably to sweeten them with the sugary tea. After weeks living off vegetable stew and stale bread, the taste of deep fried food was wonderful.

Behind the lines of food stalls were shacks with corrugated iron rooves peddling household goods: plastic containers, soap, and bottles of cosmetics, all adorned with the faces of Asian women. I guess they'd come straight from China's factories to this distant part of Africa.

But it was the back row of the market that was intended for visitors like Annie and I: stall after stall offering the same, crammed with tourist goods. Leatherware, carvings made from ebony and jewellery from silver. Agadez was famed for its silversmiths and their work was on glorious display here; everything from ornate crosses and earrings that would reach to the shoulder, to tiny daggers. I bought a dagger as a gift, thinking it would make an unusual letter opener.

Every time we looked up from the dazzling displays of silver a gang of children would arrange themselves into a comical tableaux in front of us, blocking our way, hands outstretched demanding a 'cadeau' in exchange for a cute photo.

Their mothers challenged our charity more directly, catching our arms as we tried to move to the next stall, holding out enamel begging bowls, signing to us the need for something to eat or the means to buy food.

Like Cockney Steve, Annie had come to take photos and had two cameras with her: one rather professional-looking one for the safari parks we'd visit later, and a pocket Olympus for times like this, when there was only time to point and shoot. Rather than put anything in the begging bowl she offered a few coins in return for photographing the young women with their beautiful faces, as finely sculpted as the woodcarvings on the stalls, but young and solemn.

They wore their wealth in their ears: as many as six hooped earrings, made from silver: stretching the ear lobes until they dangled uselessly, like thin plaits.

Eventually we sought refuge from the press of people in a café where others from the group were sprawled out behind glasses of Pepsi.

As my eyes adjusted I saw that every inch of the wall was covered in pages torn from Western magazines: curiously, at least half of the photos were pornographic but stuck in their midst were pop posters dating from my teens, Abba, Suzi Quatro and the Bay City Rollers.

There was no menu. When the owner came for our order she said she had meat and rice and Pepsi. So that's what we ordered. The meat was tough and fatty, and not something I recognised - probably goat. All the same, like the dough balls, like the noise and bustle of both Arlit and Agadez, the visibility of people, the colours and smells, I was feeling high on life. THIS was the Africa I had pictured, the continent I'd imagined. This was where our faltering expedition would finally take flight and become something pleasurable rather than something to be endured.

CHAPTER 9

The trucks were always surrounded when we passed through remote villages such as this one in Niger

Ever since we'd come south the wind had been building, whipping up the sand, flattening the tents in Tamanrasset, howling through the mountain tops in the Hoggars.

In Agadez it increased another few notches, pushing against Annie and I as we fought our way back to the campsite.

It looked as if a hurricane had hurled through. Not a single tent was standing; washing lines had been transported across the site to tangle on the fence, and equipment lay scattered for hundreds of yards around, half-buried by other debris carried by the wind.

In the middle of this chaos a large bundle of what looked like sleeping bags was huddled in the grass. It was only when I went to retrieve them I realised that beneath the pile was Will, dazed, incoherent and shaking.

His symptoms had continued to get worse and that morning I'd urged him to find a doctor as soon as we reached a sizeable town. Through half-closed eyes he told me the doctor diagnosed bronchial pneumonia but had doled out antibiotics, anti-malarial tablets and aspirin, presumably on a kill or cure basis.

I wasn't convinced. The more I thought about Will's early drinking, and the worsening of symptoms while we'd been in 'dry' territory, the more I wondered if this wasn't some kind of reaction to sudden withdrawal.

There was no question of trying to re-erect the tent over him while the wind raged. So Tom and I collected armfuls of other sleeping bags, tossed willy-nilly during the onslaught, and did our best to cover him up again.

***

It was a rampaging wind, a killing wind, whose meaning became clear as the next day we journeyed on towards Niger's capital, Niamey. Everywhere we drove we saw the wind had been there before us, scouring the soil from the land and sucking any moisture skywards.

Blasted trees stood bare like skeletons and many of the huts were roofless. In the streets, shrunken animals seemed merely draped with skin rather than living things. Everything was blown to a crazy angle and the fields lay empty and desolate.

The sky above us was the colour of gravy, as though the wind had turned everything on its head so that the earth now sat above these broken villages.

We stopped just once, hoping to find something to buy for that night's supper. But there were no shops, no market, and no cooking smells. Only more begging bowls thrust at us as we ventured down streets where empty buildings had already begun to disintegrate.

It made me uncomfortable to be here; to be a tourist in a place where people had nothing. Yet it turned out I still lacked enough empathy and compassion to act on those feelings. As I tried to re-board the truck, in my hand a chunk of bread I'd brought with me from Agadez, an old woman grabbed it from my hand. For a moment we wrestled stupidly with the dry bread. The eyes that met mine were dull and empty.

Two men appeared from somewhere, one at each of her shoulders. There was shouting: I didn't understand it. But then the old woman let go and one of the men pushed the bread towards me, a half-smile on his face, apologetic. The old woman continued to stand between us, staring at her empty hands, mumbling incoherently, chewing on the air.

I would like to tell you that I changed my mind and handed back the bread; that those of my companions who watched this little scene play out emptied their lockers of personal food supplies and shared it with the stricken village. But I didn't, and we didn't.

We hadn't yet grasped that our expedition was moving relentlessly towards a part of the world where drought and famine were devastating lives. We only sensed that we were in unknown territory, and responded from a base level of self-preservation, believing we should hang onto what resources we had.

That doesn't make my confused failure to hand over a lump of bread right of course. It only means that the sides of the trucks closed in on us a little tighter.

Ironically, when we reached our next proper stop, Niger's capital of Niamey, we re-entered a land of plenty. I hardly needed my chunk of stale bread when a day later there were bakers and markets stuffed with food.

Looking back now I wonder at how very different from these starving villages Niamey was: that wealth could exist so close to abject need and poverty. I think perhaps we were in Africa at a turning point, as Chinese and other foreign investment was doing its best to build new outposts which would help them capitalise on Africa's natural wealth.

It was a new age of colonialism, visible in the structures that were rising from Niamey's red soil, the half-built conference centres and hotels which would attract more investment and catapult the continent into the next century.

And yet a stone's throw away people were starving.

Even in Niamey the new wealth rubbed shoulders with a more traditional Africa, though we didn't see poverty there. Sleek cars with foreign plates raced past us, but in their wake came local people still walking everywhere with everything from baskets of fruit to an entire double bed balanced expertly on their heads.

Among those cars came the president's own cavalcade. Seyni Kountche had been in charge of the former French colony since leading a coup in 1974.

He ruled Niger as military head of state on a promise of seeing food aid was fairly distributed and morality returned to public life. However, by the time we arrived in the campsite beside the presidential palace, Niger beyond its capital was, as we'd seen, in the grip of famine. The closing of Nigeria's borders was another crisis, a blow to his ambitions for the country, cutting off a key trade and supply route.

No wonder, perhaps, that whenever Kountche needed to use the purpose-built highway connecting his palace to government buildings – it was far and away the best road we had seen in Africa – the road was closed to any other traffic. I noticed people pause to watch the convoy, but there was neither applause nor opposition: their expressions remained completely impenetrable.

I knew enough to realise that power in most of Africa was a slippery thing: often hard won and, equally often, brutally lost. In Niamey's city centre the shops sold plastic beach balls adorned with the head of Nigeria's most recently-deposed head of state - Shehu Shagari - who had been replaced in a military coup by Muhammudu Buhari (himself deposed just over a year later: I told you power was a slippery thing).

Niamey's colonial past was evident in the billboards still advertising French products, and in public buildings, such as the banks, built in a European style. There were even – oh joy! – the first supermarkets we'd seen, small by European standards and patronised only by other white faces, presumably some of those directing the capital's transformation into a modern metropolis. The chatter of cash registers joined the symphony with drills, diggers and all the other sounds of rampant construction – unfamiliar, half-forgotten noises after two months on the road.

Alongside shops catering for Europeans and wealthy Africans Niamey's outdoor and indoor markets operated and thrived as they'd always done – rich with choice, in such stark contrast to what we'd witnessed in that drought-stricken village just one day before.

***

I am writing these things now with all the benefits of hindsight but at the time all I felt was delight at the abundance of choice. Pyramids of yams, tomatoes, chillies and sweet potatoes, their sellers moving only occasionally to idly flap at the flies that buzzed around all this bounty.

I bought tomatoes for my lunches, but also for the pleasure of watching the market woman serve me. There was a hypnotic quality to her slow, easy movements as she transferred the tomatoes, one by one, into a crumpled brown paper bag she then folded into a cone. Her whole way of being was what we now understand as mindfulness, and go to classes to learn: being present in the moment.

While she served me this was the most important thing in her world, worthy of her full attention and care. It was the perfect antidote to the way Terry had been pushing us from the very first moments, with the all-night drives and constant talk of needing to make up lost time.

Time meant something different here in the market. As did competition - which seemed to be an unknown concept. Traders selling the same items sat together. There were five other tomato sellers watching and smiling at this sale, and next to them a line of women, each crouched behind a bowl of home-made peanut butter, chatting to her neighbours.

Whenever a customer came the chosen seller scooped out a spoonful of the mix, rolled it between her hands into a sticky ball, and handed it over to be eaten on the spot. It seemed to me a strange way to operate, sitting so close to your rivals, yet no-one seemed to mind when another woman's goods were chosen.

***

Once we'd enjoyed the market a small group of us went in search of the river which shares its name with the country of Niger.

We didn't have to look far. The river's presence was signalled by the huge monolith of a Hilton Hotel, towering over everything around, offering its European and Chinese guests a flavour of familiar comforts - a stone's throw from a scene that had probably changed little in the last century.

Guests who bothered to look out of their windows, beyond the end of landscaped gardens, would see the Niger, like a huge artery, serving the city.

The river's far side was a thick, unbroken fringe of tall leafy trees, palms and bushes stretching to both horizons.

On our city side, glistening black bodies strode in and out of the water, naked as the light. Some were office workers, spreading white shirts and grey trousers out on the bushes. Others took their bright cottons into the water, pounding and scouring the fabric clean on smooth round stones. They used little squares of hard soap which left a fringe of creamy scum lapping at the Niger's banks. And as they waited for their clothes to dry, spread out on more stones, they crawled slowly out into the sluggish current to wash themselves, or stood easily on the shore, toasting their skins the colour of polished teak.

We joined them, stripping to our underwear and laying on the bank, listening to the sounds of life going on around us. I was very aware of my body, slimmer and harder than it had been just a few weeks ago, before camp life began to make demands on my physical strength, at the same time as removing me from the saturated calories of a western diet.

Turning my head slowly, I studied Tom's figure, his eyes closed, chest rising and falling peacefully. I could see he'd also lost weight and his ribcage was evident under pale skin. But his arms were turned a deep brown beneath hairs that shone gold in the sun. And where he had stretched them back to form a cradle for his head the muscles stood out clear.

All around us were bathers, naked and un-self-conscious, enjoying the feel of sun and water on their skins and the sensuous murmur of the river moving along. I knew Tom was interested in me. Lately I had noticed his eyes on me often. And yet I also knew how many complications always seemed to accompany my relationships with men.

I turned my head away and closed my eyes too.

***

Later, back at camp, it seemed the market's bounty and a chance to rest had done nothing to bring calm to relationships on the truck. We walked straight into a row about whether that day's cooks must sacrifice a chunk of their £10 budget to buy wood for the fire. We no longer had gas and there had certainly been no wood to collect in the stricken countryside we'd travelled through to reach the capital. Kitty Chris was definite on this point, and since he held the purse strings he got the last, bitter, word.

Terry was equally intransigent when it came to our route. We knew Niamey was the final point at which he might offer an alternative to trying to navigate a way through Chad and its desertified lake bed. There *were* alternatives according to Tim who'd been carefully consulting our Michelin maps ever since Morocco.

Terry was having none of it. "It's not my fault the bloody border's shut," he said petulantly. "If we go into West Africa it'll add 1000 miles to the trip."

"I hadn't planned for that. It'll mean we have to make up time later on. Missing out on the wildlife parks and a trip to the coast, etcetera."

"Fine. I've already seen most of East Africa. Let's do it," Tim said defiantly.

"Hang on old boy," Will interrupted. "A lot of us want to see the parks in East Africa."

Terry seized the initiative back. "Well we can't do both. And remember, you're already moaning yourselves stupid over the amount of driving. Do you want to add another thousand miles?

"Take it from me", he jutted his chin out defiantly, "I've been to Benin and Togo. They're the same as everywhere else. Nothing special to see."

Terry had certainly changed his tune since that meet-up in Barnet but I decided not to get involved in the row about the route. He'd have his way whatever any of us said.

That night Will returned to our tent with the news that Tim and a group of three others from Q truck were leaving the expedition in the morning, to travel into west Africa. They might or might not meet up with us later but were confident that free of the handicap of two trucks, and fifty companions, they could find a way through to the beaches for Christmas.

I think Tim probably hoped his announcement would provoke a mass walkout which might persuade Terry to change his mind. Whereas in actual fact I imagine nothing would have delighted Terry more than the prospect of driving two empty trucks straight to the east coast with only his couriers for company.

So, Chad it would be. Chad the unknown and unvisited since its Civil War.

As a sop to our disappointment, and to prove that doing things his way would give us more time, Terry announced that the rest of us could have an extra day in Niamey in order to prepare properly for whatever lay ahead. None of us knew what would be available during the three or four days Terry estimated it would take us to cross the old dried lake bed to reach Chad's capital city: it was better we carry as much as we could.

Besides, Christmas was coming, and even if we couldn't spend it on the beach we planned to celebrate somehow.

On G truck there was one couple amongst all the singles. Tony was an architect in Australia and his girlfriend Sue (renamed Cookie to distinguish her from Reading Sue), a nurse.

Perhaps it was being in a couple that gave the pair the confidence to take on the role of organisers from time to time. Or perhaps travel was in their blood and held fewer of the fears than it did for rookies like me.

As we discussed how to celebrate Christmas, Cookie and Tony announced they'd happily take on shopping for a decent festive meal, as well as organizing a Secret Santa so we'd all have a gift to open on the day. They set a limit of 500 CFAs – equivalent then to about 50p (Central African Francs were the currency used throughout this part of the continent, a throwback to French colonization).

By the time we were ready to leave Niamey the trailer was stuffed with dried fruits and nuts, meats and treats, to go with the two plum puddings, plus tinned fruit and evaporated milk carried from home.

CHAPTER 10

In the face of pretty much permanent diarrhea on board, several books in our library had been sacrificed as emergency toilet paper. But there was one book that there was no question of vandalising.

Africa on a Shoestring was our Bible, a far better source than Terry on where to play the black market, the idiosyncrasies of various border posts, and the sad recent histories of the places we were travelling through.

Only on Chad did *Shoestring* fail us. I don't recall how old the edition we carried was but it had only two pages on Chad, mostly dedicated to an account of the civil war which lasted for 14 years up to 1979 – when it merged almost seamlessly into equally bloody conflict between a number of Chadian groups, Libya, French troops and occasionally other foreign nations - right up to the present time.

All of this meant, according to the book, that travel in Chad was dangerous and unpredictable: military camps peppered the countryside and desperation and lawlessness led to banditry. In short, *Shoestring* concluded, "Chad is difficult and dangerous and no sensible traveller would go there".

In the back of the truck we passed the book around and wondered whether we should, after all, have joined Tim's splinter group. Perhaps their's had been the more sensible choice. It certainly sounded the safer…

***

We did several all-night drives in order to reach Niger's final useful outpost, the tiny town of Zinder, in time for its Thursday market – a last chance for restocking on-board supplies and refilling water containers before we headed into the unknown.

We knew we'd be on water rationing which meant again devising meals that didn't need any water so we could save what we had purely for drinking.

Cockney Steve and I had another cooking duty coming up and at the back of *Shoestring* I struck gold: a recipe for chicken groundnut stew. If, as I expected, there were chickens for sale in Zinder market, we were in for a treat.

I guess the little search party of Steve, Will, Tom and I who set out in search of chickens had 'mugs' written all over our foreheads. So many people in Niger and neighbouring Chad were struggling to feed themselves; why we thought they'd have the means to feed and fatten chickens is beyond me now.

Just the same, if you are of a vegetarian disposition, or even slightly squeamish, I'd skip ahead a page or two.

Will, who spoke more French than any of us, led the negotiations in the market for three chickens, for which we paid the princely sum of £4 – 2000 CFAs – ignoring the fact that they were the sorriest, scrawniest of their species any of us had ever seen.

Back at the truck, the problem was what to do next.

Luckily, Mark was on guard duty. I knew little about him other than that he was a builder at home, in business with two brothers, and that, like Wayne, he was hugely practical. Once or twice I'd seen him assisting with repairs on the truck, and it was almost always Mark who dug the toilet and rubbish pits when we stopped to camp.

Where others talked…talked…and talked, Mark usually just quietly got on with things.

"Give them here," he reached for the sack in which we'd carried the poor birds back to camp.

I fished in the lockers for a penknife but Mark shook his head. "I don't need an actual knife. You pull the heads off see."

I did see and didn't like the thought, but since it was my idea to cook the dam stew I could hardly object. "What about the mess? Won't there be blood?"

"Shouldn't be. It's quick. Hold the sack open," Mark ordered.

He moved so quickly it took me a moment to realise he'd grabbed one of the birds and twisted its' neck so expertly the head was now in one hand while the body in his other hand continued to kick and flap. A thin fountain of blood spurted from the corpse like crimson wool onto the truck's floor and seats.

I dropped the sack, desperate to move people's bags and coats out of the line of fire. That only panicked the two remaining birds and now on top of blood there was shit oozing from the sack, and alarmed squawking.

Those poor birds. Their executions were even more messy as we hurried Mark to get it over with before anyone returned to the truck.

We were too late though. As I scrabbled on the floor, wiping chicken shit and blood from a couple of journals, two heads popped up at the back of the truck – two of Q truck's vegetarians.

"Don't spose you can lend us some money can you?" one asked. "Can't find Terry to unlock the safe and there's something we need to buy."

We gaped back at them stupidly, guilt written all over our faces. It was Tom who had the presence of mind to stand up and try to shield their gaze from the impromptu abattoir happening behind him.

"How much do you need?"

"A few hundred francs. There's this pigeon. We rescued it from a cat but then a boy said it was his cat and it was trained to catch pigeons for his family to eat. So we said we'd buy the pigeon from him..."

Her voice trailed off as she registered that right behind Tom Mark was holding a decapitated chicken in his hands.

"Oh." With a shocked little yelp she and her friend disappeared from view as suddenly as they had crept up on us. We later heard from Heather that they got the money from someone else but when they tried to free the pigeon it was only able to stagger, dazed, a few inches, before the boy's determined cat caught it between its jaws again.

All the same, the chicken groundnut stew was a triumph.

If I'm honest the delicious flavour owed everything to a lone packet of dried chicken soup I found buried at the bottom of the trailer - rather than to those unfortunate birds who yielded almost nothing in the way of meat. But combined with peanuts I'd fried in oil, onions, aubergine and tomato puree, it was not just heavenly but pronounced the best meal so far. I was happy – even if the chickens weren't.

***

We spent our last night before Chad camping in the grounds of a Catholic mission, the first of many we encountered in central Africa. I fear the missionaries' motivations were mercenary rather than altruistic because there was never any warmth in the welcome we received and we were always charged through the nose for extras such as showers and European-style toilets. Some of the most enterprising missions even came round asking for donations for their work - on top of what we'd already paid in camping site fees. They always made it clear that donating was compulsory.

More objectionable to me were the cutesy pictures pasted on the inside of the toilet doors, so that as you performed your ablutions you were watched by a white-skinned Jesus, surrounded by little white children and small animals.

We learned that because it was market day there'd be live music at one of Zinder's bars that night. So we polished our faces and set out for a final fling before Chad.

Funny how bars all over the world have the same smell: a mix of smoke and sweat and stale beer. What made this bar in a remote corner of Africa different was the enthusiasm of the band who were belting out raucous music from one corner of the room. It was nothing like the pop we were used to: this had a beat that reverberated deep inside my body, like another heartbeat. It was irresistible.

Along one wall a few African men stood nonchalantly, dressed in the same slacks and bright shirts they wore during the day. Only their hair had been especially dressed, combed flat with thick oil.

As soon as we started dancing they moved out onto the dance floor to join us. Soon we were moving in one huge, hot, friendly and un-self-conscious rabble, bouncing and swaying. The band, delighted to have such a lively audience, cranked up the volume even more and began writhing along to their own tunes.

I suppose I knew from the moment someone proposed we prepare for Chad by having this final fling that tonight would be the night I'd have to decide whether or not I actually wanted an on-board romance.

Tom and I had been spending more time sitting together. Telling each other stories from our lives and looking out for each other. I felt he was interested, and I was too. But there was a small voice in my head warning it would change the character of the trip for me if I were to experience it as one half of a partnership. Looking around my companions it was clear that Sue Cookie and Tony, and Kathy and Keith, somehow belonged less to the group experience than those of us who journeyed alone.

The trouble was, of course, that any clear thinking I might have done had been muddied by alcohol and the feel-good effects of the music. Inevitably, when I told the others I was feeling a little light-headed and needed some air, it was Tom who followed me out into the dark street.

A moment later we were kissing and gripping onto each other, tight against the building's wall to support our unsteady legs. When we surfaced for air we told each other breathlessly how long we had waited for this to happen; how much we wanted it. Then we grabbed each other again and resumed the kissing.

I was 28 years old and felt about 14, out of control, hungry for touch and the adventure of a new love. My early interest in Will was forgotten. I'd had weeks to get to know all the men on G truck and Tom was the only one I could imagine being with.

Yet back at the camp, climbing on board to sleep over the lockers as that night's guarding rota, even through the haze of alcohol a small part of me felt edgy rather than exuberant; a tiny murmur of regret.

Was this what I really wanted? How would it change things if we were now seen as a couple? Would other people treat us differently? Would I have to sit next to Tom on the truck; share a tent with him? More importantly, how would it affect my experience of travelling through Africa? Already I was wondering if I'd been wise to let things go so far. But the next morning I packed my doubts along with the tent. What's done was done, besides which there were more immediate concerns: Chad lay ahead.

Into Chad: heading along a track as insubstantial as a pencil mark, passing only isolated huts whose occupants sat idle and inscrutable on the sand outside. Occasionally a hand raised in salute; more often the figures remained still as statues, only their eyes tracing our progress.

Once, a group of children appeared to run after the trucks. They raised their arms and we cheerfully waved back. Next thing there was a cracking noise and one of the women on board dropped into the footwell, head in hands, blood dripping out between her fingers.

Those raised arms had not been waving but holding stones. A moment later another missile hit someone just below their eye, then a third stone hit someone's tooth, chipping the surface. Those sitting at the back scrabbled to unhitch the back flap. It collapsed down across the tailgate, but we could still hear stones snapping against the plastic.

From that point on it was understood that one of the duties that came along with sitting at the back of the truck was to be our eyes and ears, carefully watching for the moment children chasing the truck, calling after us, bent to the ground to collect ammunition. Then to raise the alarm with a cry to 'duck'. We were to make many more ignominious exits throughout Central Africa, heads ducked low in the back while stones whizzed over our heads.

I never really understood why people wanted to stone us. Was it because we were strange, the first overlanders many of them had seen, or because to them it looked as if we had merely come to sit and stare; if we had stopped to meet them would it have been different?

Or was it because we rode in ex-army vehicles and these people's lives had been so pummelled by military action over far too many years?

If so, they weren't the only ones who feared the military. Terry, too, was anxious to avoid getting too close to any of the encampments we'd been told were scattered across Chad – not least because these outlawed groups might very well covet our vehicles.

It was the reason he was choosing to head away from any established routes and try to traverse the dried bed of Lake Chad. Since the 1960s the lake has been shrinking rapidly, partly due to desertification, partly because so many neighbouring countries relied on it for a water supply. By the end of the 20th century Lake Chad had lost 90% of its volume and surface area.

But to navigate the former lake safely and stay clear of any military outposts we'd need a guide.

***

Nguigmi is the last village in Niger before Chad, no more than a handful of huts and a few families clinging on to a place where their families grew up.

Annie and I poked a way down empty streets until we spotted a hut boasting a faded coca cola sign outside the door. Suspecting this was a bit too good to be true we nevertheless ducked through a gap in the wall into a dark room with two polished benches running across the middle. There was no sign of anything to eat or drink but we weren't alone. As our eyes adjusted to the dim light a young man walked across the room to where we were sitting.

He was dressed in a clean white robe trimmed with gold braid, a pillbox cap of the same colours perched firmly on his head. There was just a dusting of dark hair on his chin; he must have been younger than us yet the confident way he carried himself made it seem as if *he* was the adult.

"Bon jour."

Annie nudged me, knowing my French was at least a little better than hers.

"Nous sommes Anglais. Touristes." I ventured.

"Ou allez vous?"

"Nous allons a Chad, vers N'djamena," I said, grateful for school French lessons.

The man's eyes crinkled with interest. "Dans quelque route? Avez vous un guide?

I shook my head vigorously. Perhaps we'd stumbled on someone who could help. "Non, nous cherchons un guide dans cette village. Nous voulons conduire dans le desert."

His hand vanished into the folds of his robe then drew out a few heavily folded pieces of paper which he clearly wanted me to look at. Apart from the name 'Mohammed' I couldn't make out any details but it looked as if we might have found a candidate for guide.

With a great deal of nodding and gesticulating Annie and I managed to convey to Mohammed that he needed to find our 'chef', Terry, by the trucks, and talk to him.

By the time we confirmed the coca cola sign was of historic interest only, and returned empty-handed to G truck, the young man had been engaged. According to Heather he'd reassured them it was definitely possible to reach Chad's capital city via the dried lake bed: he'd done the trip himself many times.

Mohammed estimated it would take us three days, which meant we'd be in N'djamena on Boxing Day.

I wandered over to where the two of them were poring over the Michelin map, wanting to tell Mohammed how pleased I was he'd got the guiding job. But when I touched his arm he moved away, turning only the blank stare of a stranger towards me.

CHAPTER 11

How very different from any other Christmas Eve I'd lived before was this one. Just possibly I'd eaten sardines on toast for breakfast the day before Christmas – it was one of dad's staples when we were growing up. But I had never emerged from sleep to such an empty landscape: nothing but sand and sky, so far from home.

We got moving straight after breakfast and managed about twenty metres before the noise of the diesel engine was overpowered by the sound of G's tyres whirring uselessly on sand. The more they struggled, the deeper they buried themselves into the sinking sand.

Finally, Wayne cut the power and we sat in the silence of this strange new world of endless sand.

A few moments passed then we heard Heather, shouting from the cab: "Are you lot going to sit there all day or what? Get out and push."

We'd done this before of course, in the Sahara, so we knew the ropes, jumping down from the truck to grab sand mats and spades. The men were first to the mats, leaving the rest of us to find a handhold on the truck's side, preparing to push.

Wayne turned the engine again.

Nothing happened. The truck sat squat in the sand like a whale marooned on the beach, too huge and ungainly to save itself.

So we worked harder with the shovels, digging more sand from the axles, using pots and pans to supplement them, carefully adjusting the mats so they entered the sand at an angle.

Wayne fired the engine again and this time the tyres sent a sand shower stinging against our bare arms and legs; the engine belched black fumes into our lungs. Nothing happened.

"Try with all four mats," Wayne shouted.

Dutifully we carried our mats forward to where Terry's Q truck was similarly bogged to its axles.

Forty pairs of hands now gripped the sides of the truck or braved the back, where the narrow gap between truck and trailer made it hard to get leverage. We shoved. The tyres wobbled over onto the edge of the mats, then gripped and suddenly Q truck lumbered forward. Terry hit the accelerator, inched ahead a few more metres, then, again, the noise of whirring tyres, people quickly jumping clear from the sides, Q juddering to a halt, as deeply bogged as ever.

All that for, perhaps, twenty metres. And now we had to do it all again for G truck.

For a second I looked up from my truckside position. All I could see ahead of us was more sand. More pushing, more heat as the sun began its inexorable journey across the sky.

Yet this wouldn't last. In the Sahara the terrain had changed. It would here too. I told myself Mohammed must know what he's doing.

For the next hour or two we continued this exhausting leapfrogging, shovelling and scrambling in the sand, mostly only hearing the engine and the whirring tyres, shocked into silence by the effort it took to move these monsters a few metres along.

Just occasionally, with two strong runners on each of the mats, we got a rhythm going: as soon as the front tyres were over the mats they retrieved them and ran forward ahead of the truck to get them placed again. It was brutal work.

There were mistakes and interruptions: we'd get in each other's way, someone would drop a mat or run onto its sharp edges, someone else would lose their footing and fall under the feet of the rest of us, tripping a couple of people up.

As the desert continued to stretch away ahead there was more torn flesh, more tangled limbs and ragged tempers. We'd hardly begun – even if we didn't know it yet – but already we had learned to dread the unmistakeable, heart-sinking sound of whirring wheels and straining gears before we all shuddered to a stop.

I've no idea what the trucks weighed but they were built to withstand anything wartime might throw at them.

Together with Q truck, we were 50 people strong – though some of our number were laid out in the back of the trucks, too weak from various sickness bugs to join the pushing. But without at least a little help from the engines, there was no way on God's earth we could shift those trucks in the shifting sands.

This was our Christmas story.

***

Eventually, towards midday, when we seemed to have been digging and matting and shoving and complaining for hours, we collapsed, one by one: a combination of exhaustion, heat and probably, subconsciously, in protest. This route had been Terry's idea: did he seriously expect us to continue pushing his trucks all day in the blistering heat while water was strictly rationed?

Heather stepped down from the cab, looked at our prone bodies and walked over to Q truck to remonstrate on our behalf with her boss. She swiftly returned, smiling, though it didn't reach her eyes.

"Mohammed says this only goes on for another mile or so. He had to bring us this way to avoid an army camp. There's one to the west," she said. "Anyway we don't have a choice. We just have to do this."

A long time ago I read that 'the best way out is always through'. It's advice that has sometimes served me well. Sitting in the sand complaining wasn't going to help matters. And there was no reason not to believe Mohammed.

But as I contemplated getting up from the sand there was a cry. To my dismay, a small group of children were bowling out across our hard-won metres of sand, towards us, curious to see was going on.

We had been pushing for about four hours and were apparently still close enough to Nguimi for these excited little children to have decided we were the best entertainment on offer on Christmas Eve.

While we registered how little distance we'd actually covered, the children tumbled towards the truck sides, pretending to push it, giggling in delight. All but one little lad who plonked down next to me and grabbed my hand.

I thought he was after money or a gift but beneath the dark hair flopping across his forehead his eyes showed concern.

He was dressed in a faded t-shirt with the name of a US college blazoned on it; underneath he wore a pair of loose cotton trousers and was barefoot.

I pointed at my chest and then, using my forefinger, wrote my name, Jane, in the sand. He nodded shyly then used his own dusty hands to trace out the name Hassan, tapping himself on the head.

Having broken the ice we tested out our French on each other. "N'djamena," I said again. "Nous allons vers N'djamena."

Hassan shook his head vigorously. "Non, non. Beaucoup de sable. N'est pas possible."

He pointed back towards where we'd come from, nodding vigorously, and I felt almost like a naughty child being directed home by a wise adult.

I shrugged, as together we watched Wayne begin to climb back into his driving seat. He was shaking his head.

Wearily, I tried to push myself up from the sand but Hassan's insistent hand would not let go of my own.

"Non, non," he repeated. "Ilya seulement de sable. N'est pas possible. Dangereux. Tres dangereux."

What could I do? I waved impotently towards my companions, already stationing themselves to push again. I wish I'd had something to give to Hassan, to show him how grateful I was for his concern for us. But I had nothing on me and no energy for searching my bags in the truck.

"Merci. Merci beaucoup," was the best I could muster. By the time we'd pushed and bogged again, and I raised my head, sweaty and red-faced, from the truck's side, Hassan was only a dot in the distance, heading back with his friends to his village.

***

We pushed and shuttled the mats for more hours, into the afternoon, becoming ever more despondent and sun-singed as the landscape showed no signs of changing and our exhausted bodies failed, more and more, to move the trucks so much as an inch.

Only Mohammed still seemed positive. Terry had ordered our guide to travel alongside him in Q's cab but each time we bogged Mohammed would spring energetically down to the sand and appear to scan the horizon. I'd no idea what he was looking for when the sand and sky seemed to me entirely featureless. But after a few moments gazing at the horizon he'd turn and urge us "allez, allez."

At some point Wayne, sensing how close to total exhaustion we were, sent Heather to tell Terry we should all stop what we were doing and empty the trailers into the back of the trucks. There was plenty of room on board because we now knew better than to try and clamber in, even if the engines seemed to be moving us forward. Inevitably the moment passed and we'd bog. It was better to save what energy we still had for pushing. Wayne said switching the big bags and stores to the trucks' interior might reduce the drag a little and shift the balance of weight closer to the engine.

Terry refused to stop - which was at least good news for our sick who wouldn't have to share the back of the trucks with the luggage. That morning Leader had developed a rampant fever and was shaking violently, all the while complaining he was freezing. Two others joined him suffering from heatstroke. We had nothing to offer but warm and bitter water from the carriers, which brought little relief - to them or us. Inwardly I fantasised about drinking a glass of cold, clear water, droplets of condensation on its sides. The thought was much more appealing than a turkey dinner.

Every hour that passed we expected things to improve. If the sand could just get a little shallower. If Terry and Wayne could find a different way of coaxing the trucks to cover more ground. If, if, if…

***

Nothing changed and the day ground on. Our matting became half-hearted and there were more accidents as tiredness dulled our reactions.

Several times people narrowly avoided crushed arms under the wheels as they struggled to yank the mats away. More flesh was torn on the mats' spiteful edges. Tempers frayed as we collided with each other, slamming into the back of the person in front when they failed to move quickly enough; or crunching heads as we raised them from the sides.

Arguments started about who wasn't pulling their weight; Kitty Chris was the chief accuser. He decided his energy would be best employed as a kind of cheerleader, standing at the front, hands on hips, issuing directions to the sand matters.

Even Mohammed now seemed to be wavering a little. He no longer jumped out to urge us on. Until dusk when he emerged again, and helped himself to a water bottle belonging to someone on Q truck. Without a backward glance he headed off to one side of the trucks, facing the direction we assumed must be Mecca, to pray.

By 7pm on Christmas Eve we'd been pushing for twelve hours and Terry, reluctantly I imagine, gave the order to stop. It didn't need a mathematician or a clairvoyant to tell us at this rate of progress Chad's capital, N'djamena, was weeks if not months away.

Wayne reported G truck had used six gallons of diesel to get us this far which made the question of reaching the capital an academic one: we'd run out of fuel long before we managed to push a way through the desert.

As Will and I put up our tent we found an empty bullet casing on the ground, its plastic cover still bright red so we knew it must be recent. Later a scorpion scuttled past, leaving its own miniature tyre-like tracks in the sand.

These were irritations. If Terry insisted on pushing forward in this desert heat I knew it was dehydration not bullets or scorpions that would kill us.

Over by Q truck, Wayne, Heather, Terry and Mohammed stood in a huddle. Soon they began shouting, though in the late dusk it was impossible to make out who was saying what. When Heather returned she reported our guide wanted air let out of the tyres. He said they were too solid for the sand. Wayne told him it was too much of a gamble. If it didn't work we had no way of getting air to reinflate them. Besides, like everything else connected with Terry's cut-price company, the tyres were already badly worn. Putting more strain on them would likely blow them.

Under the lockers we were carrying a brewery-load of wine and beer to toast Christmas Eve, but none of us felt like getting drunk. It wasn't just exhaustion and despondency. We knew we couldn't afford the dehydrating effects of alcohol with no spare water.

Plus Terry wanted a 5am start so we could make the most of the hours before the sun rose high and the sand was just a little harder.

There was no talking around the campfire once supper was done. One by one we peeled off to collapse in our tents. I fell asleep almost before my head hit the padded jacket I was using as a pillow now the nights didn't require me to be fully dressed.

I woke briefly when Will joined me, coughing as if his guts wanted to be released from his body. But soon even he was asleep, moaning softly, beads of sweat visible on his forehead.

It was shaping up to be a Christmas to remember. Or maybe to forget.

CHAPTER 12

> I learned how to braid hair to deal with the sand and lack of water

"Happy Christmas my dear." Will's voice woke me from my dreamless sleep and I struggled from my sleeping bag to plant a stale kiss on his whiskery chin.

"Happy Christmas right back. Let's hope Santa shows up with his sleigh to give us a tow."

"Doubt he'll find us here," Will grinned.

For the first hour of the day it looked as if the worst might be over, and that Mohammed was right about the tough stuff lasting only a few miles. Though the trucks continued to bog at regular intervals, once we'd shoved them free of the deep sand they sometimes managed to lumber almost a quarter of a mile before shuddering to a halt again.

During those times when they *were* moving we jogged silently beside them, holding our breath, fearing that to climb on board would be to jinx their progress. The only sound other than their groaning engines was the patter of flip flops on the sand.

Q truck got stuck more often than us – something I suspected was down to redundant notions of chivalry. Three of their men had joined Tim's breakaway group yet those that remained insisted sand matting was not women's work. That meant fewer men were doing more work and quickly became exhausted.

Their other handicap was Terry, who seemed close to losing control of himself. Whenever his truck bogged he stuck a red-face from the window and screamed at his passengers for not pushing hard enough.

Wayne's approach was different: he coaxed our vehicle as if it were a sensitive animal and gently coached us, suggesting what would help us manage an extra few meters between boggings. And believe me, to borrow a well-known advertising slogan, in those difficult circumstances, every little truly helped.

***

Inevitably, as morning progressed the sun rose higher, leaching the energy from our aching limbs. The later it got, the more the sand softened and slid away from the tyres' grip so that soon we were back to the previous day's see-saw pattern. Q truck would limp ahead with help from all of us, then we'd troop back, ever more despondent, to G truck to use all four sand mats to edge it up to where Q sat marooned – the only speck of colour on a faded, hostile landscape.

Searing heat from the climbing sun created mirages on the horizon. In the distance the sand and sky shimmered together, dancing with unsteady light. It was possible to imagine anything might be waiting for us there: water, maybe even a village or road - the end of the sand and sweat.

But of course the nearer we came, the further away the mirage skipped from us. There never was anything other than more desert.

For all my exhaustion, my mind would not be still, chuntering on about Terry and his terrible trip, teasing me with thoughts of Christmas at home where I knew the table would be groaning with rich foods and, underneath a sparkling tree, there'd be stacks of gift-wrapped packages waiting to surprise.

For the first time since setting out I felt wave after wave of homesickness as memories of Christmases past played in my mind. What if this was my last Christmas? If I never made it home?

The idea of dying out here seemed ridiculous and melodramatic, and yet a small part of me recognised that we were in uncharted territory and, with the dubious exception of Mohammed, none of us, not even Terry, actually knew for sure that there was a way out of this mess.

These were the tricks of an overheated mind. One minute I would have given everything I had to be holding my sister, sharing our familiar Christmas; the next I imagined telling my family I had discovered the secret to life: it was really so much more simple than we made it. You just had to get up and get on and do whatever was in front of you. We didn't need to work so hard at being happy.

***

Of course in reality even the simplicity I imagined was no more than part-truth. There is nothing simple about dying when death is caused by drought. Back home, unknown to us, the media was reporting a drought and famine of Biblical proportions. *Do they know it's Christmas?* had just reached number 1 in the UK on Christmas Day 1984. *We* had food but the water carriers were less than half full and dwindling by the minute as we pushed ourselves harder and harder in the relentless heat.

But a Christmas miracle was just around the corner. It came in the shape of two wise men riding camels across the desert, diverting to greet us as the desert code dictates they should - just in case we were in trouble.

We were, and pointed out to them the water carriers. One of the men nodded his understanding, then swivelled around to point directly away from the trucks, off towards a horizon that looked the same as every other in this place.

Though no words were exchanged we understood him to mean that there must be some form of help in that direction: a village perhaps.

Once we'd thanked the men, bowing our bodies in gratitude, Terry and his couriers consulted with Mohammed. They decided it was better to save our strength in case this mysterious help was a long way distant. One truck would remain where it was and the other would be emptied of everything, including the sleeping bags on the roof, the trailer it towed, and the sick lying on their backs on the seats. A very small party of us would accompany it in search of whatever lay beyond that horizon.

I was keen to go, if only for a break from this new exhausting pushing and matting routine. We pooled what water remained into a few of the carriers and set out with the empties, hardly daring to believe that, in this wasteland, there might be a water supply.

Without its customary load, G truck proved more able to navigate the dried lake bed surface without bogging. Even more miraculous, the camel riders were right. Around 20 minutes' drive from the trucks we saw the promise of a few green shoots, then some bushes, and, further on, a solitary tree. A few minutes more brought us to a small spring gushing and foaming from the ground like a miniature volcano.

At some point, when perhaps there was a village here, people had tried to harness this lifegiving water. There were still bits of old pipe, holed and broken.

Light-headed from a mixture of heat and relief we stepped fully dressed into the water spray, scrubbing at our sunburnt skin, feeling our bodies tingling to life.

When it was my turn I ducked my head down into the water, rubbing at the grittiness in my scalp, certain that no Christmas gift would ever be so thrilling.

It didn't matter that we then had to drag eight brimming water containers back to the truck. Nor that their weight meant we had to walk the distance alongside the truck back to camp, rather than risk bogging. It was a price worth paying for those moments of cool, life-giving water. At least I knew we wouldn't die of thirst for the next two days.

***

It was still only early afternoon and Christmas or no, Terry planned another four or five hours of pushing and matting duty for us. My legs were leaden, but my spirits were high with the relief of having full water containers again.

Those who'd been left behind to rest, but mostly swelter, in the heat had none of our revived spirits and it soon began to show. We had scarcely been moving for five minutes when I heard a loud jagged cry. My cooking partner Cockney Steve was on the ground, lying awkwardly where he'd fallen, the sand mat half across him.

Tell me, if you were running a five-month expedition across some of Africa's most remote places what would be one of the first things you'd pack?

A decent first aid kit possibly?

We had a first aid kit on board but all it held were a few old plasters that had long since lost any adhesive. That was it: another Terry equipment fail. It was his good fortune that among his 50 passengers were three nurses, all of whom had made a better fist of assembling a first aid kit than he had.

"Lie still. Don't move in case something's broken," Sue Cookie warned Steve.

Gently she probed each of his limbs, lingering over his right shoulder. "What do you think? Feels to me like there's something floating loose under the skin."

"It's a broken collar bone I think. Did you pack a sling?" another of the nurses asked.

"No need," volunteered Will. "You can use my shesh."

"That's one way to get out of cooking duty," I teased Steve, but behind the smile he returned I could see he was fighting hard not to scream out in pain.

***

Not long afterwards, when we were once again stuttering forward, there was another accident.

This time someone on the other truck fell, crashing forward onto the sand mat he was holding and knocked himself out. There was a lot of blood running from the tear in his skin. His floury complexion was perhaps more scary.

A group of the men lifted him on board where he lay until nightfall mumbling incoherently, tended to by one of the nurses holding a wet flannel against the wound.

These new casualties joined Leader, whose fever was no better, and the youngest passenger on Q truck, a lass called Sally. Both were now a serious concern. In the back of the truck Sally lay on her back, wheezing and choking, struggling for each breath. When the breath came it sounded as if it had been wrung from her lungs. How much longer would she have the energy to force her breath?

Someone loaned her an inhaler but it made no difference. I noticed the nurses whispering between themselves, with the grave expressions reserved for critical care units. They sensed she was in serious trouble; I could see that.

Leader seemed to have had a relapse of the malaria he'd suffered two years before. He lay prone across the benches inside, alternately delirious then pleading that he was cold. All three nurses were excused from pushing since they were more urgently needed in this desperately under-equipped sick bay.

It wasn't sustainable, whatever Terry believed, and eventually, Heather broke ranks to remonstrate with him.

"Can't you see they've had enough. Chrissakes it's Christmas Day."

"We can't stop yet," he shouted back. "There's nothing here. We don't know when we'll find water again. Or food. I don't think any of you realise how serious this is. No-one's coming to rescue us. And I don't plan to end my days stuck in the desert with you lot."

It was too much for my Aussie friend Gai: "We're already stuck in the desert you idiot."

"So long as we've got the light we need to keep going. I'm not arguing."

This time Heather grabbed his arm: "I'm serious Terry. If you make people go on there'll be more accidents. If you're not careful you'll get someone killed."

Others waded into the argument but a few of us knew better. These arguments had a way of sprawling on for hours. Quietly, we took matters into our own hands and began hauling tents out of the trailers.

***

In the circumstances it ought to have been a sombre Christmas meal. We had little enough to celebrate other than another day's survival. Sometimes though, when you're in a painful situation the temporary absence of pain lifts you to a strange high.

So it was for us that Christmas night, feasting on dried goat meat, cold pasta and coleslaw, all prepared and cooked by Cookie and Tony back in Niamey days earlier, and sweeter to our exhausted bodies than any turkey dinner we might once have yearned for.

As for the cold Christmas pudding served with evaporated milk, it was as if our tastebuds were discovering flavours for the first time. Dulled by porridge, dried bread, and endless vegetable stews, they were suddenly fired into life again. Food had rarely tasted so good.

Afterwards we sang a few Christmas songs, and Israeli Jacquie donned a paper crown she'd made and delivered her version of the Queen's speech.

Tom disappeared to stick a pillow up under a red tee shirt he'd borrowed and dole out the Secret Santa gifts, and we toasted each other with cans of Fanta brought from Niamey market: to Wayne for being the best driver, to Kathy and Keith whose rows were such an effective alarm clock, to Will for being the most generous person on board, and, to my discomfort, to G's newest couple, Tom and I.

I smiled and raised my can along with everyone else but felt again that unease at being singled out and paired off.

In the two days since Zinder there had been too much else on our minds for me to worry much about whether we were actually 'together' or not. And almost no time sitting on the truck when I'd have to decide whether to plonk myself down next to him or carry on, as I had been, finding somewhere different to sit each time.

How to handle this felt like a decision for another day; a day when we wouldn't be pushing for our lives.

CHAPTER 13

Boxing Day began with a triumphant fourteen miles on the clock, due to one heady spell early morning when we hit a field of hard, flat sand, darker than the rest.

Up close the surface was made of millions of grains of splintered shell fragments, ground to dust by heat and wind and passing centuries. Clearly this part of the desert had once been covered by tropical waters, forming Lake Chad - though Mohammed seemed uninterested in confirming that this was so.

We only saw him now when there was food on offer and though we knew his French was as adequate as ours he shrugged off any questions about the route and how much longer it would be to the capital by pretending not to understand.

By mid-morning the brief honeymoon was over and the trucks once again ground to a standstill. Grudgingly, we climbed out and began the hellish Groundhog Day routine.

The only difference now was that there were fewer of us still fit to push. If anything, the sun seemed even hotter today and one by one people were succumbing to heatstroke and having to be lifted on board Q truck – the G truck sick bay was full. The rest of us had no choice but to form a single pushing party, taking one truck at a time.

It was the hottest part of the day when our group turned back from G to rescue Q, stranded some distance behind. I was on mat duty and puzzled at the mat's weight, especially as Tom had hold of the back behind me. The mat seemed to be pushing us deeper into the sand, as though we were walking through toffee. The sun scorched onto our heads and the air all around felt solid and dead. Ahead, the truck shimmered and disappeared then reappeared further away.

By the time we reached Terry everything had become hazy and insubstantial. I could see people were talking because their mouths were moving but all I could hear was a loud hum inside my skull.

My body felt as corpse-like as the air we'd walked through, nothing to do with me. And when I looked down at my legs I wanted to laugh hysterically. They were shaking like jelly and covered in hundreds of little white spots. But no, that was wrong. The spots weren't on my legs; they were everywhere I looked.

Then I lost consciousness.

I came around in the back of Q truck, someone holding a warm flannel to my forehead. But it was too much effort to ask what happened so I stayed still, drifting in and out of dreams and silence. Only when the heat subsided at the end of the day was I strong enough to get back on my feet.

***

I wondered if I might still be hallucinating when, the next morning, we spotted a white Landrover bouncing across the sand towards our once-again stricken vehicles.

But it was no mirage and the effects on all of us of seeing a red cross on the vehicle's side was like a shot of pure adrenaline. The Landrover skidded to a halt and out onto the sand stepped three immaculately dressed Europeans, a team of French doctors, working with Médecins sans Frontieres in a part of Chad where civil unrest still raged.

Pleasantries scarcely finished, one of the nurses was ushering them on board to review our sick bay. And this, dear reader, was our second Christmas miracle for I have no doubt that the appearance of this mobile clinic saved at least one if not two lives that day - just as the camel riders had saved us on Christmas Day.

The doctors quickly established that Sally's asthma had deepened into severe bronchial pneumonia. She was very poorly. They injected her with massive doses of antibiotic, remaining at her side until her temperature began to drop out of the danger level. Next they treated Leader for malaria, complicated, they suspected, by a relapse of his glandular fever. They removed the scarf supporting Steve's broken collar bone and set it properly with industrial strength tape so it was completely immobile. Then they turned their attention to the heatstroke patients and one or two whose wounds from sand-matting were suppurating and infected.

The rest of us waited and hoped, like expectant fathers fearing the worst and praying for the best outside the delivery room.

It was several hours later that the doctors stepped down from G and Q truck, satisfied that they'd done as much as they could. They spoke to Terry and Heather, urging that Sally, Leader and Steve should abandon the trip and travel with them in the back of the Landrover to Niamey where they could catch a flight home for proper treatment.

I watched Mohammed jump down from Q truck's cab to join the discussion. He was pointing energetically towards the horizon, shouting in French, appearing to reassure everyone that N'djamena was less than a day away now and our patients were closer to the airport there than in Niamey. Besides which, they could travel in comfort, flat out in the back of our trucks, rather than scrunched up in the back of the Landrover.

All three decided to stay, mostly from faith that Mohammed was right I think. But perhaps there was also something about being so far from home, in such strange circumstances, that made them crave the familiar. We weren't family but in some ways we'd become so, simply through sharing the difficulties of the last few days.

There was a palpable shift of mood, as if their choice to stay confirmed how close we were to escaping the desert, to reaching civilisation. And doing so without running out of water.

The doctors shook their heads disbelievingly, but handed more cartons of antibiotics to the nurses, before skidding away off into the sand. Somehow it seemed of less importance that with their departure we had to resume pushing. We now knew this was temporary. And to prove it, after just two more hours of pushing and matting we spotted a few huts ahead: not N'djamena but a tiny desert community. If people lived out here in this remote spot then there must be water. We knew we were safe for another day.

Perhaps that knowledge caused us to shove a little harder and a little more enthusiastically. In any case, this was the moment - after days of maltreatment - when G truck's back finally broke. Wayne had coaxed and cajoled, bullied and beaten it through choking sand for three long days. Not counting all the days leading up to the Chad desert with pitted tracks, the breakneck ride up into the Hoggars, and sand – always sand.

As the first children emerged shyly from the huts, drawn by our noise, there was an almighty crash.

Wayne jumped down from the cab and took only a few seconds under the vehicle to reach his diagnosis.

"Something's gone in the gearbox mate. Might as well get the tents. We're not going anywhere."

CHAPTER 14

Mechanic Mike and our driver Wayne crashed out after another all-night shift trying to fix the truck

Through the skin of the tent I was surprised to see it was light outside. I'd slept through the whole night and felt only relief that our breakdown meant there was no pre-dawn start.

Will was already up, though he'd not gone far: I could smell cigarette smoke. He must have heard the rustle of my sleeping bag for the next moment his head was poking through the flap. "Cup of tea old girl?"

"Yes please. I'm so glad I got you for a tent partner!" I grinned. "Any news about the truck? How's Wayne getting on?"

"Been up for hours. It's not good news from what I heard. Doubt we'll be going anywhere soon."

When I emerged I saw Wayne was lying flat on his back beside the ashes of the campfire, snoring loudly with his mouth wide open, arms, oil-black, splayed above his head.

It was Mark who filled us in as we breakfasted on stodgy rice pudding made with dried milk from the stores and the little sugar we had left: Mohammed's taste for ten teaspoons of sugar in every cup of coffee he drank had decimated supplies.

"Worked all night," Mark said. "What it is is the spare see. A tooth's gone in the gearbox. They packed a spare back in London cos Terry said both trucks have the same gearbox. We got the old one out at four-o-clock. Went to fit the spare parts and it's no good. Wrong model. Doesn't fit."

"Shit. What now?" Cockney Steve, nursing his broken collar bone, had more reason than most of us to be anxious.

"We had to put the old one back. Can't do anything else see. The spare's quarter of an inch out. Might as well be quarter of a mile. Wayne reckons he'll just have to get us going in third gear. That's where it's stuck."

"And get a replacement in N'djamena?" Steve asked.

"Maybe…" Mark shrugged.

"Let's hope Mohammed's got it right and we're close," I said.

It hadn't escaped our notice that, having predicted we were only a day away from the capital the appearance of this desert village seemed to surprise our guide as much as us.

Mark had news about that too. "Heather forced it out of him this morning. What it is, he's never been across the actual lake before."

"Well there's a surprise. So he's no more idea than us about the route?"

Mark nodded. "Yep. Heather and Terry are deciding what to do about it now."

"So you're telling me he's as lost as us?" Steve asked.

"Yeah, only difference is he's getting paid for it," Will said.

***

While Wayne slept on, we idled in the sand, watched by a circle of women and children. We knew we were lucky to have reached a village that had a water supply but it was clear their lives were far from secure. Some of the children's bellies were distended, malnutrition blowing them up until the skin stretched thin as paper.

Hunger made them easy prey for other diseases too. Some had eyes half-closed with pus; one boy dragged a dead limb after him like a piece of useless luggage. Few had hair and the scabs on their scalps swarmed with flies. It was hard to look at them – and harder still to deal with the guilt when we looked away.

We decided instead to explore the village – apparently it was called Liwa - removing ourselves from those children's blank stares.

The cause of their swollen stomachs became clear: a building with a baker's sign outside, but as empty as the desert; an empty market place where the only sound came from stalks of straw blowing across the surface of abandoned tables; and finally one small shop that still operated. Its shelves held only cans of famine relief tomato puree, sardines plus cigarettes, priced so far beyond the means of Liwa's local population they had clearly been there for months, if not years.

We bought up everything there was, refusing to see the need all around.

But every night we were stuck in Liwa the children came after dark and dug up our rubbish pits, taking away the empty cans and used teabags to extract what they could: existing on first world leftovers as so many have been forced to do since our ancestors 'discovered' Africa's bounty.

***

But I'm getting ahead of myself, for at this point we were stuck not only in the sand, but with a guide who was as clueless as Terry himself.

Heather had news when we got back from raiding Liwa's solitary shop. "Mohammed claims to have a friend here who knows the way and we've got to bring him along too."

"Another guide?" I asked.

"Well yeah, that's what Mohammed says. You can imagine Terry's reaction."

"He's not going to pay for two guides, especially not when one of them has got us into this trouble already." She swept a few tails of blonde hair from her forehead, looking anxious.

A part of me was thinking it was at least as much Terry's fault we found ourselves stranded somewhere in Chad pushing vehicles that clearly weren't up to the challenge of the dried lake bed.

"Terry says when Wayne's had a sleep we're going to make a quick getaway with the new guide and get shot of Mohammed. He's told him to go and have a coffee and that his friend should come and meet us for an interview as soon as he can."

Like all of Terry's plans, this was always going to end badly. It wasn't just the very obvious handicap of two noisy army trucks, accompanied by a battalion of weary travellers, attempting 'a quick getaway'; we hadn't managed to go anywhere in a hurry at any stage of this trip and now he was expecting us to do so with G truck in third gear.

When the new guide arrived my instincts told me he was more trustworthy than the man he was replacing. His name was Abduhl and he had a shyness about him. His expression was earnest, a permanent slight frown between his eyes. He spoke so softly you had to draw close to catch his words. Like Mohammed he spoke French to us.

Abduhl was a little older though, dressed in the long protective robes of the desert, quietly shaking hands with each of us to introduce himself. After the introductions he followed Terry to the Q truck cab, seemingly unsurprised that we appeared to be leaving without any sign of Mohammed who had, after all, offered him this shared gig.

"Get Wayne up," Terry ordered Heather.

***

The problem was our escape route lay through the village, down the narrowest of unmade tracks, separating two lines of straw-rooved huts.

Wayne revved the engine in third gear while we pushed for all we were worth, scrambling aboard delightedly when somehow G picked up the momentum we'd started; our truck began to rumble along behind Q.

On both sides of us the huts vibrated with the noise of our motors, shaking people from their dark interiors to see what was happening and what it was that was scraping against their rooves.

Naturally Mohammed was among those propelled from the huts.

He burst out, spouting a torrent of angry dialect, then raced ahead to Q, flinging himself at the cab.

We leaned out of the windows to watch the spectacle as our former guide latched onto a wing mirror for all he was worth, legs dangling helplessly, trying to get a footing on the stairwell.

From the driver's window Terry's arm appeared, hitting at Mohammed's arms to try and make him let go. My fear was he'd fall under the tyres but Terry seemed unbothered by that prospect, swerving slightly to the left to try and unbalance him and force him to let go of the mirror.

There was a loud yelp; in swerving Terry had caught Mohammed's back and legs on the sharp straw of the adjacent huts. The guide let go, pressing himself against the walls of the hut, only to then launch himself at Wayne's mirror on G truck.

Who knows what would have happened if we'd been able to keep going with Mohammed clinging on for dear life? As it was, our little convoy suddenly shuddered to a halt, G truck stuck behind a stranded Q.

Wayne and Terry cut the engines and we heard only the deafening silence of failure.

It lasted just a few moments. Then all hell broke loose: we were still very much in the middle of Liwa and not only was our sacked guide furious, Terry's clumsy attempts to shake him off had infuriated the rest of the village. Seconds later the first sting of a missile hit the truck.

"It's the fuel line on Q, as well as the sand this time," Mark told us when he got back from consulting with Wayne and Terry over this latest breakdown. "Wayne's looking at it now."

Call it karma, but Mohammed now had plenty of time to summon support to back up his claim on Terry. I doubt he wanted to be on board any more than we wanted him on the truck; however he did want the fee he'd agreed at the start.

As Wayne laboured under Q's bonnet, and we scanned the crowd to see where the next missile was coming from, there was a commotion. Mohammed appeared with a couple of men at his side, and a third man dressed in army fatigues, a red and yellow flash on each shoulder. Worryingly, he carried some sort of whip and a very serious-looking rifle slung across one shoulder.

As Mohammed's eyes fastened on Terry, stooped and sullen, watching Wayne work, he began jabbering excitedly, pointing Terry out. The army man fished in one pocket and pulled out a small silver whistle which he blew sharply in Terry's general direction.

It took a moment for Terry to register that the whistle was meant for him, a summons to stop what he was doing and come over.

His always-pained expression seemed to come alive: first puzzlement then utter fury at the impertinence of our former guide and his cronies. How dare they treat him like a naughty schoolchild? Terry marched over, thrusting an angry finger at Mohammed, calling him a conman, shouting that he was a waste of space, and how he had no intention of paying him a penny.

It was hard to know whose side to take: the hopeless guide or the man whose lack of preparation and general arrogance had lost any loyalty we might have once felt.

It didn't matter anyway. We were bystanders, and watched, both exhilarated and horrified as Terry's shouting escalated and he brought himself nose to nose with Mohammed, still calling him names and swearing he wouldn't get paid.

This was too much for the man in military fatigues who clearly thought the fact he had a whip and gun meant *he* should be in charge. For the second time he blew his whistle and when Terry failed to come to heel he strode towards him, poking his whip repeatedly into Terry's ribs to try and establish his authority.

It was a red rag to an already enraged bull of course. Terry grabbed the whip and you could hear the sharp intake of breath, not only from us but from the watching villagers wondering who'd win this escalating battle of wills.

For the longest time we watched as they wrestled with the whip, poking at each other, voices getting louder and louder. I saw the whip slip from Terry's grip and then the soldier whacked him across the face. Terry raised an arm either to grab it back, defend himself, or attack the other man: it was unclear. But this was too much for the old soldier: in a moment he'd let go of the whip, hoisted his gun from his shoulder and pointed it straight at Terry.

There was a deathly silence. For the first time since Mohammed's reappearance Terry was quiet, standing still as a statue. The soldier held the gun high, still pointing it at Terry's chest, as if trying to decide whether to shoot him anyway. Wasn't that a fair price for disrespect and besides, who would stop him? We were completely off-grid.

None of us noticed that our new guide had slipped down from the cab and, with gentle authority, stood alongside the military man with one hand resting on the gun's barrel.

He said some words, then nodded towards Heather who stepped forward to Terry.

"For chrissakes, it's not worth getting yourself killed for. Just give him the bloody money."

"I'm not scared of them. Lying little creep," Terry hissed.

"Terry?" I had not heard Heather speak with such power before. "We need to do whatever they say."

She was right of course. With both trucks out of action we were stuck in Liwa, guests of a community that had turned hostile towards us, and under the jurisdiction of an old soldier with a gun.

This really was the wild west and justice apparently belonged to the one with the biggest weapon - and the willingness to use it.

While we piled back into the trucks, Terry and his couriers were shepherded to what Abdhul told them was a 'court', presided over by a serious-looking old man.

He listened quietly to Mohammed and Terry and pronounced that our useless guide must be paid off before we were free to take on Abdhul.

There had to be something in the whole business for 'the judge' too naturally. Once Mohammed's honour, and wallet, were satisfied, the judge disappeared with Terry and Wayne to organize the sale of a couple of barrels of diesel he seemed to own – perhaps confiscated from other transgressors, such as ourselves, who'd happened to stray into his jurisdiction.

Though the price was hyper-inflated, the rest of us thought it was good news. We now had more diesel supplied after burning through so much of our limited supplies as we navigated the sands of Lake Chad.

***

After justice, of a sort, had been seen to be served, people melted away. We were left little better off than when we started the day, still stuck in Liwa. Wayne managed to fix the fuel pipe on Q truck quickly and for the sake of removing Terry from the scene of his crime we decided to push both trucks clear of the last huts. Unfortunately, there was a new obstacle in our way.

Liwa, it seemed, was built in the shelter of a large dune, guarding the village's exit like a vast sand amphitheatre. For those who lived in this bleak little outpost, the dune offered a little barrier from the rampaging desert winds. For G truck, stuck in third gear, it represented an insurmountable obstacle.

Both trucks took one look at this wall of sand and whimpered to a halt.

"Righty!," Wayne emerged from his cab like the lone ranger. "Let's at least try pulling Q truck clear. No way we'll push either bugger *up that*. 'Fraid we're stuck here with G. Not a chance we'll get her shifted in third gear."

Out of the trailers came some old, frayed ropes which Wayne attached to Q's frame. The rest of us clambered up the dune. It took an age, the sand slipping away beneath our flip flops almost as fast as we tried to climb skywards.

Eventually, when those of us still able to help had conquered the summit, and Wayne had knotted three ropes together to cover the distance, we lined up like a tug o' war team abandoned by its opposition.

Wayne took over from Terry at Q's wheel. Our leader was still sulking and in no mood to provide any more spectacle for anyone who should happen to be watching. Deep at the foot of the sandpit Q's engine roared into life and revved itself like a dragon being woken from a 100-year sleep.

We tugged. We dug our heels into the slippery sand and tugged some more. "PUUUULLLL. Together!" for once Kitty Chris' self-appointed cheerleading helped us find some kind of rhythm.

Inch by inch, with help from the groaning, complaining engine, the truck teetered uphill. But as soon as we relaxed our hold on the two ropes it slipped back down, almost as far as it had come. We had to learn not to let go of the tension on the ropes at the end of every exhausting tug.

This time it worked. Slowly, painfully, we made progress.

Two hours later, with most of us crimson-faced and blistered, Q finally reached the lip of the sand mountain and with one final effort came lumbering over the top.

If there had ever been any doubt about Wayne's verdict on our own truck, we now had proof it would be impossible to shift G without the engine's power to assist. We were going nowhere, and there was nothing for it but for Wayne to once again remove the gearbox and somehow try to adapt the unsuitable spare.

"How's he going to do that?" I asked Mark who stood at the top of the dune with me, hands on hips, surveying our truck with a look of utter despair.

"D-d-dunno. He says he packed a hand drill by chance. Think his plan is to drill some new holes in the spare box so it can be made to fit."

"Sounds impossible. How d'you drill holes through metal with a hand drill?"

Mark looked away, towards the sand mountain. "No idea. Never heard of anyone trying it…"

***

In the entire five months we were travelling I think this was the only time I envied the other truck.

Up to this point I'd thanked my lucky stars to have been drawn on G, travelling with people I mostly liked or found interesting, in the care of a driver who was clever and ingenious, rather than the bad-tempered, anti-social Terry.

But oh, those extra meters Q truck put between herself and Liwa that afternoon would have made a world of difference.

None of the locals bothered to follow them up the dune to watch them or harass them. There was no need when half of the circus was still in town, beached at the foot of the sand mountain.

As Mark and I descended we had to step around children and adults who had gathered to watch. The hostility was palpable: we had lost any goodwill we might have had when Terry tried, in their eyes, to double-cross one of their own.

The eyes that studied us were resentful and bitter.

To make matters worse, we had nothing more to do than sit in the sand and wait under their watchful gaze.

Only Wayne, Mark, and Q's mechanic Mike had a purpose, laying under the truck, drilling and filing away, spelling each other when their hands seized in cramp.

We'd discovered the trucks were carrying only one jack between them which made it too dangerous for any of us, even the invalids, to stay on board – just in case the additional weight or movement sent the truck crashing onto our mechanics' heads. So we idled in the sandpit, our soundtrack the insistent whine of metal on metal.

Looking back now I wonder at our arrogance in not asking local people's permission to help ourselves to their most important resource – their water.

Liwa was an anachronism, a rare survivor in a land of drought. They had water and therefore they had been able to remain, at least until they starved. Then we arrived: fifty of us, drawing from the same well they queued for hours to use. Hauling up their precious water not only for cooking but for washing our clothes and our skin with no sense or care that we might be taking too much.

When dusk came around they showed us how they felt about our greed in the only way open to them - creeping around our encampment under cover of darkness and pelting us with camel dung.

Squatting behind the truck, never out of sight or range of the onlookers, I was quite sure things couldn't get any worse.

And being stuck at the foot of a huge sand cliff seemed a fitting symbol of our plight: we had hit rock bottom from which the only way was up.

CHAPTER 15

For three more days we languished in that sandpit. One of those days was my birthday, a date I shared with Terry of all people. But celebrating couldn't have been further from my mind. Celebrate what? The heat, the sand, the flies? The stench of our toilet pit with its improvised toilet paper – no longer from books but now letters, pages from journals and even – misguidedly – the leaves of a mystery succulent which was one of the few things growing anywhere.

I later read in *Shoestring* that the sap from this plant is highly toxic and can cause blindness if it touches the eyes. It only needed one or two people to experience the agonizing pain of this sap on their most tender parts for the rest of us to abandon any notion of using the plant as replacement loo paper.

I've always considered myself lucky to have a December 30 birthday, not just because people are mostly around to celebrate with me but because it adds extra weight to the usual new year rituals of letting go of the old year and welcoming in the new.

This year, however, I had no interest in thinking about all that had happened during 1984, the heartbreak and the loss and the way the people I loved most in the world had struggled. Nor was there any point in thinking ahead to 1985 and what I wished for the new year. I knew that even if I survived I would still be sitting in this sandpit a year from now, swatting flies and numb with boredom.

***

As my 28th year slipped ignominiously away, Wayne continued his drilling and filing - and someone came up with a bright idea for celebrating the final day of 1984: we were each to put our names in a hat, then draw out someone else's name and dress as them for our New Year's Eve supper.

Unexpectedly, given our plight, having something different to put our energies into proved a tonic. Mark looked even skinnier than usual in my pink cotton shift with 'Jane loves Tom' scrawled in biro on his thigh.

Will dressed as Annie, his unkempt hair tamed into cornrows. I slathered suncream into my legs to try and emulate Kathy's deathly white Scottish skin. And Annie drew thick glasses on her face and sported a debating society badge to represent Tom.

We were almost too busy admiring each other's ingenuity to spot that Wayne had emerged from under the truck, straightening himself up with a pained expression on his face.

"Reckon it's time to test her," he mumbled, then blinked hard, registering the pink dress his right-hand man was wearing.

No-one needed telling twice. It was early evening on 31st and we'd been resigned to a fourth night in the sandpit. But the smallest prospect of pushing our way out, and seeing in the new year from outside Liwa, was like a shot in the arm.

We must have looked like the worst-dressed Pride march ever, a motley collection of drag queens and pantomime extras, securing a tow rope to Q truck so it could assist the effort, then taking up position alongside and behind G, as Wayne once again switched on the engine.

What a sound. I felt like cheering aloud. Could we make it up and out of the dune?

Yes we could.

Perhaps our truck had needed that long rest. Perhaps – the squits notwithstanding - we were a fraction stronger after our enforced break from pushing and matting in the heat. But most likely it was Wayne who was the reason for our success; Wayne who had worked miracles with the wrong gearbox and almost no equipment.

G felt stronger, crawling its way painfully up the dune's sides, faltering almost as much as it moved, but then straining, recovering strength and inching forwards.

As we shoved, and, above us, Q truck pulled, a block of wood hit me hard on the back; beside me Will took a hit to the head.

In donning each other's clothes we'd only made ourselves even more strange to the people of Liwa. But tonight it didn't matter. We were moving - and 90 minutes later G sat squarely alongside its mate, while we tucked into celebratory onion soup.

Perhaps, after all, this was a New Year's Eve worth celebrating.

Even Terry, wearing one of Heather's dresses, joined in the dancing when we switched on the cassette player. And he was still up and willing to join hands with us at what we thought might be midnight. The words of *Auld Lang Syne* rang out from our camp.

A world away I thought of my family listening to Big Ben's chimes. I could no longer imagine myself back there, among familiar places, so present was I with these people I'd come to depend on as they depended on me. Singing together under that vast black African sky the only thing that mattered, the only thing I wanted to celebrate, was that we'd escaped Liwa and could once again start believing N'djamena was around the next corner, urging us on.

***

Every new year I wonder how long the adrenaline of Christmas and New Year will last and carry me forward into January before I succumb to the same-old, same-old.

In Chad the answer was ten minutes into January 1st.

We had toasted our escape too soon and should have known better. No sooner had the day started and we got moving than Q truck broke down: Terry was apoplectic.

"It's the fucking fuel pipe again. You need to fucking fix it properly this time. I won't put up with this. It's ridiculous." He sloped off into the sand, the nearest he could come to slamming a door I suppose.

Wayne simply shrugged and rolled up his sleeves, telling us the fuel wasn't getting through because the timing was out. It shouldn't take long to fix.

But an hour turned to two turned to four and then word went around that we might as well pitch the tents because it was not a straightforward job after all and we'd certainly be stuck all day.

I wish I could have been like Wayne, able to shrug and just do what needed to be done.

I couldn't. After all the difficulties and delays of the last nine days, the worry about whether we'd make it, my exhaustion from pushing the trucks all day in desert heat, I was flatter than a battery with a broken alternator.

Some of the others found a place to sit where they could watch the latest scene playing out. I only wanted to get away from them all, but there was nowhere to go. I certainly didn't fancy the trek back to Liwa and everywhere else I looked there was only more barren desert.

Eventually I grabbed the onboard copy of *Lorna Doone* and crawled into my tent, preferring its oppressive and airless heat to sitting with other people.

My skin crawled with irritation and every part of me felt filthy. I knew I'd lost a lot of weight. I could feel my ribs through my tee-shirt. Inside my mouth the taste was permanently sour, as if I was waking every day with a hangover.

I didn't want company – I didn't even want to be with Tom. I had nothing to say to him and no desire to listen to him either.

Instead, I chose to lose myself in Blackmore's classic book, conjuring from its pages a vision of green and lush valleys and simple pastoral beauty in which to imagine myself.

***

We started afresh on January 2nd. Most likely I was imagining it but I convinced myself the engines of both trucks sounded stronger, even though they continued to bog ever hundred metres or so and the old routine of sand matting was once again the shape of the day.

Still, the crunching noise had gone from G's gearbox and if I tried hard I could believe the landscape was changing fractionally. Occasionally the empty horizon was interrupted by a lone tree, branches spread like open arms supporting a fringe of green thorns. Possibly the sand was whiter and finer, hard to tell, but each tiny shift planted a seed of hope.

Most exciting of all was Q truck's discovery of a shallow round hollow in the sand, the width of a frying pan lid.

"Elephant," our new guide Abdhul announced, looking worried. "They cause much damage. Bad," he shook his head, perplexed by the way we'd all reached for our cameras. And why shouldn't we be excited: we thought we were lost but now we not only had evidence of plant life but animal life too. Maybe the ordeal really would end soon…

Except for the realization that elephants could move through this terrain in a way that seemed impossible for us.

Another day passed in relentless and oppressive heat and we were no nearer to finding N'djamena, or indeed any other signs of life, including those elusive elephants.

The next morning brought deja vu as a nut sheered off G's gearbox. We endured another wait in the sand while Wayne fiddled, wondering why we'd bothered to get up that day if all it held was more waiting.

But after a few hours he got the truck going. There was an ominous new knocking sound which we pretended to ignore, but it meant none of us was able to relax, much less believe we'd get through this endless desert crossing. Mombasa, which we were supposed to reach after five months travelling, might as well be the moon.

***

"Land ahoy!"

The cry came from Q truck's passengers and we strained to see what it was that had caused the shouting. Not land, exactly, or an end to the desert, but a couple of brick buildings, stark and alone, solitary on the distant horizon.

"Well fuck me. Looks like this guide knows what he's doing," Kitty Chris said when Heather leaned out of the cab to confirm that by some miracle we'd stumbled on other human life. It wasn't N'djamena though, as we'd been promised. Apparently this desert outpost was a town called Bol.

We were too grateful for the sight of brick buildings to ask Abdhul why he'd not mentioned this and where the heck was Chad's capital city?

Bol once thrived on the banks of Lake Chad. Now the settlement ahead of us was merely a shadow of itself, taken over by the military to guard against incursions from Libyan troops.

Apparently our guide knew of Bol, and knew we needed to travel via it, in spite of the risks, if we were to find fuel and water to replenish the almost empty carriers. He just hadn't explained this to Heather and Terry until now.

Yes, Bol was controlled by an army, and there was no way of knowing which side they might be on nor whether they'd take kindly to our arrival. But without water, or filling the empty fuel tanks, we had no hope of reaching N'djamena.

As we approached the buildings a group of men emerged in army fatigues, guns in their arms: the hairs on my arms prickled with fear.

We shuddered to a stop and suddenly there was shouting and activity - orders in a language we didn't understand but the meaning was clear. The men waved their guns at us, demanding we get out of the trucks and line up in front of them.

There were four soldiers watching with the same intent I might watch a snake blocking my path. While one guarded us with his raised gun, the rest of their group piled on board and began turning everything out, hurling bags onto the sand, ripping the seat covers from the benches and plundering the lockers beneath.

It was like a crazy rummage sale, the pile of discarded luggage and garments rising like a pyre on the sand.

We watched helplessly, wholly intimidated by their guns, as items were slipped into pockets, down the front of shirts, or openly displayed to each other, assessing their value.

These boots which were supposed to protect us from snakes and scorpions vanished more quickly than a cold glass of water might have done. Each of the soldiers chose a pair and I was glad my feet were too small to make my boots of any use to grown men. Sunglasses were also popular, and a couple of thick jackets were 'confiscated'.

There was no question or remonstrating with them. This was the price for our passage into Bol.

****

Despite the unwelcome welcome committee, and Bol's remoteness, there was more to the town than we realised: low rammed earth buildings organised into streets and a few people on the streets.

Our latest problem, now we'd reached 'civilisation', was that we had no local currency with which to pay not only for the provisions we'd need, but for the local taxes our military friends decided to impose on us. Until they were paid, they insisted, we were going nowhere.

We tried offering French francs left over from Europe but Bol's small population were not ever likely to leave heir village, and merely looked on suspiciously and shook their heads.

The advantage of remote outposts, of course, is that everyone soon knows everyone else's business.

As we pottered around the field that was to be our campsite until we could pay our way back out of Bol, a tall, bearded European wandered in to find us. His skin was red and blistered beneath a grubby baseball cap, but his manner was confident and business-like.

He said he worked in the town for an American aid agency, running famine relief projects from Bol. His employer paid him in local currency which was pretty useless since there was nothing here to buy, and his plan was to travel in Europe when his stint in Chad ended. He would gladly swap the piles of local notes he'd accumulated for French francs.

With local currency in our pockets, we wasted no time heading into the centre of Bol in search of kitty food and anything resembling drink cans or bottles that might be stowed for when we continued our journey.

Tom and I joined up, abandoning any attempt to compete with the rest of the group as they descended on the 'market' where there were only two stalls among the empty tables. They held the usual fare: onions, fresh chillies, plus cans of tomato puree and sardines, again clearly labelled famine relief gifts.

Instead, we poked our way down unpromisingly deserted alleyways – and struck gold: a small, dark building with a dusting of flour on its walls.

There was no sign, or indication than anything might be happening but when we poked our head inside the darkness a man appeared, beckoning us in, his mouth set in a broad and semi-toothless grin, indicating that we should follow him.

The man led us through the empty building and out into a little enclosed courtyard, bare except for a rush mat and a low table made from three short planks.

Still grinning, he thrust his hand at the mat several times, so we knew we were being invited to sit down. And then, with a flourish that would do credit to any magician, he produced a small loaf of bread, two plastic mugs and a flask of cold water.

Our host looked just as delighted as us when we smiled our appreciation and placed our hands on our hearts to thank him. Some things do not need language. We were thrilled at the fresh bread, even more so perhaps at the clean water. Pouring it as carefully as the finest vintage wine we allowed its clear coldness to sit on our tongues and the back of our throats, as if we had never tasted anything like it before.

The man disappeared but he had not quite finished bringing gifts. When he reappeared he was holding a tiny battery-operated radio.

Face frozen in concentration, he fiddled with the dial, looking up every so often to nod frantically, reassuring us that it would be worth the wait.

Eventually he found what he was looking for and the unmistakeably authoritative tones of the BBC World Service boomed out into the little courtyard.

The baker nodded at us in a 'didn't I do well' sort of way and we could only agree – even though, in our heart of hearts, we'd have preferred the peace. The plummy voices blaring from the radio seemed like echoes from another world and time, with no relation to our lives now.

But to show anything other than gratitude would have been churlish when our host was so clearly thrilled. We determined that one practical way to show our gratitude would be to send the rest of the truck his way to spend their recently acquired currency at his café too.

Before that though, we'd munch our courtyard picnic in thoughtful silence, any conversation we might have had, drowned out by a voice from the other side of the world droning on about community centres in Northern Ireland.

CHAPTER 16

Mark collecting water from an abandoned well in which we found a dead goat

Once we'd paid the local taxes we were ready to leave, but Wayne begged another day in Bol so he could get as much sand out from under the bonnets as possible.

Our driver also organised the rest of us to help him swap tyres around. Each truck carried two spares on the roof and they were now urgently needed to replace the tyres scoured almost bald by the endless skidding in sand, and cracked by days of desert heat.

Lack of adequate preparation had been Long Haul's biggest failing so far. Wayne wanted to do all he could to prepare us if we encountered more of the same beyond Bol.

For the umpteenth time, Ahmed assures us that the capital was a mere day or so away but by now none of us believed that.

Instead, we did what we could to prepare ourselves, snapping up every single drinks can in the small town, stowing them as personal insurance inside clothes at the foot of lockers, hiding them in bedding.

The reason we hid them was because a few of my companions on the truck had reported money and other items going missing from their belongings. One of us on board G was a thief, and in the desert, where liquid was infinitely more important than money, we feared our personal supplies might not be safe.

Unable to quieten the chatter in my head telling me worse was to come, I sought out Mark. Wayne seemed to trust him more than the other mechanic, Mike, and certainly more than Terry.

"What do you think? Will we make it to N'djamena?"

"That's the plan."

"I know it's the plan, but what's your opinion. I heard Abdhul says it'll take us a day or so, but I've heard that before."

"You don't really want to know," Mark shrugged. "What difference will it make?"

"I don't know. I suppose I just want to prepare for the worst."

"Alright. I'll give you any odds we'll breakdown again in the next two days." He put a sympathetic arm on my shoulder. "Well you asked."

***

Mark was wrong, but not by much.

We weren't far from Bol when the oil pressure gauge burned out but as there wasn't anything that could be done about it the trucks lumbered on, grinding to a halt in the sand at ever decreasing intervals.

That first day out of the town we clawed a heroic ten miles on the clock over a day lasting fourteen hours.

The following day we managed twelve miles by setting out just after 5am.

But on the third day we managed only a morning pushing the trucks before my ears detected a change in the engine noise, from its usual roaring and grinding to a flat pfutting sort of sound.

G truck's engine spluttered for a moment then everything went silent. Stillness descended on us like a cloak. No-one spoke. No-one had the heart to.

All I could think was that we were three days out of Bol, which lay in God knows which direction. We were three days into the water supplies we'd replenished there. How long would what we'd got left on board last?

Like some sort of ghostly parade, moving automatically without speaking to each other, we went through the motions of setting up camp around the two trucks. The only thing differentiating this new breakdown spot from all the others was a small bank of sand where a few bushes and a spindly tree survived, enough to offer a little shade from the heat. Bizarrely, under the tree was a bed of straw, perhaps left there by local traders, who had passed this way and used the opportunity to stop.

That at least suggested we were not entirely off the beaten track, but still there was no sign of life or resources, or the water we'd need if we were to be here more than a few hours. Judging from the grim expression on Wayne's face, as he dipped down under the truck again, that was likely.

None of us had the heart to ask him what was wrong this time or how long the repairs would take. Wayne had succumbed to the sickness bug and every ten minutes or so would re-appear from his labouring to dash behind the bushes, his face pale beneath the grubby oil stains he wore like a mask.

Soon bits of the fuel pump lay alongside the vehicle: apparently Liwa's judge was exacting a second penalty on us, having sold Terry fuel that was dirty. Clods of goat hair, dung, straw, had clogged the fuel injectors. The only way to clear them was painstakingly by hand. This was going to be a long haul – just as the company name promised, though the irony no longer amused me.

***

"We need to see if there's water anywhere close. Otherwise some of us are going to have to walk back to Bol with the containers," Tom said.

"Thirty miles? In this heat? We'd have no chance, even supposing we could find the way." For once I thought Kitty Chris had a point. Everywhere looked the same as everywhere else and we already knew that heat does strange things to the mind. Bol was no metropolis and we'd only have to be a half degree out in our calculations to sail past it into more of the same desert we'd barely survived before.

"Let's split into search parties. None of us should go off alone here," Will suggested. "And make sure you leave decent footprints in the sand so you can follow them back."

"Wind permitting," Annie said grimly.

We paired up and headed off, at least those strong enough to do so, drawing a kind of compass in the sand so that we had six search parties heading out at different angles, hopefully covering all bases.

Tom and I went what we assumed was north, though who really knew since none of us carried compasses and this was long before the era of mobile phones with their apps.

Our only guide was the sun, but in the bleached sky even its trail was deceptive, often lost in a white haze of dust, sucked upwards from the parched ground. We walked for around an hour without spotting the slightest change in the scenery. We saw nothing but sky and sand and eventually had no choice but to turn back.

Others were already back, sitting despondently by the bushes again. We barely had time to join them before someone spotted our Scottish couple, Kathy and Keith, yomping through the sand back to camp. "Got it! Got it!" Kathy, always the spokesperson for the two, yelled - the closest I'd ever seen her to excitement.

Quite how they'd spotted the small hole in the ground in the middle of an endless plain of sameness I have no idea. Any structure that might once have existed around this tiny well had long since vanished.

What caught their eyes, Kathy said, were a few dried sticks on the ground which they thought might be useful as firewood. Only when they reached them did they see they were laid in a pattern around a hole, as if some other travellers wanted to be able to find the spot again.

***

We celebrated with a mug of warm Bol water each, trusting that we now dare dig into our meagre supplies because we could replace them. Then we established a chain of people stretching from the camp to the well to refill our containers.

Tom, who went with Keith the whole way back to the well, reported that its walls were half-dissolved, the water itself the colour of toffee. It was too narrow to leverage the containers down into it so they used cooking pans to carefully dip into the water and decant it from there into the first of our water carriers. Each time they pulled the pan up animal turds and dead insects bobbed on the surface of the water; the deeper they went the more sludge came with it.

But now at least we had something to do other than sit in the sand and feel sorry for Wayne: we'd been using water sterilising tablets on and off but the foul state of this abandoned well called for a great deal more. While the fittest carried water back to camp the rest of us set up our own laboratory to do the best we could not to kill ourselves with it.

Firstly we siphoned the water through a pair of thick jeans, which removed at least some of the shit and wildlife. It dripped slowly through the denim into a cooking pan which was then boiled with a lid on for twenty minutes. Finally, sterilising tablets were added before the water went back into the container.

I can see the problems with this system now: the water was going back into the same containers it had been carried in before all this cleaning took place. And none of us had thought, or actually would have been able, to clean those containers of any lingering microbes of disease. But what the heck; at least we weren't going to die of thirst today. Nor the next day or however long Wayne needed for his repairs - so long as the well held out under the demands of our very large group.

We didn't realise that was a possibility until the next morning when we began the whole routine all over again. The first people to the well found the bloated, stinking corpse of a small goat floating on the water's surface.

From the level of decomposition it had reached, it had clearly been in the water some days if not weeks, its corpse dislodged from somewhere under the surface by the disturbance we'd caused. There was nothing for it but to haul the body out and resume panning the water into the containers.

The best we could do was increase the cleaning regime by boiling the water for even longer and adding double the recommended level of water tablets. The well had been the death of that poor goat; we would do all we could not to let it be the death of us.

***

Yet somehow the thought of dying had ceased to worry me, I realised, as I returned to the bank in the shade after a long stint on water filtering.

We had been stuck in Chad for something like nineteen days and I'd spent much of that time in fear: fear of running out of food or water, fear of being stuck here forever, fear of being shot or attacked by people who seemed hostile to us, fear that the man leading our expedition was hopeless and capable only of leading us into more disaster.

I don't know why the fear quietly melted away after all that time. It makes no sense to me now when I look back: nothing had changed.

These days when I lead workshops I counsel people to name their fears on the basis that however grim our fears are, they have a fraction less power over us when we shine a light on them. Rather like the tricks used by film directors who terrify us with dark sets and creepy music until the moment the monster is finally revealed and somehow we are less scared because we know what we are dealing with.

I had travelled from England with my own demons. Even before Chad I was a little scared to be in places I had no sense of, among peoples I had no cultural connections with. Nor was I alone in that when I considered the ways in which we'd allowed the plastic walls of the trucks to separate us from the peoples we passed – people who in all likelihood only wanted the same from life as we did.

For the first time since leaving England I could see the monster right in front of me. But now it wasn't about strangeness but something purely practical: the fact that we needed food, water, health and shelter to survive. Over the last almost three weeks all of those things had been in the balance. They still were but somehow we had survived; were still surviving.

However much I might struggle with the oppressive closeness of the truck, with this new discomfort over whether Tom and I were in a relationship, the fact was that most of us were pulling together.

Finding and cleaning the water was a group effort every bit as much as pushing the truck was. We all wanted to survive and in helping each other we were naturally helping ourselves. Whether we made it out of the Chad desert would depend on us all. Which meant I could ease up on the controls a bit.

Back home, being in control was my way of handling a mistaken belief that I was responsible for everyone else's happiness.

It sounds crazy because there was a very real possibility we would die in Chad. But there was also this peace, almost relief, that now I'd accepted the only thing I could do was my best - along with everyone else - then the rest was out of my hands.

***

On our third day marooned in the desert this new peace of mind was tested by the arrival of four men riding on camels travelling towards our camp. They were like a throwback to our weeks in North Africa, dressed as the Arabs do for desert conditions, faces and bodies entirely swaddled in cotton robes to protect against the sand and dust.

They rode two to each camel and strapped to the saddles were huge sacks stuffed with something – presumably to sell. Their animals made the weight look effortless, every step a soft glide gobbling up the distance, soundless. Even as they came close the only noise was the creak of the leather saddles.

The men stayed where they were, sitting high above us, only their eyes showing through a narrow gap in the cloth so we could not tell what expressions they wore. For long minutes we stared back, until, eventually, someone must have alerted our guide to the visitors; Abdhul emerged from Q truck's cab to greet the strangers.

It was the first time since he'd joined us that I'd seen our guide flustered. He exchanged some words with them in a language I didn't understand but his body language betrayed a certain nervousness; as though he was unsure of these desert visitors.

"Do they want a cup of tea?" Annie suggested, reaching for a mug and raising it towards them, pretending to drink from it, a question in her expression.

Still the men remained sitting on their camels above us, moving their heads to survey the camp and tents and the vehicles off to one side.

Finally, they spoke a few words to each other and our guide. We watched as they ordered their camels to lie so they could dismount, sliding silently and gracefully onto the sand. Abdhul led them to where we had a fire burning so we could boil our filthy well water; then took it on himself to collect a few abandoned mugs from the ground nearby and thrust them at Annie indicating she should indeed make tea.

All the while he was moving around, assisting Annie with pouring and adding dried milk, his eyes were shifting from one visitor to another, then to the loads on the back of the camels: watching, assessing, we knew not what.

Eventually the men began speaking to Abdhul again, in their own language. From the staccato tone of their words, and his garbled responses, I sensed they were questioning him. Every so often they and he would turn their eyes towards the trucks, or over to the edge of the camp where Terry sat with his couriers. But without any comprehension of their language we were helpless to join the conversation so we simply sat in silence, watching the men as keenly as our guide seemed to be doing.

***

An hour merged into two. The mugs were topped up. The questions and careful studying continued. I began to wonder whether the desert code meant we must ask these sullen visitors to stay and eat with us.

I hoped not. Though I couldn't put my finger on it their arrival had shifted the whole atmosphere: it felt tight, edgy, as if we they and we were waiting for the other to make a move. It struck me how not being able to understand words forces you to pay greater attention to what gestures and facial expressions are communicating. The energy I was picking up was uncomfortable: an undercurrent of suspicion and distrust. I didn't know which side it was coming from.

The visitors finally made a move, after a particularly loud - but equally incomprehensible to us – exchange with Abdhul.

They walked softly over to the bags attached to their saddles, pulling from them a whole collection of ornate swords and daggers, their shiny silver blades decorated with script and carvings. I assumed we were being invited to buy them but before any of us could get close to look Abdhul began shouting, waving an arm as if to say they should be off. It no longer looked to be a friendly gesture.

Barely were they mounted and gliding away before our guide, red-faced and sweating, ran over to where Terry had remained throughout this encounter. We heard more raised voices though we couldn't make out the words. Then Heather strode over to the campfire.

"What's this all about?" Will asked.

"He's worried about those men. He says they were too interested in the trucks; much too interested."

She seemed to be weighing something up in her mind. "OK, so he says he believes they'll return and kill us so they can have the trucks."

"What?!!!" A collective gasp from the rest of us.

"But that's mad. They couldn't kill all of us," I said.

"They wouldn't need to would they?" This was Mark, sensible as ever. "They'd only need to kill one or two and the rest of us would give them the trucks."

"Shit! What the effing fuck do we do now?" Kitty Chris asked.

"Abdhul told them we were moving on now. That's why he said they couldn't stay and eat with us. Because we're expected in N'djamena and we're so late we know there'll already be people searching for us. He said we'd be leaving right after they did and if we didn't make it to the capital tonight search parties would come and find us."

"Can't we do what he wants then? Move a bit away from the camp? We haven't pushed the bloody trucks for three days. We've had a chance to get some energy back," Will said.

"Nope. I've checked with Wayne. The fuel pump's in bits and if we push now we'll just get sand in all the exposed parts and ruin everything he's done. Be back to square one."

Heather looked over at the truck where Wayne continued to labour. "I suggest we arrange an all-night guard. We should have eight people awake at all times, two looking in each direction. Take turns through the night.

"And you need to look on board and find anything you can we can use as a weapon if we get attacked."

I could hardly believe we were having this conversation. It seemed so much like something from fiction. And yet a part of me understood that however badly off we considered ourselves in this broken, famished, lawless land, our trucks had real currency.

If they could be made to work they could make the difference between power and subjugation, strength and weakness, wealth or death. There was the personal wealth we carried too, meaningless to us in these surroundings where only water and safety counted, but valuable trading currency for people who learned to do whatever was necessary to survive during the long years of civil strife.

I drew an early guard as the light faded, jumping at every sound coming from one of the tents where I guessed no-one was actually sleeping. I knew when it came my turn to be relieved I would no more be able to sleep than fly.

In fact being inside the tent was in many ways worse because I could now only imagine what each whispered instruction between the guards meant, conjure up footsteps moving just around our circle whether or not they were really there. I could hear Abdhul pacing - a sound that went on all that night - endlessly patrolling the borders of our little encampment, even while the guards sat, alert to any slight shift in the light or the darkness on the horizon.

***

The night stretched to an eternity, as nights sometimes do when anxiety stalks our minds.

I'd say it was the longest night of my life except that at some point I must have slept for it was light coming through the cotton of the inner tent that woke me. Dawn was here. And we were still here, and still alive.

We had made it through the night and daylight made everything seem a little easier.

Suspicion still lurked that the bandits might be back, perhaps even with reinforcements; after all, our helplessness meant there was no need for cover of darkness. They could just as easily attack us during the day, especially if they had gone somewhere to get back-up or more modern weapons to subdue us with.

I saw Terry on his knees, talking to Wayne under the truck, perhaps persuading him it was more important to put things back together now than to clean every last grain of grit and debris from the engine and fuel system. It was worth the risk to put more miles between us and this camp, where we were sitting ducks.

By midday Wayne gave the signal that we could pack up, load the tents and water containers, restack the bags on board, prepare to leave. Moments later he fired the engine and for the first time in three days G's engine roared into exuberant life. We were underway once more.

CHAPTER 17

Bullet-pocked buildings in N'djamena

Not just underway. We were, finally, approaching the end of our desert ordeal.

It seemed unbelievable after more than three weeks of struggle. But sometime that afternoon the ground beneath G's tyres became firm enough for the truck to move forward under its own power rather than ours.

We weren't done with the pushing but the periods in between, when the trucks rolled forward at a few miles an hour, became longer.

Each mile we covered allowed us to breathe a little more. I hadn't realised the extent to which I had been holding my breath for weeks, not daring to relax for a moment in case of some fresh disaster.

Yet we continued to move, slowly and uncertainly, but increasingly without the familiar sounds of bogging and stalling which had been our accompaniment for so long.

We never did catch up with the elephants, but on Sunday 13th January, three long weeks after entering Chad, we spotted a colony of monkeys chattering in the tops of a clump of trees. Soon after, someone pointed out a griffin vulture, huge as a bush, squatting in another tree, perhaps waiting for the next group of clueless travellers.

A flock of marabou storks flew overhead, wings flapping a thunderous beat. And then, most thrilling of all, we watched a herd of gazelle flying through the air in a graceful stampede away from the noise of our trucks.

After that we drove through the first settlements since Bol, and the first that felt as though they might be a part of a world we half-recognised. People came out to greet us, pleading for cadeaux; we merely waved and called back to them, heady with the promise of an ending to our journey across the lake bed.

Then, incredibly, a road. Not much of one but we didn't care. If there was a road then it must lead somewhere, to people and maybe even to the capital. It lay across the middle of an empty savannah, an unlikely thread of tarmac with no signs or road markings. But to us it held all the promise and thrill of an airport runway, about to spirit us somewhere new.

For once Terry raised no objections when we asked for a photo stop. I think we wanted to record our survival, how we looked after three weeks in the desert wilderness; a way of remembering because of course memory fades and our stories get rewritten.

It would be so easy to convince myself I made it all up; we were never in any danger. Privileged westerners such as ourselves always come through, get assistance, can buy their way out of trouble.

Perhaps the demons I've described were really in my head, a dramatising of what amounted to not much more than the usual, expected ups and downs of overland travel.

That was why I wrote it down at the time. That is why, when I look back through the pages of my journals, I can still hear my doubts as loudly as I did then: I didn't believe we'd survive.

It may also be why, almost four decades since we were in Chad, some of us are still in touch with those with whom we shared that scary desert crossing.

Once I asked Heather was it really so bad? Were we ever in danger of dying? She, after all, as a courier, was in a better position than me to know what Terry and Wayne were saying.

"Oh yes. I thought that too sometimes," she said. "That we wouldn't make it," and her eyes took on a faraway look as she too remembered.

***

Before we climbed back into the trucks we emptied the footwells of luggage, stacking the bags and cooking equipment back into the trailers.

Next we collected wood. Terry really seemed to believe that N'djamena was not far and we should get enough firewood to see us through the couple of days we'd spend in the capital.

We also changed out of our desert clothes. N'djamena was a city that had been under siege and was only just emerging from that time. It was likely there would be police checks and military stop points. The better presented we were, the less likely it was that we would be mistaken for insurgents.

We were wary, especially in light of *Shoestring*'s warning, but nothing could dampen the surge of expectation running through the back of G truck when we were once again fully underway, tyres biting easily on the tarmac, more and more evidence of life as we passed through another village and then another.

Even Cockney Steve, his bandaged shoulder gripped across his chest, managed a triumphant smile as the first rooftops of the capital shone into view.

Somehow, with enough luck to last several lifetimes, we'd made the crossing.

***

Our first glimpse of N'djamena was a salutary reminder of how lucky we'd been. No building we saw had escaped the crossfire of battles between government troops and Libyan-backed rebels from the north of Chad. Every façade of what must once have been an elegant city was scarred with the grey pockmarks of bullets. Deeper into the city some buildings had not survived at all, but sat with their skeletons and innards on show, ugly holes between the concrete and steel.

Those structures that still stood were mostly covered in political graffiti, words painted like red gashes across their once white surfaces.

Yet some semblance of normality was returning to the capital. Alongside the main road was a line of fruit stalls, their surfaces piled high with rosy tomatoes, lemons brighter than sunlight, and fat bananas.

The juxtaposition was incongruous, - and in some ways a reminder of the past three weeks when our lives hung in the balance and yet we'd continued to eat and sleep and talk to each other.

Life goes on in even the strangest circumstances and perhaps, after all these years of turmoil, the city's people no longer thought their circumstances strange. They had grown used to the child soldiers on street corners, fingering gun belts aggressively as though to ward off their own fear. Nearby, the few trees that had survived N'djamena's battering were embarking on their annual cycle of growth and change: bright carpets of fallen pink and yellow blossom contrasting with the greyness.

Between these two worlds local people went about their everyday marketing, undeterred by the soldiers' brooding presence and the shell-shocked buildings that were their backdrop.

We received a military escort to the main police station where officials needed to see our passports: an army truck led the way while another followed close behind. Heather collected our passports and vanished inside a concrete building. She returned empty-handed with the news the police needed to keep our documents overnight and we'd be placed under 'house arrest' at a holding site while we waited to hear if we'd be allowed to remain in the country.

So the army vehicles formed their escort again and led us deeper into the city, tantalisingly close to all the sights and smells and sounds of a world that we weren't going to be allowed to enter. We hardly had time to lament our misfortune – so near and yet so far – before the convoy began a slow turn, up an avenue and then through high locked gates – into the manicured and elegant grounds of the Chadian Hotel.

As house arrests go, this one took the biscuit: not only did the hotel have proper toilets, a washroom, laundry and restaurants, it had a beautiful terrace overlooking a large swimming pool. We were instructed to pitch our tents in the gardens but no-one had the patience to fiddle with tents and cooking equipment right away. Within a few minutes of arriving every one of us, except for those whose turn it was to guard the trucks, was in the pool, or sitting with ice cold beers on the terrace. We could scarcely believe our luck.

It didn't matter that the only meal on the menu was chicken and chips nor that, as we looked closer, the hotel's paintwork was peeling, its windows dusty and opaque. It didn't even matter that thieves prowled the gardens, looking for a chance to snatch whatever they could from our tents and trailers.

We had coped with much worse, as had N'djamena, and knew this was no more than we should expect from a part of Africa that had come through things we couldn't even imagine.

There were other guests, among them a team of French vets - and, bizarrely, an American air crew, whose self-appointed spokesman, introducing himself as Larry, was obviously delighted to have a new audience, especially one that included women.

Larry was a bland looking character, pale flesh squirming from the top of his swimming shorts, cropped hair that sat flat as a plate on the top of a pink scalp. He had a habit of talking with his mouth open while he tucked into a huge serving of fries.

I couldn't bring myself to watch the food churning about in his mouth while he held forth, preferring to move my chair away to watch the pool where Annie was swimming lengths up and down, hardly seeming to stir the water.

Still, there was no escaping his voice or the fact that some of the others found the prospect of baiting Fat Larry irresistible.

"So what are you really doing here mate?" Cockney Steve coaxed him.

"Told you. We're working for Esso. Can't tell you what. It's all top secret," he smirked

"Aaw, come on. We're supposed to be on the same side. Special relationship and all that."

Larry continued to chew. I could hear him. "OK. Put it this way right, we're not supposed to be involved over here. Not our fight and all that."

"And?"

"Someone wants to know what's going on. Just keep an eye on the news is what I'll say,"

Larry's voice dropped to a stage whisper. "A few months' time you'll see what we're doing here. Take it from me."

"Important business then?"

"You betcha."

***

The only Africans in evidence were those serving us at the bar or sweeping the white paths which criss-crossed the hotel gardens. Until the evening that is, when the hotel's basement transformed to a nightclub.

It was sticky and smelt of bodies the way pubs used to do before they got gentrified. The later it got, the louder the music, the more Chadian women appeared, apparently looking for someone to pay them for sex.

Any time I moved someone would sidle up to me asking if I'd like to go to my room with them. It became impossible to sit at the bar, or to dance.

I thought the restrooms might be quieter and went to escape the press of bodies for a moment, but the women were there too, loudly arguing with each other, presumably about who was charging too little or stealing who's business.

It was hot and sticky in the toilets and wet underfoot. I assumed the sinks had flooded but as my eyes adjusted to the bright lights I realised I wasn't wading through water but urine. None of the women were bothering to use the stalls; rather they squatted against the far wall to wee.

I gave up trying to pretend any of it was ok. After the emptiness of Chad it felt like there was too much noise, too much press and too many people. I went back to my tent.

Hours later, when Will woke me stumbling into the tent, he told me by the end of the night competition had become so intense the girls were asking customers just $1 for sex.

He also claimed some of our group had found the offer too hard to resist. This was still early days in terms of our understanding of AIDS. It had only been diagnosed in the UK a couple of years earlier. Still, I was surprised to hear any of my companions wanted to take the risk.

"Something I need to tell you though," Will went on.

"Hmmm," I was still half asleep.

"I'm going to leave the trip."

"What for good?"

"No, just for a couple of weeks. I'm out of cash. Reckon I'll fly ahead to Bangui. It'll give me two weeks to get some money sent from home before you lot turn up."

"I'm sure Tom will lend you money if that's the reason." There was a long silence. "Is it?"

"Part of it old girl," Will seemed to be considering.

I waited in the silence, just reaching out one hand to rest on where I thought his must be, so he knew I was listening.

"I feel better when I drink. People seem to like me then. But I've been getting sick so in the end I saw the doc. He said the drink's killing me. Said I have to dry out.

"He wanted to send me to some clinic somewhere, but that's not really my style."

"So, Africa?"

"Yeah. So Africa. Only it was hard because the rest of you were getting drunk all the time, especially in Europe, and then when we couldn't get booze any more it was like a ton of rocks landed on my head.

"I wish you'd told me, told us. Maybe we could have helped you a bit more." Memories of our whiskied tent and Will struggling with what he said was bronchial pneumonia came back to me. I'd been helpful to him but I hadn't been the good friend he needed. Amazing what we choose not to see when it inconveniences us.

I squeezed his hand a little tighter. "It sounds like you're doing the right thing. I'll miss you though."

***

Will was not the only one departing. As soon as the police released our passports, satisfied we were who we said we were, Cockney Steve headed to the airport - only to return later because his flight was stuck for 24 hours in Zaire. He finally got away two days after that.

We got a letter from Steve once the trip reached East Africa. His UK doctor said the collar bone had set beautifully which made me wonder if he might have regretted leaving when he did. When we all met up back home, however, he was certain he'd made the right choice and was saving for a return trip, this time with a more reputable company who might get him to the wildlife parks in one piece to take the photos he'd come to Africa to capture.

Will disappeared the next morning without a goodbye. I could only pray we would see him again. There was something so very vulnerable about him, for all the bonhomie. I wanted to know he'd be alright.

CHAPTER 18

N'djamena was a carnival and, let loose by the local police, we plunged into everything it had to offer: elegant mosques with towers reaching almost to heaven; government buildings designed in recent years to mimic centuries-old Islamic architecture, domed and ornately carved with sparkling white forecourts; the Christian church which had not fared well – only its façade survived, like a cut-out silhouetted against the sky.

At the heart of this cultural mish-mash was the city market, colourful as a circus, crammed with cheap imports from bright yellow plastic buckets to toxic skin lighteners.

Like every African city we'd encountered, N'djamena in the 1980s was caught between past and future, old and new, wealth and poverty, western and African values and norms: the clinically clean pharmacies, shelves fully stocked with every drug modern science has dreamed up, a stone's throw from street stalls peddling traditional cures such as dried animal pelts. The shoppers and traders too were as vibrant as the things they bought and sold, living their lives alongside the dour, threatening and ever-present soldiers and police.

My favourite pastime was people-watching from one of the stands where they served fresh milk shakes. After the weeks of near-starvation, these were as welcome as a lottery win, made from plentiful fresh fruit: mango, banana and paw paw which went into a blender with generous amounts of sugar, dried milk powder, ice cubes on top. The mix that came out was as thick as ice cream and as invigorating as the pulse of this city after the empty desert.

Like many things that we taste when we are away from home, I was never able to make such amazing shakes for myself again, despite using all the same ingredients.

***

Some aspects of city life were less welcome. We quickly learned it was better not to venture out alone. One of the women on Q truck narrowly escaped being raped when she decided to head into town by herself.

On her way a man jumped her from behind, wrestling her into the shell of a house from where they couldn't be seen. As she struggled he began to rip at her clothes, completely unbothered by her shouts, as if certain there was too much fear still in N'djamena for cries of help to be answered. Remarkably, she kept her head and allowed her attacker to force her to the ground.

Once they were there, him fumbling on top of her to open his trousers, he lost the advantage of greater strength. With one arm now free she thrust an elbow up into the man's nose as his face hovered, expressionless, above her own. It was enough to stall him: as he reflexively pulled both hands away to encircle his bleeding nose she pulled herself out from under him and made a frantic dash back out into the street.

She heard the man scramble to his feet to come after her but at that very moment a guard emerged from the steps of the US consulate, just up the street from the derelict building she'd escaped. It was this guard who delivered her, shaky but relieved, back to our hotel camp.

Annie recounted this story to me. "I got off lightly it seems," she said.

"What do you mean? Were you attacked too?"

"Only for my money, in the marketplace. Look…" She peeled back the edge of her t-shirt and I saw a deep red weal.

"What's that? What happened?"

"Someone grabbed my purse and it took a long time and a lot of force for the leather to snap. The guy wouldn't give up, even though I was yelling."

"How much did you lose?"

"Oh not much. I never carry much cash on me. But I'm annoyed. I liked that purse and it's seen me through loads of walking trips."

"Sounds like word's out that we're here now. Mark told me the guys chased away some men who'd got into the hotel grounds and were trying to steal some of the big bags."

"Yeah. Shame, because I like this place. I'd love to have been able to spend more time wandering around with my camera."

***

The knowledge that we'd become a target meant we were pleased to learn our paperwork was sorted, and we'd shortly be ready to resume our travels, was greeted with relief. We were heading across the border into Cameroon, grateful for the time we'd had to rest and recharge after Chad, and not the least put out when Terry announced we'd be making an early start to get to the ferry.

Unfortunately, our willingness to sacrifice a few hours' sleep was wasted. Having rumbled down to the water which formed the border, we waited for what seemed like hours for something to happen. Finally we learned the ferry was broken so it was back to the Chadian Hotel for another night.

Most of my companions decided to head to the market for more milk shakes but the thought of the sticky liquid now brought a wave of nausea lurching up into my throat. I retreated to my tent to lie in the shade.

As the day wore on the nausea sunk lower, down into my belly. My arms and legs felt leaden, solid as tree trunks, and so did my head.

Sometime later the hot flushes started, searing up my throat and face until sweat was pouring from my forehead.

My tee-shirt and shorts were quickly sodden, though I was not coherent enough to know if this was sweat or I had somehow wet myself. Everything was burning up: as though I was lying inside a bread oven.

When the others got back, Tom came to check on me. He took one look at my white face and the sweat pouring from my forehead and ran to fetch a bowl of cold water from the hotel washrooms. He raised me up so I could rinse my hands and feet in it, then damped a cloth for my forehead. For a while I felt a little more human but as night fell the cramps began - like hot needles piercing my insides and turning everything to liquid.

When I could no longer hold everything in, I pulled a sarong around me, planning to dash into the reception to use the toilets. But even before I'd unzipped the tent I'd messed myself. Shamed, I swapped the sarong for a towel, bundling the soiled material into a ball, and gingerly made my way around to the washrooms to try and clean myself and the sarong up.

I did what I could but my legs were shaking and scarcely seemed able to support me. I needed to lie down again. I could rinse my clothes properly in the morning.

No sooner had I made it back to the tent than another cramp shuddered through my guts. This time I made it to the toilets but my bowels had turned entirely to liquid, burning like acid as everything poured out of me.

All night long the cramps continued, preventing me from getting any rest; and with each new episode I felt I had even less control. Three times I had to change my clothes until, on the fourth occasion, I found the front door of the hotel locked against me. I was forced to squat behind one of the trees in the gardens, praying I could do enough to cover the evidence.

In truth, there wasn't much left to come out. But those early hours of the morning, when the only sounds are of others lost in sleep, when the darkness has its own secret quality, were among the loneliest I had experienced since starting out from the UK.

***

The next morning someone packed my tent up for me since I no longer had Will to do so.

Then Tom and Annie helped me on board the truck where the departure of Will, Cockney Steve and another of the men meant there was room to make me a kind of bed along one of the bus seats. I lay on Aussie Gai's sarong while she and Tom took turns to wipe a wet cloth across my face.

Even through the haze of nausea and fever I was aware the mood on G changed as we crossed the border into Cameroon.

In rare moments of consciousness I glimpsed advertisement hoardings written in English, promoting familiar brands. There were petrol stations too, and then the excitement of a game park: my eyes were shut but my companions reported seeing a herd of elephants, monkeys darting from the verges, and even a lioness in the distance.

I could hear their cameras clicking, sense the renewed energy on board. This was, after all, what so many of them had signed up for – the wild side of Africa. But I slept through most of the park, taking only occasional small sips of water. I was afraid that anything I put into my system would come straight through me and lion country was not a good time to ask the truck to stop so I could find a bush to squat behind.

That evening we simply pulled off the road to camp and again someone put my tent up for me. Later, Tom came by to let me know a local man had visited our makeshift campsite to warn that the area was full of scorpions and we should take care.

His warning played over in my head when the cramps began again at midnight. I'd eaten nothing but a few spoonfuls of soothing soup cooked up especially for me. But apparently my system couldn't even cope with that. I fought the urge to get up and squat for as long as I could, torn between the fears of soiling myself again and the scorpions.

Eventually, knowing there was no chance of sleep unless I emptied my guts, I reached for the torch Will had left in my care when he departed. I found a place a little distance from the camp where I could squat, playing the torch all around me like a prison searchlight: sure enough, three scorpions scuttled away from its beam. Perhaps they were even less tempted by me than I was by them. Either way, I made it back to the tent without being stung.

***

The following morning I began to pass blood. My insides were beginning to devour themselves. There was no mistaking the fat black clots which lay on the soil where I had squatted.

The sight of them scared me and when we pulled into a town, and Heather said we had two hours to shop for food, I determined to find some medical help. None of the anti-diarrhea tablets the nurses had been feeding me had touched the sickness.

"I'll come with you. You might need help," Tom suggested tentatively.

He had no need to be shy about it. I was grateful for his company, glad for this strange understanding we'd established which had somehow stopped short, perhaps because of the Chad desert, of turning into a proper relationship.

It was Tom who hailed a passing cab and told him to take us to the nearest medical centre, and Tom who kept his arm around me as we slowly walked into a low white building where the only other people were three African women sitting on a wooden bench.

There was no sign of a receptionist, or any staff, nor any sound to indicate that there were surgeries in progress. The women simply shuffled up to make room for me at the end of the bench, hoisting the babies they held closer to their breasts.

Tom set me down then stood alongside me, preparing for us to wait.

I knew, however, that when Terry said we had two hours he would not hang about if we were delayed. We'd be expected to catch up with the trucks under our own steam. I looked up at Tom, hoping perhaps he might go in search of someone, but he seemed oblivious to my impatience. As the minutes ticked by, fear of being left behind overcame fear of being a nuisance: I hauled myself back up, using Tom's arm to pull on, and went to investigate whether there might be anyone working down one of the corridors.

There was no-one down the first: just a row of closed doors and silence, but around the corner I could hear the quiet tapping of typewriter keys. I followed the sound to an open door, spotting a European man sitting there, casually dressed in slacks and a short-sleeved shirt. I cleared my throat and he turned to see what the interruption was, clearly irritated at being disturbed.

"Quest'ce que vous voulez?"

For the life of me I couldn't remember any of my French so I stood there with my mouth open, stupidly silent.

This time his voice was softer. "English, American?"

I nodded and the fact he'd spoken to me in English, kindly, was all it took for the tears to start flowing down my cheeks. "I think I need help. I'm sick."

Now he looked pained. "I'm sorry. The clinic is shut. You must come back on Monday. I am only here to do the paperwork I don't have time for."

A sob escaped me then. I didn't know what to do. Monday was still two days away.

The poor man spoke again. "What is the matter? Monday is not a long time to wait. Is there pain? Tell me what is the matter?"

I shook my head: "No pain but I'm scared. I am passing blood. There was a lot of blood this morning. I can't eat or drink."

The man turned fully to face me now and started firing more questions: where I was staying, what I was doing here, how long had I had this condition?

I was too lost in my own misery to properly appreciate his kindness in breaking off from the office work he'd given up his weekend for on in order to help me.

"You need tests. Perhaps the others will wait for you for a few days?"

"I don't think so," for the first time I almost smiled. The thought was preposterous.

"Then I cannot do much more than give you medicine," my Good Samaritan said. He turned and scribbled on a piece of paper. "You must take these, eight a day, and four of these. With food or they will be too much for your stomach."

As I reached for the prescription he held onto it for a moment. "But I do not advise travel. It is dangerous for you. If you vomit, if these medicines do not work, you must go to hospital straight away. Immediately."

I nodded to show him I understood, then reached into my money belt to pay for the consultation. He shook his head and gently patted the hand which now held his prescription. "No money. The clinic is closed and I am not working. Just promise me you do as I say. You are very sick."

Only later, lying inside the truck again as we headed deeper into Cameroon, did I wonder about those three women. The doctor had said the clinic was closed. Did that mean they were there waiting for it to open on Monday, as he'd initially advised me to do? Two days wait to see a doctor? All those people who queue overnight outside Selfridges to snap up a Boxing Day sales bargain: they have no idea...

Not that I was in any position to judge, having somehow wept my way into jumping the queue of patients, by virtue of my accent and pale skin.

CHAPTER 19

While everyone else tucked into a breakfast of fried bread and tomatoes I swallowed down a few teaspoons of rice to cushion the effects of the Flagyl and Bactrim - both hefty drugs used for treating dysentery, malaria, pneumonia and plenty of other things that the doctor presumably wanted to attack since, in the absence of blood tests, it wasn't clear what I was suffering from.

It was no good. A few minutes later the whole lot came up. As did the small amount of soup I tried, and later a simple glass of water. Dimly I was aware that if I couldn't keep anything down, especially the medicine, I had no hope of getting better.

After that the hallucinations began. I could swear I heard the others talking about my death and how on earth they would get my body home. A moment later I knew we were under attack from a herd of elephants, about to be crushed underfoot.

The images came and went, each weirder and more scary than the last. I realised I was getting worse not better, and that for all my fear of leaving the truck, I'd got to the point where my life might depend on me doing so. I needed to regain consciousness for long enough to ask them to stop so I could track back to the last town or settlement we'd passed through.

"I'll come with you," Tom said when I told him I needed someone to ask Wayne to stop so I could get off. I was pathetically grateful that I wouldn't be alone. Annie and Gai packed a few of my things into a daypack, the truck stopped and suddenly it was just Tom and I, alone beside a track somewhere in Cameroon.

I suppose it was a blessing that I was too ill to worry more about what it might mean to strike out alone in the heart of Africa. I let Tom support me while he hailed the first vehicle that came by after G truck departed – a lorry transporting live chickens.

The nearest town was apparently called Garona, where a police point on the edge of the town ordered the driver to drop us at the gate of what looked like a brand new hospital, pristine white walls and clear glass windows.

Maybe it too was the result of foreign aid for it looked incongruous and out of place next to the homes and dusty streets we'd passed through.

It was Sunday and the hospital was closed, its gates padlocked, something I didn't understand until the next day when we returned and discovered there were no patients and therefore no need to keep it open at the weekend. It's likely none of the local people could afford such a shiny new hospital for their medical care.

So Tom led us back into Garona to find lodgings for the night.

I am not kidding when I say that what he found for us was the most luxurious accommodation we'd had since leaving home, a replica of the African huts of western imagination, with a wide straw roof, and mud exterior, but inside fitted with a hot shower and huge double bed shrouded in a mosquito net.

Just before I fell into a deep grateful sleep it occurred to me that this probably wasn't how Tom imagined our first night sharing a bed would be: lying next to a comatose skeletal version of the woman he'd fallen for - though I did snuggle into his back, grateful for the warmth of another human being.

***

We were at the hospital gates at 8am anticipating a queue but there'd been no need to rush. I was the only one there and as soon as the reception checked me in I was asked to follow a smiling porter down the corridor to a room.

The room was bare other than for a hospital bed with no covers, and a single chair. There was no sign of any medical paraphernalia. In the corner was a second door that opened to a private toilet and shower. The white walls were bare and the windows, looking out over a school field, curtainless. Still, its cleanness was reassuring and the very existence of a flushing toilet so close to the bed soothed me.

I nodded at the porter, hesitating. Was I supposed to get onto the bed or would he fetch sheets and make it up for me. "The doctor will come," was all he said, so I sat and waited on the edge of the bed. Tom plonked down on the chair.

Eventually we heard footsteps, the first sign of any other human life since the porter had departed. A man breezed in as if he were in a hurry, stethoscope around his neck and a few papers clutched in his hand. He was short and unsmiling, wearing a white coat over dark trousers, so I assumed he was a doctor. When he spoke it was in French, and directed at Tom rather than me; only occasionally did he glance over towards me as though I were an exhibit.

He asked to see the tablets I was supposed to be taking and nodded sagely before slipping them into the pockets of his pristine white coat. Then he left us.

"Did you understand any of that?" I asked Tom.

"Only the word amoeba. I wonder what happens now?"

"Please don't go. I'm not sure my French is up to this at the moment."

"Don't worry, I can stay," Tom said.

When several hours passed without any sight of the doctor or porter I asked Tom to see what there was in my pack to lay on the plastic cover of the bed, which was sticking to my feverish body and making me sweat more.

Luckily Annie had packed my towel and sarong in the small rucksack I carried so I lay on one and pulled the other over me, drifting in and out of sleep. Eventually, around early afternoon a young nurse came singing into the room trundling a chrome trolley.

While she swabbed my arm and hooked me up to a drip she smiled reassuringly and spoke the only English words she knew - "London" and "Queen" over and over. Tom tried to ask her what was wrong with me but she'd reached the limits of her English and didn't appear to understand his French. Still smiling she reached in her pocket for a bottle of pills which she pressed into my hand, assured me of "London" one more time, and left us alone again.

"What now?" I looked at Tom.

"I think I'd better go and get you some water. It looks like they don't provide food or drink here. I'll go and find you some; I need to get somewhere to stay tonight anyway if you're going to be here."

Many years later, reporting on Save the Children projects in Uganda, I spent time in Kampala's hospital and discovered it is usual in parts of Africa for relatives to provide everything other than the actual medical care. Some families even camp out for days in the hospital alongside their loved ones, so they can be a part of patient care. But we were not to know this and there was no-one to ask, which added to the strangeness of the whole scenario.

***

Tom returned with a bottle of water, and later in the day nurse London returned to change my drip. I kept expecting to hear the sounds of a hospital: bottles clinking, trolleys wheeling up corridors, people calling out for the nurse or doctor. But everything was silent, cloaked in an almost eerie stillness, and so it remained the whole time I was there.

I did see the porter who'd bought us to this room again, towards the end of the day, when there were no more children's voices coming from the field outside and Tom had departed to find something to eat.

He was still smiling as he had been when we arrived. "How are you miss?"

"You speak English?"

"Oh yes. Little English. We learn in school. One day I want to go to London. I have friend there. You live in London miss?"

London again! I didn't want to talk about London. I ignored his question.

"Can you tell me what is wrong with me? What is my sickness?"

"Of course. This sickness comes from bites. From flies."

"You mean malaria?"

"Oh yes miss; that's it. Is very bad. You must stay here."

I hadn't spent enough time talking to Africans by then to know what I know now: that out of politeness some may tell you what they think you want to hear or, if they don't have an answer, make something up rather than appear rude by not answering your question.

The doctor put me right the next morning when he reappeared to check on me and change the medication again because I was still vomiting up the tablets. In stumbling French I asked if I had malaria. He looked amused and pulled out a pad from his top pocket, writing down something in French that I interpreted as amoebic dysentery.

It was as likely or not as malaria since – somewhat to my relief – there had been no bloods taken. But the good news was that finally, as the day wore on, it seemed *these* new tablets were finally making a difference. Not only was I able to keep them down but I even began to feel a little hungry, despite the fluids still dripping away into my blood.

For the second night on the trot I tried to keep Tom talking as long as I could. There was something very scary about the thought of being in an empty hospital at night, alone.

I soon found I wasn't alone. That night, after Tom had gone back to his lodgings, and I'd locked the door behind him, there was a faint knock.

"Miss? Are you alright miss?" The friendly porter had returned.

"I'm fine. I'm sleeping now thank you."

The footsteps retreated but half an hour later there was another knock. "Miss? Can I be your friend?"

I stayed silent, pretending to be asleep, praying he didn't have a key. Why was he here when the previous night there hadn't been anyone on duty? I held my breath tight.

"Miss. Can I come in? I like to be your friend."

It may well have been innocent, a genuine wish to make another friend in London, but I didn't dare risk opening the door, knowing there was no-one else around if that wasn't the case.

It was another achingly long night as my wannabe-friend returned at half hourly intervals long into the early hours, knocking the door and suggesting we become good friends. Morning could not come quickly enough for me.

***

When it did arrive it brought Tom bearing gifts: fresh bread, a hard boiled egg, triangles of processed cheese and some tomatoes. I promise you, that after almost a week of not being able to eat anything, and certain I'd turned a corner with the drugs and the drip, no food I've tasted before or since had so much flavour as that simple egg.

I might not be fully recovered but now I was not only eating but able to keep food and water down, and with the correct drugs at hand, I felt ready to begin the challenge of trying to catch up with the trucks. I expect my enthusiasm for leaving also owed something to not wanting to spend another night awake and alert to my night visitor.

Tom didn't argue but packed my things and assured the doctor as soon as we caught up with the trucks I could continue my rest and recovery. In the meantime I would take it gently and continue with the tablets.

The doctor nodded his agreement, perhaps keen to return the hospital to its normal empty state so he could get back to growing vegetables.

He said we should ask for the bill at a little office by the entrance gate. My treatment came to 6000CFA, the equivalent of £12, something it took the clerk at the gate a full half hour to process.

I'm sure that having a paying customer was such a novelty he wanted to make the most of this and took his tim,e typing me a receipt in triplicate, lingering over an array of rubber stamps as if he had no idea which to use. In the end he used them all.

We emerged blinking into the bright light of a Cameroon morning. We were now at least four days behind the trucks. The only thing on my mind was catching them up.

CHAPTER 20

Tom catching up on his journal while we wait for a lift

At the hospital gates Tom and I unfolded my Michelin map of Africa. We knew the trucks were heading through Cameroon into the Central African Republic, and on to its capital Bangui. It was pretty clear that there was only one main road running along this route.

Unfortunately, however, Tom hadn't seen any buses on the roads during his to-and fro-ing from the hospital. Even if he had, I doubted a lumbering bus would be able to close the gap that had opened up between us and Long Haul.

That left us with only one choice: hitching a ride.

We were making our way out to the edge of town together, beyond the last of the stalls and huts when, without warning, two tall boys appeared from nowhere, blocking the path. Before either of us had time to react the boys each grabbed one of Tom's arms, using their free hands to begin wrestling the money belt out from under his tee-shirt.

It took me a moment to register what was happening – that this was literally daylight robbery; as it dawned, I felt a wave of fury surge through me. I rounded on the boys and with a satisfying thwack slapped the one closest to me across the face.

It was enough to convince them we were too much trouble and they scarpered as quickly as they had come. But the incident was a reminder that now we'd left the trucks we really needed to start looking out for ourselves more carefully.

***

It was easy to convince the police that we had legitimate reasons to be heading south. All I did was wave the doctor's note and they signalled us through the checkpoint.

A half mile further on our luck was still in. A huge lorry carrying crates of Guinness rattled past us then, having registered our outstretched thumbs, slammed on the brakes and came screeching to a halt in a crash of protesting bottles.

"The others won't believe this! A lift from a beer lorry. Wonder if he'll offer us any free samples," I grinned at Tom.

We clambered up into the lorry, squeezed together on the passenger seat to avoid tangling with a massive gear stick.

"Thank you. Merci beaucoup," I turned my grin to the driver but he returned only a blank expression showing no hint of acknowledgement. My attempts to speak French dried up. I'd been expecting to make conversation but it was clear from the rigid way the driver held his body, how quickly he turned away, that talk was the last thing he wanted.

He looked young yet the skin of his face was marked by black lines and smudges, signs he had been in his fair share of fights. His mouth was clenched in a tight line and the eyes he'd turned away from me were an unhealthy yellow. Without waiting for us to settle in, the driver wrenched the vehicle back into the road and we realised it was going to be too noisy to talk, even if the driver had wanted it.

The next town of any significance, according to our map, was N'Gaoundere, around 200 miles to the south, and, despite our sullen driver, as we rattled along, gobbling up the miles, my spirits rose. I could visualise us as if on an aerial map of Cameroon, the trucks lumbering along at their usual 4-5 miles an hour, stopping for loo breaks photos and kitty shopping, while we narrowed the gap by travelling at maybe four times that speed.

The road began to climb and that too was a cause for celebration because I knew those great blue beasts would struggle even more on hills. On either side of the road the fields were replaced by forest; the air felt cool and through the lorry's open windows we drank in the smells of lush vegetation and forest life.

Once or twice I glimpsed flashes of colour as birds darted through the sun dapples.

We sped on for hours until the light began to dim, and the first weak lamps of a town came into view.

N'Gaoundere seemed to be very much a one-street town, with all its life clustered close to the main road. Without speaking the lorry driver pulled into the verge, outside a low wooden shack with the word 'hotel' scrawled in white letters across a roof made from corrugated metal.

Stiffly, we clambered down from the cab, preparing to thank the driver for the lift. But even before we'd had time to hitch our packs onto our backs he was in our faces, a hand thrust forward touching Tom's stomach.

"You pay me now."

How foolish we were to think the lift had been anything other than a business transaction. With so little public transport, and few people owning their own vehicles, paying for lifts on passing trucks is a way of life in Africa. I was embarrassed by my naiveite.

"How much shall we give him?"
"Dunno. A thousand CFA each?" Tom suggested.

"I suppose if the hospital cost 6000 that's fair."

But when we handed the driver four notes he angrily shook his head and spat into the dust.

"You pay now. This is not enough."

"How much then?" Tom asked.

"Ten thousand. That is the price for this road."

I'm sure it wasn't, but by now a handful of interested spectators were gathering around. I was anxious to avoid them thinking we were rude westerners trying to exploit one of their own. After all, we'd be staying here tonight and something about the gloom of twilight, the roughness of all the buildings, made me fearful. My gut was telling me this was not a safe place so we shouldn't make enemies.

"Forget it," I said to Tom. "Next time we'll agree a price before we get in." I handed over more notes which the driver resentfully stuffed into a tee-shirt pocket. He climbed back into the vehicle, tyres screeching to show his contempt for us as he departed.

"Suppose we'd better see if they've got room for us here," Tom looked doubtfully at the wooden shack. Nothing about it made me want to go in, but it didn't occur to us to look for another place. It was dark, and besides, I was far from fit and being bumped about in the lorry had taken its toll on my energy levels. Really I just wanted to lie down.

"Let's make sure we ask the price first though," I smiled ruefully.

We had to duck to get through the doorway, which opened into a bare bar where a few men were drinking, their eyes turned curiously to study us.

From another doorway a man appeared. Without waiting for us to speak he thrust out his hand and asked for 3000 CFA for a room for the night. We were grateful it wasn't more, even as we registered that in charging three times that amount the lorry driver really had taken us for a ride.

The owner indicated we should follow him down an unlit hallway, past a foul-smelling shower and out into a yard.

In the centre of the yard was a sort of storeroom, made of concrete, with no windows. Clearly this was the room they kept for really unwelcome visitors: inside, it was dusty and humming with insect life.

There was only one item of furniture – a narrow iron bed whose mattress was stained and covered in straw and plaster that had fallen from the ceiling above.

There were no sheets; just a single pillow, yellow and sticky with what I guessed was hair oil.

"Where's the light?" I asked Tom when the owner departed, taking his oil lamp with him.

"Don't think there is one. But I've got my torch."

The thin light made the place look even more depressing but at least we had my towel and sarong to lie on and cover us up - and it was only for one night.

"Thank God there's a lock on the door," I said, relieved we could keep ourselves safe from thieves if not the buzzing insects who were sharing our accommodation. "I'm going to have a shower."

I returned almost before Tom had had time to lock the door after me.

"No water?" he enquired.

"I don't know. I didn't get that far. I'm not even sure it is a shower; it looks like people have been using it as a toilet."

"What?"
"Yeah there's a hole in the concrete and shit all over the floor. On the walls too. And it stank of urine. I'm not going to be showering. And if I need the loo I'll do it behind this hut." Nothing would persuade me to enter that dark and stinking hole again.

"Not much point sitting here in the dark. Shall we find some supper before we crash," Tom suggested.

"I may have just lost my appetite."

***

The clean jeans I shrugged on hung from my bottom and waist. I couldn't recall ever having been so thin.

But when we ventured out onto the shabby street there didn't seem to be anywhere to eat. Everything was closed up apart from, curiously, a couple of music stores from which wonderful African beats blared out into the darkness.

It took no more than a few minutes to exhaust the possibilities of this strange part of the town, drawing a blank. So we returned, dejected, to our even more shabby hotel to see if the blank-faced owner could be persuaded to serve up any food.

When we enquired he looked at us in the same silent way he'd greeted our arrival, simply shrugging and disappearing back into whatever room led off from the bar. We could hear banging and, hoping it might be a sign he was preparing something to eat, stuck it out.

Eventually two plates of sticky rice were plonked down in front of us, heavy and stolid, and smothered in cold chilli sauce. I've eaten better.

I fished the plain rice out from under the congealing sauce and ate what little I could manage.

It was a relief to get back behind the locked door of our storeroom sleeping quarters, knowing we just had to survive the night and could be on our way again in the morning. The whining flies and stuffiness made sleep difficult but somehow, at some point, we both fell into an uneasy slumber and woke only when light began to creep through the cracks in the roof and walls, and under the door.

Perhaps you know the feeling when you wake, aware that something is wrong, but unsure what. There's a heaviness in the stomach, a reluctance to come fully awake because it will mean facing whatever is responsible for that sense of dread somewhere deep within.

That was how it felt to wake the next morning. Something was not right.

It came to me the moment I reached under the grubby pillow for my money belt. Wearing it all day everyday I knew its' shape and weight like I knew the back of my own hand. It was too thin.

Tom registered the look on my face: "What's wrong?"

"My money. Something's missing from my money belt." I unzipped it. Not just my money, CFAs and, more importantly, US dollars, but all my travellers cheques were gone. Every penny I had.

"But how? Do you think someone's been in the room?"

"They couldn't have could they? It was locked," I said dully. This really was it then. I'd got through sickness but if I had no funds the trip was off.

"What about last night. When we were eating?"

"It's possible I suppose. Maybe I was careless when I was paying for our drinks. It doesn't matter anyway," I shrugged. "Whether I lost it then or someone has a key and came in while we were asleep, I've got no money. Might as well find an airport."

"Well I'll lend you money." Tom was so matter of fact it took a while for his offer to sink in and for me to readjust to the idea that I might not have to leave the trucks after all. "It's not much anyway. What did you lose? A few hundred quid?"

"About that. I bought what Terry suggested: £100 for the kitty and £400 spending.

"Let me sub you. We can find a bank and cash one of my cheques for you. And then you just ask when you need more."

I didn't need much persuading. The prospect of flying home just at the point this trip might really be opening up to us, and certainly before I was ready to return to my old life, felt far worse than the fact of having lost all my money.

Nor did I relish the prospect of heading off alone to find an airport. For all my reservations about the strange status of our relationship, I found Tom's presence reassuring and felt stronger and more myself because of it.

As we set out from the dingy hotel, heading beyond the music shops and emerging into a tree-lined street where the houses were brick-built with gardens, I realised our mistake had been stopping where the greedy lorry driver had dropped us in the shanty town, no doubt with his 'friends' in order that the exploitation could continue. As indeed it had. We had been well and truly fleeced.

Had we just walked on a little we might have been safer and had a better experience of this Cameroonian town which, in the bright daylight, looked friendly and prosperous.

Nowhere more so than the bank which commanded one corner of the main street, tall and self-important outside; inside as hushed and formal as a church.

We were first in the queue, much good it did us. This was still Africa, after all, even if the surroundings owed much to the country's colonial past. Once Tom has signed two travellers cheques we were waved to one side and had to wait, and wait, and watch as what seemed like the rest of the town came in to do their banking.

Five minutes turned to fifteen turned to fifty and still we waited, half-wondering if the cashier had disappeared with the signed cheques never to be seen again. Tom seemed to take it in his stride but inside I could feel myself beginning to boil up again: bloody Africa, bloody African bureaucrats. Even to myself I sounded just like Terry but I couldn't stop the soundtrack running riot in my head.

Finally our cashier returned to his seat, only to serve a couple of other customers first before signalling we could at last approach the metal grill. He reached for a pile of notes, possibly the grubbiest, most dog-eared the bank's safe held. It certainly looked that way to me.

Slowly, with agonising care, the cashier counted them out, then recounted and finally nodded to Tom to pay attention. For the third time he counted the notes pushing them towards him in batches, each as torn and tatty as the last.

Were they even still legal? Would anyone be willing to take them off our hands?

***

I'm not proud of what happened next but, having accused Terry of racism, it's only fair I tell you that at this point something in me snapped. As everyone else went peacefully about their business that morning I turned into the kind of furious, raving idiot I have always despised, accusing the cashier of rudeness, of deliberately keeping us waiting, of trying to palm us off with notes that had been deemed unfit for circulation.

On and on I went, asking why they were being so horrible to us, did they think we were fools, angry tears spiking in my eyes. Poor Tom looked on in horror while the hapless cashier merely greeted my tirade with a look of incomprehension. Because, of course, it wasn't personal. It was just the way things happen in Africa, and I'd been there long enough and should have known that.

In my defence I suppose what was really erupting out of me was four weeks of fear, sickness, frustration and anxiety: the weeks in Chad, the fallout of being seriously ill, and then the final straw of losing all my money.

But to everyone else in the bank that morning it must have looked like white privilege, another tourist expecting preferential treatment or at least kindness for no other reason than the colour of her skin.

I still feel shame when I recall my outburst.

And yet there was in all of this a glimmer of something positive. As I have learned many times since, allowing emotions an outlet, releasing them – hopefully not in such a rude way - is hugely empowering. It is as if all the pent-up energy that's been diverted to keeping a lid on difficult feelings is suddenly available to be used in much better ways.

As I strode out of the bank, leaving Tom to do his best to paper over the cracks of my bad behaviour, assuring the bank staff of his gratitude for their help and patience, I felt stronger than I had at any point since leaving the UK.

I had survived drought and danger, sickness and robbery, so I knew now I could survive anything else this journey would throw at me.

I bowled along the road, looking for a place where it would be safe to stop and throw out a thumb for our next lift, the lift that would take us as far as those Long Haul trucks.

I knew, without a shadow of doubt, this morning, this experience, was a turning point.

CHAPTER 21

Yousouffa

An hour later I was doubting myself and my optimism. The main road out of town was worryingly quiet. Tom and I took turns standing at the verge, raising a thumb hopefully whenever a vehicle passed. But that wasn't often: during that first hour we counted a measly four trucks, every single one of them already dangerously overloaded with people, animals, equipment, crates and luggage.

Though it was pleasant sitting by the roadside, listening to the sounds of birds and humming insects I wondered if perhaps we'd have done better staying in the town centre; that was clearly where all these trucks had collected passengers.

On the other hand, the thought of travelling in any of them, crammed in and forced to stand while the trucks rocked and rolled down bumpy road for hundreds of miles, was not an attractive one.

It was my turn to be lookout when vehicle number five appeared, its speed sending a cloud of red dust skywards so it took me a while to realise that, unlike the other vehicles we'd seen, this was a private car.

Not only a car; it was a sleek blue Mercedes. And, incredibly, it was stopping.

Tom and I were still rooted to the spot, gaping in disbelief, when the driver door opened and a young African man stepped out into the dust. He wore a light blue suit over an open white shirt, and polished leather shoes on his feet. As he approached, hand extended, a shy smile on his face, I caught the unlikely scent of aftershave.

"Voulez vous voyage avec moi?"

"Oui, merci," I stuttered. "Ou allez vous?"

"Vers la frontier. Republique Centrafrique," he said.

"Perfect! Nous allons aussi a la frontier," I hoped I made sense. "Je suis Jane et mon ami s'appelle Tom." Thank God again for O level French.

"Je m'apelle Yousouffa. Bonjour." Pointing a beautifully manicured hand the man indicated we should climb into his luxurious car, sinking into comfort with space to spread out. I could hardly believe our luck: surely with Yousouffa's help, we would quickly close the gap with the rest of Long Haul?

***

I'm not sure I can accurately convey how it felt to be travelling along, at speed, in an air-conditioned Mercedes, with a guide who was every bit as polished and lovely as his vehicle. Yousouffa looked younger than us, yet his manner, a quiet confidence as though he had no need to convince anyone of his importance, commanded the respect due to someone much older and wiser.

His voice was soft and thoughtful, and whenever he spoke he looked up into the rear mirror, smiling reassuringly at me – Tom had taken the front seat on the grounds his French was better than mine.

Yousouffa wanted to hear about our trip and about our companions and the company running the expedition. He also wanted to hear about our lives at home, our occupations, our families and more.

We asked about his life too and learned he had two homes, one in Cameroon and the other in the Central African Republic – CAR. He was married and also mentioned a business, though I was never clear what he was trading in; only that it involved importing and exporting between the two countries.

Yousouffa also talked a little about his Moslem faith but, as the day wore on, it became clear that mostly he just lived it.

He was one of the first people I'd ever met who behaved as if his religion ought to make a difference to the way he lived. Of course, he was already our Good Samaritan, but all day long, as we drove through little Cameroonian villages, he'd pull over to put a few notes in the hands of street beggars.

Those villages were few and far between: mostly the red dust track wound a way through lush jungle vegetation, only occasionally giving way to a river or a few huts.

The air fizzed with noise from creatures we couldn't see – except for the baboons who scuttled across in front of the car from time to time.

Once we came upon an accident. Two men flagged us down – their car was wrapped around a tree though they looked unharmed. Yousouffa fished into his wallet again and gave them money so that they could get the car towed and rent a room for themselves while they waited for repairs. There was no ostentation about his generosity: I felt he would be doing exactly the same if we hadn't been in the car.

Around lunchtime Yousouffa pulled into a small village to buy us meat skewers from a stall beside the road. The smell was heavenly. Another time he pulled in at a stall to buy us cans of cold coke. He refused Tom's offer of payment as if it were an insult.

***

Mid-afternoon he made a stop for prayers, producing a prayer mat and flask of water from the boot.

Then we resumed, chatting away to each other in broken French, smiles cementing this new friendship. I felt the optimism in me returning tenfold. Despite all the stops it felt as though we were skimming through the countryside, drawing ever closer to our missing companions.

Beyond the car windows the scenery was changing, proving how far we had come. Instead of green forest and the occasional distant hill the landscape was becoming bolder, craggier, with rocky outcrops. Sometimes we all sat in silence for a while, comfortable just watching the world unfolding beyond the car windows, lost in our own thoughts. At other times we started a new conversation, respectfully listening to each other's views on some of life's big topics – even things that I might have ordinarily considered taboo, such as our understanding of each other's countries' politics, religions, and attitudes.

Day subsided into a cosy dusk and it was a shock to hear Yousouffa say we'd covered so many miles we had reached the last significant village before the border with CAR. The village was called Garoua Bolai and he said he planned to stop the night here and wait until morning to cross: it was always to do so in daylight.

Yousouffa warned us that Garoua was not a safe place, because of its proximity to the border and to CAR which was, he said, 'difficile'. He would find us somewhere trustworthy to stay the night in safety, and he would meet us outside our lodgings in the morning.

I never doubted for a moment he would be as good as his word; after all, he had looked after us all day as though we were precious charges placed in his care.

The lodgings he took us to were small and clean and cost the equivalent of £1 for the night. We were shown into an airy bedroom, this time with bedcovers, and then taken to a shower stall in the yard, supplied with several enamel jugs of cold, clear water.

I could hardly wait to get clean and once we'd thanked him and said 'au revoir' I headed straight back to the stall: watching as the water trickled down my dusty skin leaving clear trails.

As the water cleaned me, so I imagined it washing away some of the despondency and despair of recent weeks. Each slow pour of water brought me back to an appreciation of why I had come to Africa, the excitement of adventures to come, and gratitude for the kindness of a stranger who had transformed our experience of this part of the continent.

By the time I felt refreshed and renewed it was dark and I paused a moment to look up at the stars pricking through the blackness, breathing in the smell of warm earth and woodsmoke. Another of Africa's gifts to me, this assault on senses that I now realised, thinking back to my life in London, had been asleep for so long.

We went in search of food, finding a bright and busy café serving tasty omelettes. But the food wasn't nearly as exciting as the news our waitress shared: she told us that our trucks had stayed in the village the previous night. We were literally now only a day away from them.

Only later did we learn the trucks hadn't made a positive impression on the village. Garoua has no campsite so the trucks were told to camp near to the town's border, away from any facilities.

This posed particular problems for stomachs unsettled by the richness and availability of fresh food after those lean weeks in Chad. All night long a steady stream of our companions headed from their tents to relieve themselves. It wasn't until morning arrived, and with it daylight, they realised they'd been squatting in a private garden, now decorated with numerous flags of toilet paper.

The owner wanted recompense and before local police would allow the trucks to go anywhere our friends were forced to clean up the resident's garden until it was spotless.

***

Youssouffa told us to be outside the lodgings at eight but half eight came and went, then nine, and nine thirty and there was no sign of him or his Mercedes. Had we got him wrong?

I should have learned by this time that Africans have a much more relaxed relationship with time than we do. Two hours later than arranged, there was Yousouffa, smiling broadly and ushering us into his cool saloon again, seemingly unaware that anything could be amiss. Perhaps something had come up but I think it more likely he was - like so many people we met - on Africa time, which was as flexible and unimportant as it was rigid and in short supply for us back home.

What did it matter anyway, now he was here and we knew how fast he travelled?

As we crossed the border there was a noticeable shift in atmosphere. It was hard to put a finger on: out of the car windows the scenery was as lush as it had been all the previous day; Yousouffa was as solicitous.

Yet the huts we passed had an air of neglect; and once or twice I noticed people watching us pass, shaking their fists or turning their backs. Behind them, in the dense cover of the forest, trails of dark smoke rose like ghostly flagpoles, evidence of fires burning unchecked: we saw blackened tree skeletons alongside the road where other fires had spat and crackled a way through.

Yousouffa no longer wanted to talk about politics, nor CAR's history - about which I only knew that having emerged from the time of the corrupt dictator Bokassa the country was now ruled by a military junta. He said that he'd been forced to move his business headquarters to Cameroon, but gave no reason why.

Perhaps the logistics of actually moving anything through the country were a factor for anyone trying to do business. For after the freedom of Cameroon's open roads we now began to encounter one police check after another. Even the smallest settlement had a sentry box and barrier across the road, guarded by boys in uniforms carrying guns as casually as if they were cans of coke.

With each halt, each time we had to get out and show our documents, Yousouffa got quieter; more than once I spotted him handing over notes to ease our progress up the road.

In some ways it was humbling to see him treated by his compatriots with the same rude disdain we'd encountered so often and had assumed to be a penalty of our white skin.

Here, in the Central African Republic, his wealth and elegance were no protection from those with the power of uniforms and guns.

Yousouffa held on hard to his feelings as we humbly waited to be allowed through each checkpoint. Back in the car he wiped his forehead with a white, laundered handkerchief while his fingers drummed uneasily on the steering wheel.

***

The only upside I could see from all these stops was knowing that every time we were delayed, Terry and his trucks would be held up for a great deal longer. I imagined his frustration at the guards' insistence on seeing everyone's paperwork and searching the vehicles for goodies they could take in lieu of the kind of bribes Yousouffa was having to pay. I knew we must be closing on them.

At midday we reached a town called Bouar which Yousouffa said was where his journey ended. This was his other home town and he would take us to the police point at its exit, but first wanted to be sure we had food and drink for our onward journey.

We stopped at another stall by the road for fresh bread and before we climbed back into the car he asked to see our map and pointed out the road we'd need to follow in order to reach the trucks on their way to CAR's capital of Bangui.

He dropped us a few hundred yards before the check point, promising to drive back this way at the end of the day, just in case we hadn't been able to pass through, or get another lift, and needed his help finding safe lodgings for another night.

It was so typical of him to think ahead, and believe he wouldn't have discharged his duty to us until we were truly underway again.

Saying goodbye was difficult and unsatisfactory because I knew Yousouffa could have no idea how much his kindness and generosity had truly meant to me at a time when I might have been forced to give up on our journey. How much he had the pervading view on the trucks of African people. Naturally it turns out they are as individual as all of us, good, bad, ugly and – like him – simply saintly.

I hoped one day I might get the chance to repay him in some way, and meet him on more equal terms.

But Youssouffa had business waiting and we had two trucks to catch so, after shaking hands and garbling the best thanks we could in our inadequate French, we turned from him and walked up the hill towards the checkpoint. I felt vulnerable to be doing so without Youssouffa's help.

Even before we reached the checkpoint a young guard emerged, hand thrust out for our passports. The whites of his eyes were bloodshot, his expression hostile.

"Nothing changes does it?" I whispered to Tom.

"Ah but when was the last time a British customs officer smiled at you?"

"Fair point…"

After the most cursory glance the guard threw our passports back at us, shouting in French and waving an arm back the way we had come. Tom asked him in French to speak more slowly.

"He says we have to go back into town. We need some sort of stamp, a visa or something, before we can go through."

"Shit. I thought Terry and Heather organised all the visas before we came away. You don't suppose he wants a bribe do you?"

"I daren't," Tom said. "If we're wrong and we really do need some more paperwork we could get arrested for trying to give them money."

"It's a long walk back into town. There goes our hope of catching the others," I said despondently. How quickly the fire had gone from me.

"Well we'd better get on with it."

We turned, contemplating the long hill we'd just slogged up. I estimated it was a mile or more back into the town, and then we'd have to find out where to get this missing stamp or visa or whatever it was. It was unlikely we'd be leaving Bouar today.

I sighed, and began the slow trudge downhill, Tom a few steps behind me. The hill dropped steeply so within a few minutes we could no longer see the checkpoint and were also, I thought with relief, past the range of those guns.

Yet I could hear something, a low sort of sound, like thunder, even though the sky was clear blue.

It was the blueness which made it hard to immediately see what was making the noise. It was coming from lower down the hill, in the distance, where the blue was actually moving. Towards us. Two bright blue trucks, lumbering slowly uphill.

"Tom!" I shrieked. "It's them. It's the trucks."

And then we were running downhill, arms waving like helicopters, hardly daring to trust that, after all we'd been through, here in the vastness of Africa, we'd found our friends again.

When we reached them, huffing from effort and excitement, they were every bit as delighted as us.

"Good God! It's Jane and Tom," Kitty Chris yelled out of the window for the benefit of those who couldn't see over the truck sides.

"Of all the roads in all the towns, you pick this one," Annie's laughing face was alongside his. "Want a lift?"

Did we want a lift? There was no question we wanted a lift!

Were we worried we didn't have the right stamps in our passport? Well yes, we were.

But it was those stamps we had to thank for us catching up with the trucks. Just like us they'd had been turned back earlier by the same guards who halted our journey and had wasted most of the day in town getting all their passports correct.

We had no intention of leaving the group again. So our companions on G cleared the entire gangway of bags and firewood so Tom and I could lay down on the truck floor. Then they piled everything back on top of us, taking care to make sure not even a tiny bit of clothing or skin could be seen between the gaps.

It wasn't comfortable but we were so grateful they were willing to risk the consequences of being found out smuggling people through a police check.

The minutes the trucks idled at the checkpoint were nerve-wracking. There would be many more such minutes to come since Tom and I didn't have the right permissions to progress. We grew used to going undercover in the footwell every time a police check loomed.

But none of the guards at any of the checkpoints were interested in searching what looked like an enormous pile of firewood and, once everyone else had been checked, we were allowed through.

It's strange how absence really can make the heart grow fonder. A month before I'd been railing at my companions, about the numbers on board and Terry's inadequate leadership. Now all I felt was warmth and gratitude to be back in the fold.

CHAPTER 22

Hiding out at the Red Cross compound in Bangui, Central African Republic

Just beyond the truck's plastic canopy the road was now a crimson gash, curling its way between heavy curtains of emerald, trees and creepers twisting together into a living and always-changing tapestry.

Sometimes the red ribbon vanished beneath the clear waters of a jungle stream, drawing a host of butterflies, black and white laced wings, to sunbathe alongside its shimmering surface.

At other times we passed fruit trees, bright mangoes and fat bananas, hanging like drop earrings from their branches.

It was a world of huge natural riches, and yet the sense of sadness persisted. When the road passed between huts the noise of the trucks shook children from their homes and they raced out to us, arms outheld, pleading for gifts, or, just as often, scrabbling in the dust for stones to throw.

***

One day, as afternoon wore on, there was a new sound: a low thrum beneath the cackles and clicks of birds and insects. It was the sound of all those streams we'd crossed coming together in a dramatic plunge through the trees down into a valley below. As the trucks bounced off the red road, following a sign to Boali Falls, the water's thunder drowned out every other sound.

On board, we scrambled for soap and shampoo, for towels and razors, and raced from the campsite to the place where all those waters gathered for a moment, drawing breath before throwing themselves off the rock face. The falls were like a giant open air bathroom, pockets and pools carved by the waters and separated by giant boulders, peaceful before reaching the hurly burly of the edge. The rocks provided places to sit and dangle our feet, or pound filthy clothes with soap.

I quickly found my own pool where I stripped to my knickers and lay back half submerged, lathered hair spread out like a fan from my head. From where I lay I could see up the gorge to the mass of green we had driven through, and closer to home scarlet dragonflies hovering above my cooling skin. On the closest rock sat a tiny lizard, black and white stripes as neat as a zebra crossing, but with a tail luminescent as the blue green of peacock feathers. It ignored me.

My ears were under water so the sounds around me were muffled, as if coming to me from far away: the shouts of little children who'd followed us here and were now offering to plait hair; the cries of men as razors met sensitive skin that had hidden under stubbly beards for months; and, always, the storm of the water plunging several hundred feet to the valley floor.

Later in the evening there was a new noise: an unearthly orchestra of toads, bellowing to each other, throats swollen like balloons, the sound reverberating off the rocks and tree wall until it seemed an echo of the thunder of the falls.

Only when real thunder struck, giant tongues of lightning stretching from the heavens to earth like illuminated ladders, were the toads briefly silent. There was no rain but somewhere, in a remote corner of jungle, the sky glowed red, the earth beneath it ignited by tens of thousands of volts of static.

It was a sound and light show like none I have ever seen before, or since. Spectacular and scary, a reminder of our smallness and nature's awesome power. No wonder the toads were silent.

***

Terry allowed us two days at the Falls and we seized the chance to spend hours at the waterfall, and explore a path up the gorge which led to a liana bridge stretching out across thin air to connect one bank to the other.

There was a very practical reason for Terry's unlikely gift of extra time. Throughout our journey Wayne had hardly ever lost his temper with the trucks or their slapdash owner. He was one of those enviable people who gets on with things, even when those things look hopeless. There was no doubt that without him we wouldn't have made it as far as Central Africa.

But for once Wayne had had enough and put his foot down with his boss, insisting on time to properly regroup after what we'd put the trucks through in Chad.

On the second night Mark and I went into the bar of the Boali Falls Hotel to sink several cold beers. We found Wayne, huddled in one corner with Mike the mechanic, white notebooks opened in front of them.

"Whatcha doing? Would you like a beer?" Mark asked.

"Log book mate. It's about time the old bugger kept one."

"Why?" I asked, ignorant.

"If he'd kept one on his last trips I could've prepared better. Known what spares to pack. What she's up to."

"You were brilliant. We wouldn't be here if not for you," I said.

"Tell the truth Jane, I didn't think we'd make it. All you folks saying what an adventure it was. All I remember is waking up every day feeling like shit thinking 'Not gonna be able to fix this'."

"Are you Sorry you came?"

"No. We'll be right from here on. And if I sign up again I'll know what I'm getting myself into." Wayne grinned shyly. It was as many words as I'd heard from him in one go since we left London. For a moment I glimpsed the shy twenty-three-year old rather than the grown-up guardian angel I owed my life to.

***

Terry had been to Bangui before and warned it was a place where every single one of us would need to be on our guard from thieves and muggers.

Like Niamey, Bangui, as we approached it, bore all the signs of its French colonial past: large houses hidden behind high walls which fronted wide tree-lined avenues, bars and hotels with French names, and, incredibly, a number of patisseries. We insisted on stopping. The lure of all those pastry confections was too much: tastes we'd all but forgotten.

We queued up in the street outside the shop – there was only room for one person at a time at the counter. So it took a moment to register someone at the end of the street was shouting. "Hi. You guys! YOU GUYS!" Heading towards us was not only Will but Tim and his breakaway group.

After all the hellos, we wanted to hear their stories of independent travel. I thought Will seemed subdued. He said he'd no luck getting money sent through from home yet, but had nevertheless been staying at one of Bangui's smart hotels courtesy of his Barclaycard. Once Tim's group arrived they'd established a system of Will leaving his window open when he returned to the hotel room so the others could shin up a handy drainpipe and sleep on his floor.

It didn't take long for the hotel cleaners to work out what was happening and the whole group, Will included, was sent packing after a couple of nights. They'd been forced to stay at Bangui's official campsite which was reputed to be the original den of thieves: rucksacks, clothing and money vanished with the same regularity as our trucks broke down.

Tim and the other West African adventurers hadn't fared a whole lot better. They'd apparently been robbed twice while they were making their way to the west coast in time for Christmas - before flying over Nigeria to Cameroon and then onto CAR.

"We went into this souvenir shop in Togo," Tim recounted. "The locals told us we could change money there. Handed the guy our dollars and then waited while he went out back to check they were genuine."

"Let me guess. He never came back," Kitty Chris sounded pleased with himself.

"Bastard did a vanishing act. That wasn't the worst though. We tried to change some money here for going on into Zaire."

"Don't say it happened again?"

"Nope, we got our notes straight away, no problem. Only thing is, we didn't know what the currency over there is supposed to look like," Tim slumped further into his t-shirt and leather waistcoat. "So we get out and show the notes to some other dudes on the campsite and they point out the thieving scum have given us Makuta notes instead of Zaires."

"What?" Chris asked.

"Pennies not pounds. Cents rather than dollars. The whole lot is bloody useless. Wouldn't even buy us a banana."

***

One useful piece of intelligence Tim had picked up on the campsite was worth its weight in gold however: the travellers' grapevine claimed that there was an alternative to the official site – run by the International Red Cross in its own grounds. It lay at the heart of Bangui's shanty town, but nevertheless was surrounded by a wall and had 24-hour guards.

We didn't need telling twice.

Terry invited Tim to climb up into the cab with him and lead us through the city to what sounded like a sanctuary.

Soon the wide avenues gave way to narrow streets between huts made of corrugated iron. There were no more patisseries: just the usual array of street sellers and children begging for presents. Under the tyres the tarmac vanished to be replaced by red dust which settled on everything.

It seemed everyone was out on the street, distracted from their conversations, marketing and drinking, by our arrival. I glimpsed cooking fires burning in the open air and clusters of people around the doors of shacks selling alcohol. As we passed the crowds hissed at us and soon the sides of the trucks were again ringing to the sound of missiles.

It was a relief to pull up to the padlocked gates of the Red Cross compound, though it appeared not to be their offices as we'd been told, but some sort of storage facility, explaining why they needed guards.

Alongside the grassed compound, which had a concrete shower and toilet block in one corner, the actual Red Cross building was mostly a bombed-out shell. Only one small portion seemed still to be intact though it had no windows or doors. The rest was just a gaping hole, open to the sky.

Bizarrely, a string of fairy lights ran from the end of the building across the compound: presumably the only lighting they'd been able to find. It made the place seem somewhat prettier than the reality, which was basic and shabby.

The whole compound was surrounded by a high brick wall which looked as if it might offer some protection from Bangui's criminal element. Sadly it was not to be.

It took Bangui's underworld only a few hours to mount their first assault on the camp, climbing over the barbed wire on top of the walls to grab onto everything that had been carelessly left outside the tents. We'd assumed that with two guards employed to protect whatever was in the Red Cross store our things would be safe. Yet the first morning we woke to find clothes, shoes, everything that had been washed and hung on lines, plus cooking equipment and tools had been stolen from under our noses.

Out on the streets the next day we hardly fared any better. Everyone who left the site to collect letters from the post restante, to revisit the patisserie, explore the shanty town, or sit in bars, had their own version of being robbed or mugged. A favourite tactic was the same one used against Tom in Cameroon: two men grabbing an arm each while using their other hands to rip off money belts or handbags.

We learned it was better not to resist if the thieves targeted you. Those who had tried now sported black eyes or bruising on their arms and chest.

Watches were particular favourites and at least a half dozen of the group had theirs cut from their wrists. It became obvious we should leave anything valuable behind before venturing out onto the streets.

Not that we were much safer in the compound, despite supplementing the official guards with our own all-day and all-night watch. Nights were a stop-start affair, with regular interruptions as the alarm went up that there were strangers moving around the tents, even unzipping them to slip silent hands inside.

Our paranoia grew in direct response. One night we were jolted awake by screams and the sounds of a violent scuffle.

In the dainty glow of fairy lights it was impossible to make out who was a part of the mound of bodies over by one of the trailers: only that more and more people who had been asleep a moment ago were piling in.

It took Heather, appearing with a torch as bright as a spotlight, shouting at them all to get off, to establish what the scrum was about. As each of the bodies unpeeled itself from the heap the person at the bottom turned out to be one of the Red Cross guards, incandescent with rage and shouting as he pointed to the torn fabric of his grey coat.

"Well he was asking for trouble, skulking around the campsite like that," Terry huffed, doubtless fearing another compensation claim. "Stupid bastard. What does he expect?"

"Isn't 'skulking' around the campsite his job?" Gai asked.

***

I've made it sound as if Bangui was just scary and hard work, and in truth it was impossible to relax there. But Bangui had another side which more than compensated for this sense that we were under attack throughout.

Tom, Annie and I made found our peace when we discovered the market hall. It reminded me of going to the theatre: everything about it ran like a kind of performance, as novel and entertaining to us, to whom it was so unfamiliar, as our arrival on those trucks always was to the local people.

We passed many hours, over the next three days, sitting at one or other of the tea counters, watching as the plump women sellers siphoned off boiling water from a huge pan into their thermos flasks. In place of mugs they had tin cans, into which they ladled half an inch of sugar.

No-one ever asked if we wanted sugar: it was as integral a part of a cup of tea as the actual leaves, which stewed in a giant teapot and turned the water the colour of soil.

Just in case the tea wasn't sweet enough the sellers added a good slug of condensed milk to the mix, before handing the brimming tin cans over with a flourish. I found the whole thing irresistible, and welcomed the chance to restore a little of the weight that had dropped off me during Chad and the sickness.

Another favourite for us was the so-called artisans' market on the dusty corner of a crossroads towards the edge of Bangui.

On the ground sat the sellers, their tourist wares spread out on blankets, coats and lengths of bright African cloth: malachite statues and jewellery, gleaming green in sunlight which highlighted the marbling within the semi-precious stone; ebony carvings, placemats, stools and animals; bone shaped into heads and necklaces, knives and earrings; and brightly coloured pictures which, on closer inspection, turned out to be made from butterfly wings.

I had no money spare to buy anything, which was in many ways a relief. The prices were so outrageously inflated for tourists that the whole haggling process might take an afternoon. Besides, some of the materials made me squeamish: I preferred my wildlife alive and kicking.

But I used the chance of Bangui's post restante to fire off a few letters home, specifically one to dad asking him for the funds to buy my flight back to the UK when the time came.

In Bangui I'd picked up a letter from him in which he urged me to 'seize every opportunity for adventure'.

That was the first time in my life I'd heard him talk in those terms and of all the messages from home, whose contents had once made me homesick but now seemed so distant and unrelated to my life, his message was the one I took into my heart.

CHAPTER 23

Wide and brown as sticky toffee pudding, the River Ubangui made an impressive border between the Central African Republic and Zaire, where we were heading next. Of all the countries on our itinerary, Zaire was the one where we were due to spend the most time – a luxurious three weeks.

But we had to get there first and in a country criss-crossed by rivers and streams, the Ubangui was only the first of many watery obstacles to our progress. The river is one of the region's arteries, surging through the jungle, dwarfing the tiny wooden canoes which ply their own trade in drinks and snacks around the single vehicle ferry.

On the Bangui side an opportunistic shanty town was scattered around the quay, sounds and smells of cooking wafting from a tumble of wooden huts and shacks made from corrugated metal.

There was room for only one vehicle at a time on a ferry which looked as if it might have been here for as long as the palm trees fringing the banks. It meant the traders had a captive audience, patiently waiting to cross.

We were soon joined in the queue by another overland vehicle with German plates, this one boasting just eight passengers and luxuries such as a fridge from which the passengers pulled cold drinks. Apparently they even had a cook on board.

The sight of all that space, plus cold drinks and no cooking duties, proved too much for some of those on Q truck: as Terry prepared to nudge his vehicle onto the ferry two of the men who'd been a part of Tim's breakaway group announced it had been a mistake to rejoin Long Haul were off to join the Germans.

I understood it must have been a shock for them, free from Terry for five weeks, to suddenly find themselves again part of a large crowd scene. I wasn't surprised they'd realised they preferred travelling with fewer people.

For the rest of us, it was time to cross. As the ferry slowly inched across the water I was happy to sit on the riverbank staring towards Zaire. The trees looked almost as if they had been painted in oils, dark, glossy and impenetrable.

Somehow our scheduling was always a bit off: we'd be arriving in Zaire just as everyone disappeared for the weekend, giving us no opportunity to swap our Central African Francs and sterling for the local currency, the Zaire.

Naturally, it quickly became clear that there were locals who could help us with this. While I sat watching the ferry's slow progress, taking Q truck over to Zaire, the rest of G truck was being mobbed by young men, pockets stuffed with notes, squabbling with each other as they tried to do a deal.

Once the black market dealing was complete I watched bemused as my friends began looking for ingenious places to hide the notes from any border guards we'd encounter. They were being stuffed into the cooking equipment on the trailer and I saw others being shoved into bras and socks.

Time passed, the hubbub died down, we snacked on peanut butter balls and coke, until eventually the ferry returned and it was our turn to board.

From the water I couldn't see where we'd be docking on the other bank. The wall of trees looked solid, apart from a tiny beach.

Eventually there was the sound of scraping, as the ferry eased its way onto the grit and Wayne switched on the engine and asked us all to disembark. The route off the beach was up an almost ninety degree ridge. One of the reasons it was taking so long for vehicles to cross was because most were not up to the challenge of exiting the beach without help. Local people had devised a system whereby each arriving vehicle was hauled up the ridge by the vehicle that crossed ahead of them. It was a relief to realise Q truck would have to do our heavy lifting and the sand mats could remain where they were, strapped to the truck's sides.

At the top of the bank we came to a small clearing with a single hut serving as the border post. Men in uniform ordered us to stay on the vehicles while they did a thorough search.

We knew what they were looking for – currency bought on the black market in CAR - and they knew that we knew. But it seemed they were in no rush to turn the place upside down looking for illicit Zaires: as soon as they boarded one of the men began miming a jig, pointing at the cassette player.

"I think they want some music," Annie said.

"Musique?" I asked them.

"Oui, oui."

I was sitting closest to the player and the box of now battered and dusty cassette cases. With my back to my companions I was oblivious to the sharp intake of breath all around me.

I flicked through the cases, settling on a bit of Bowie. The official reached out a hand, wanting to put it in the player himself.

This time I couldn't miss the tension; no-one was breathing as the uniformed border guard fumbled with the plastic case and took an age to get the cassette into the player.

Suddenly Bowie's wonderful voice blasted out into the back of the truck, and beyond, to the waiting jungle. A few of my companions stood up and began to dance, and soon the officials joined in too.

I whispered to Annie. "What was that about?"

"We hid money in all the cassette cases. Seemed like a good idea at the time: I mean who's heard of playing music at the border?"

"You got lucky," she whistled. "That must be the only bloody cassette of the whole lot that isn't stuffed with Zaires."

***

I think we'd all have loved to put more distance between us and CAR but after the ferry shenanigans, and the extended search at the border, it was nearing dusk. So we decided to camp that night at the first village we came to, the prosaically named Zongo, a few hundred meters up the road from the crossing.

Zongo was like every village we would encounter on the long and beautiful drive through Zaire: it consisted of two long rows of huts teetering either side of the narrow road, squeezed between it and the wall of wildness behind.

It wasn't clear if people were holding the jungle back or just borrowing a bit of it. But what it meant for the population here was that villages were forced by the geography to spread towards each other.

The deeper we went, the fewer the gaps between settlements. When the rains came, relentless and ferocious, the single track would turn to mud and nothing could get through for weeks on end.

That night, around the campfire, I could sense the jungle encircling us, breathing down our necks.

Its heartbeat was the rustling of the air and unseen life deep within the trees; its smell the rank odour of drenched vegetation dripping in the darkness. And its rhythm was the sound of Zongo's drums, broadcasting our arrival along the track to other villages. I felt an overwhelming smallness here: as though the jungle was merely crouched, waiting to pounce and swallow up any evidence that we, or the villagers surrounding us, had ever existed.

***

One practical drawback of Zaire's geography was that there was nowhere away from human habitation to pitch the tents; we'd have to find somewhere to camp within the villages, which meant seeking permission from the chief.

But such an important conversation could not happen without a great deal of sitting down and sharing a few drinks plus smoking a certain amount of weed as an expression of mutual goodwill. My only experience with drugs up to this point had been an unfortunate episode with some red leb baked into a cake. This ended badly with me pleading to be taken to hospital, certain I was dying. The Zairean variety was like dolly mixture in comparison, harvested from the jungle, and mostly harmless. We felt perfectly safe with the people of Zongo.

It is hard to explain what made the difference, why we automatically felt we could trust them, but then so much of the way we communicate and make up our minds whether we like or dislike someone happens at a gut level. In CAR I had picked up suspicion and distrust and therefore I had returned those things.

The people of Zaire had, in contrast, a sense of being comfortable in their own skins; a warmth and almost childlike openness towards us that opened our hearts to them.

Plus strangers like us brought a bit of variety, as well as the chance to trade, barter and sell.

Having shared tea and bananas with the chief we set up camp for the night. Since Cockney Steve's departure I'd been allocated yet another cooking partner, my third, a tall good-looking Australian called Lloyd who never anything seriously – least of all cooking! It happened to be our turn to guard so after supper I crawled onto the luggage trailer, doing my best to cover all the bags. It was more comfortable than it sounds, at least in comparison to the ground.

I quickly fell into one of the deepest sleeps I'd had and at some point began dreaming that someone was yelling, pulling at my arm, telling me to get up. I struggled to consciousness, still bleary, realising this wasn't a dream - but unable to work out where I was or what was happening.

"Bloody great guards you lot make. Wake up for Chrissakes."

"What is it? What's happening?" my words were slurred with sleep.

"We've only been bloody raided again. That's what's happened while you were getting your beauty sleep," Kitty Chris spat. Dimly I registered he was wearing only shorts. Behind him I could see Terry hopping about, wearing only a pair of navy underpants.

"What do you mean?" I said stupidly, but Chris had already gone. So I pulled myself up on the plastic trailer cover and blinked around me.

"Bastards have got my flip flops."
"And my walking boots."

"Fucking hell. My jeans have gone."
"Shit, they've been onto the trucks. There's stuff missing from there."

One by one the chorus swelled as people woke to the commotion and realised none of us had been exempted from this raid. The thieves had been bold enough to unzip several tents and steal money bags and clothes from inside them. They'd taken mugs and toothbrushes, almost anything that wasn't nailed down, as if it all had currency here. And they'd been lucky enough to find a camera bag left in the gangway of Q truck rather than stowed in a locker which people were sleeping on.

It was a pretty comprehensive haul.

Most galling was that we knew we'd been careless. While we were no longer behind a high wall with security guards at the Red Cross, we were still only a canoe ride away from the same people who'd followed and mugged and robbed us in Bangui. Why wouldn't they try their chances one more time by crossing the river?

If you've ever been robbed you'll know that one of the most unsettling things is the way you keep discovering other items that were taken, long after the event. When daylight came the air was blue with swearing and exclamations as my companions discovered other items of clothing and personal stuff that was missing.

The Zongo villagers took it personally and as soon as word reached the chief he came to talk with Heather and confirm that, as we'd guessed, the thieves had come across the river.

Much later on, when our paths crossed again with the German overland trip, we learned that, as they waited for their ferry across the Ubangui the day after our crossing, they'd been offered the chance to buy back some of our goodies. They even got as far as agreeing to ride with their informant in a canoe up the river to meet the thieves, but turned back in a hurry when shots were fired – apparently from a group of soldiers watching the border.

I, of course, was luckier than most in that I had nothing much of value left to steal since my money vanished in Cameroon.

***

When we got moving the exuberance of Zaire was the perfect antidote to any upset about our losses. As we drove on through the jungle people spilled out of their huts to greet us. Sometimes they offered fruit for sale: bananas costing less than a penny for three, fat red mangoes and paw paw whose flesh was the creamy consistency of ice cream. Children grinned cheekily and demanded 'cadeaux' but somehow for the sake of it rather than from any expectation they'd get something in return.

We passed women moving along the track, huge buckets of brimming water balanced perfectly on their heads. Or carrying bundles of sticks, longer than they were high, for firewood.

Sometimes we saw family groups, crouched around small fires made simply from three stones and a few twigs. Bare-breasted women stirred whatever was in the smoke-blackened pots while their men dozed alongside. The children entertained themselves playing with make-believe cars, constructed from an empty tin can attached to the end of a stick.

They seemed so comfortable yet I knew I could not claim to know whether that was true. Did their lives really happen at the slow pace I imagined? How much did they know or care about life beyond their village? Were they as childishly happy as they seemed, living totally in the moment?

Their country was effectively a dictatorship under the rule of Mobutu, none of whose personal wealth trickled down to the kind of places we were passing through. And what did they make of us, perched loftily high up in our vehicles, waving at them, not unlike a royal cavalcade?

Yet this impression of contentment persisted, even though they appeared, to my western eyes, to have so very little in the way of wealth or material possessions; not just that but so little diversion from the daily imperatives of collecting water, hunting food, and gathering together to share it all.

I am somewhat ashamed to say that I had reached my late twenties without questioning the values and beliefs I was brought up with, initially by deeply conservative parents, within schools and Sunday schools which taught the Christian orthodoxy. I had never, as far as I recall, looked around and wondered whether this path I was taught to want – school, university, career, acquiring first possessions and later a home (and probably a husband and children) – was the only way to live my life.

Naive, I know, but then like so many women of my era I was also brought up to be a good girl. And being good meant doing what I was told, believing what I was taught, and wanting what everyone else thought I should.

Even at the time, those long hours watching the Zairean people (as they then were) living very different lives, I was aware of something shifting inside me: a question mark, like a little bubble of possibility, growing inside. Maybe there was more than one way to live?

Now, as I look back to those days, a sort of coming alive again after our near-death experiences in Chad, as well as the true mid-point of our journey across Africa, I am so grateful for them. So glad that the journeying allowed me to, finally, open my eyes and consider for the first time that peace and simple joy might be the goal rather than conformity. And that beliefs, social norms, are no more than stories passed down from one generation to another.

Once you see *that* you can choose your own story.

***

One day, perhaps a week into Zaire, we drove into a large village which was entirely deserted: no-one greeting us, no escort of excited children: just a few wisps of smoke from abandoned cooking fires.

The explanation was just around the corner as our ears picked up the sound of faint chanting and, beneath it, the thump of drums. The beat got louder as we drove further into the village until we reached a clearing where all the trees had been cut away. Not that you could see the ground because the whole place was moving and undulating, a sea of dancing bodies, dipping and rising as one, around and around, almost as though they were in a hypnotic trance.

Across the clearing I could see the only instruments were two drums made from hollowed tree trunks, beaten with canes.

The rest of the music was coming from the crowd repeating the same few notes of a chant over and over. Looking more closely I could see that actually they were hardly moving at all; certainly scarcely more than walking pace. Yet the lightness of their feet, the ease with which they rocked and curled their bodies, turned every movement to dance.

Within the mass, smaller snakes of people, hands on each others' waists, weaved a different pattern to the rest. They were all ages, from small children jogging to the beat to grey-headed villagers, moving with the same grace and mesmerising purpose as everyone else. Some waved sticks with palm leaves attached while others held seed pods aloft.

The celebration could not have been going on for long as there was none of the sour smell of weed we'd come to expect here, nor any sign of the bitter palm wine they brewed: a milky fluid which stung the tongue and kick-started cross-cultural friendships as dramatically as jump leads. This village was high only on the jungle beat.

Suddenly a warm hand grabbed my arm through the side of the truck. An old woman, skin like bark, grinned toothlessly, indicating I should step down to join her. I didn't need asking twice. The moment I entered the throng I ceased to be an individual, becoming part of this vibrating whole, feet, bodies, heads and minds, perfectly in tune with each other. Others came down from the trucks to join in too, all our differences dissolving in the music.

CHAPTER 24

There were dancers on other days as we continued to rumble an unsteady route along the pitted and often broken red track.

On one occasion we were suddenly surrounded by young men, skin blackened as if they had rubbed charcoal from the many fire embers into their pores.

They darted around us like forest spirits, headdresses made from green creepers accentuating the whites of their eyes and mouths crimson as blood. Once the men had dipped and arched for the benefit of our cameras they ducked into their huts and emerged with nick nacks to trade with us: bows and arrows too frail to have ever killed anyone's supper; carved afro combs whose teeth were unblunted by use, and musical instruments carved from the forest so recently that flecks of sawdust clung to the strings.

In return we offered our own cheap trinkets: plastic sunglasses, digital watches that cost a few quid in Woolworths, bras we no longer fitted since Chad had shrunk our figures, and faded tee-shirts which nonetheless still bore the faint logos of prized western brands.

I'd seen villagers wearing what were obviously western tee-shirts: the sight of ET emblazoned on one man's chest above the short sarong he had around his waist was only one of many surreal moments. Presumably each overland truck that passed this way was like a mobile supermarket, giving both cultures the chance to acquire things they prized.

***

Zaire continued to feel like a safe haven in a way our previous destinations hadn't. Each morning a group of us would skip breakfast in order to walk ahead of the trucks for an hour or so, until the rest had eaten and packed and could catch us up.

It was a chance to see this beautiful country at an even slower pace, to get up close to the termite mounds which were so fantastical, like giant desserts made from melting caramel. To linger in places where jungle streams pooled between rocks and a myriad of butterflies sunned themselves. And to shake hands with people who came out from their huts to greet us.

I felt more comfortable at their level, rather than waving at them from the trucks: there was something about the height that made me feel as though we were spectators and they the exhibits.

There was another reason to go ahead without the trucks – in search of the Bare-faced Go Away Bird.

Our resident ornithologist, Steve 'Birdman' had taken a lot of ribbing when he announced it was one of the species he hoped to see in Africa.

But he'd had the last laugh by showing us a picture of the strange creature in one of his reference books. Now there was a competition on to see who would spot it first – even though Birdman thought us all mad. Its habitat was East rather than Central Africa.

Still there was plenty of other wildlife to enjoy – not all of it welcome. Tempting as the waters always looked, I held back from dipping so much as a toe in the shimmering water. One of the things I clearly remembered from Terry's mostly inadequate joining instructions, was a warning that the vast majority of Africa's rivers and lakes are home to the miniscule bilharzia worm.

Apparently the worm is able to burrow through human skin to feed from its victim's internal organs. It was a gruesome enough story to warn me off even the tiniest of the streams.

Another health hazard was that in the wet heat the wounds we acquired from camp life refused to heal, festering into tropical ulcers. Even the smallest scratch rapidly swelled to an open sore, oozing pus no matter how many times the nurses on board wiped it with boiled water and dressed it.

The other thing we learned to be wary of was one of the new tastes Zaire offered: a local staple called manioc – long misshapen tubers whose insides looked chalky and fibrous. Vegetable stews remained the usual fare for each day's cooks with the welcome addition of sweet potato and plantains which were in plentiful supply in Zaire.

Manioc, which was the most plentiful of all, was more problematic: it seemed not to want to cook down. Annie probably came closest to cracking it when she boiled the manioc for three hours then chopped six entire bulbs of garlic into the pasty mix. But it was like eating wallpaper paste and impossibly bitter.

Fortunately, after her failed efforts, we gave up the fight and focused our appetites instead on the plentiful fruits and rice fritters we were offered whenever we stopped. When I got home I read up on manioc and learned that it contains cyanide compounds: it needs to be prepared and cooked properly to avoid cyanide's toxic effects. Many of the people we passed must have had as little understanding of this as we did: I was worried by the huge goitres swelling the throats of some of the villagers, as bulbous as the puffed-out skin of grunting toads. Apparently cyanide poisoning causes these goitres which, at that time, were endemic in parts of central Africa.

***

Every so often the streams merged to collect into a wide arterial river, even more vital to Zaire's transport system than the tracks we were travelling on because, unlike the roads, the rivers didn't dissolve during the rainy season. Where track and river intersected, they were served by ancient ferries, slogging between the banks a few times each day, loaded with freight transporting grain or battered drums of cooking oil, or an impossible number of paying passengers, clinging to the chassis for dear life.

Terry hated these ferries with a vengeance. Like almost every other aspect of African life, he seemed to believe their sole purpose was to be an obstacle between him and his itinerary. The antipathy was mutual: the captains of these ferries always reacted to his impatience by becoming even more obdurate and laid back – if that was possible.

The day he almost lost Q truck was just one example of how this mutual dislike played out. We'd made a 5.30 am start so we could be first in the queue for the ferry, even though we'd been told it wouldn't start running until 7am.

Every ferry halt had its own ubiquitous shanty town, made up of refreshment stands selling the thick syrupy chai so beloved of central Africans, hot and oily rice fritters and dough balls to dip in condensed milk. This was no exception: the place was bustling when we pulled up. Alongside the quay was a visiting container barge whose deck was like a campsite, covered in African cloths spread out for sleeping and eating. Above the deck washing lines flapped like bunting.

Seven o clock came and went and Terry, pointedly pacing up and down outside the food stands, seemed to be the only one expecting the ferry to get moving on time. By the time his watch showed ten past his face was redder than the road we'd travelled. He shouted at Wayne to get into G truck and follow him onto the ferry: that ought to raise the ferry captain and his crew to their posts.

The rest of us watched from the bank, still sipping our cups of chai, as Terry revved Q's engine unnecessarily loudly. When no-one stirred he allowed the truck to roll down the slipway onto the ferry's ramp. But as the front wheels clanked onto the metal the ferry, which had only been loosely secured to shore, seemed to shudder - and then began to slip away from dry land. I guess Terry must have reflexively slammed on his brake which sent a shockwave through the ferry sending it even further out into the water.

Naturally the experienced ferry crew tethered it loosely, so it could ride any wash coming from the large barges which plied this river. I could no longer see Terry but could imagine him sitting in his cab, powerless and scared, wondering whether the river's force might somehow scoop up the stranded truck and carry it away.

Our leader was forced to remain where he was, straddling river and ferry ramp, unable to get out of the cab without getting soaked.

I was glad to be on the bank, laughing along with the locals rather than have them believe this ridiculous man was anything to do with me.

The only one not laughing was the ferry captain. He abandoned his chai to race to the slipway yelling abuse at Terry, gesticulating wildly. You didn't need to speak his language to know he was not amused at having his breakfast interrupted.

Wayne quickly stepped in front of him, signing that he'd fetch our tow rope and use G truck to try and drag Q and therefore the ferry back to the jetty.

Several of the African crew took the other end of the tow rope and waded into the flowing river to tie it to the ramp.

The moment Wayne fired G's engine and tried to reverse the rope snapped. The impact sent another jolt shuddering through the rope to the ferry which seemed to bridle, then begin a slow turn towards the current, as though poised to make a bolt for freedom.

The captain had had enough of our games. He ordered his crew to untether a chain, wide as a human neck, which was attached to a winch at the top of the slipway. It took them a long time to pass the chain hand to hand across the water and secure it to the ferry. Slowly, painstakingly, they brought the ferry, and its unruly cargo, back to shore.

***

I suspect the captain wanted to punish Terry for causing so much disruption. The only way open to him was to prevent Terry's second truck from joining all the other freight and passengers on board for this first crossing of the day.

So after Q truck crossed and loitered on the other bank, we had to wait for the next crossing, which wouldn't take place until the captain and crew had enjoyed a second breakfast. We weren't worried: the slipway was a perfect spot for people watching. I looked on bemused as the captain strolled past us to the stands, helping himself to a plate of food and a large beer, before settling at a shady table with a bunch of noisy lorry drivers.

Terry, on the other bank, was unaware of this. As we whiled away yet more waiting time – one hour's break became two and still the captain stayed where he was – Tom spotted a canoe paddling across the river towards us. There was a strange contrast between the motion of the little boat, constantly having to correct its position as the current tugged it downstream, and the silhouetted figure, distinctively hunched, sitting stationary behind the canoeist.

"It's Terry. What's he doing?"

"Someone tell Heather and Wayne."

Terry barely waited for dry land before he was out of the canoe and splashing towards us, red-faced and furious. "What the hell is going on? Where's the fucking captain? We haven't got all fucking day. Where is the lazy BASTARD?"

If the captain heard Terry's tirade I guessed lunchtime probably just got another hour longer, but Heather stepped swiftly in front of her boss, almost nose to nose.

"They've gone for lunch," she said. "Now sod off."

One of my fondest memories of Long Haul's founder is of his return journey in that canoe, having been given a flea in his ear by his own employee. There was something deeply fitting about the sight of his bent body, sitting alone in the centre of the canoe, separated from us and everyone else by the vast expanse of river, hazy in the heat, isolated by his own sense of being ill-used; beaten once more by the continent he loathed but somehow could not stay away from.

***

Our own crossing, late in the day, was uneventful and brought us a step closer to the next major stop on our crossing of this beautiful land: the city of Lisala, birthplace of Mobutu, and our first encounter with the Congo.

We camped near to it and, without bothering to unpack, headed straight to the shore to catch our first glimpse of a river whose very name seems synonymous with so much history and mystery.

That first sighting filled me with a deep awe, and not only because I had never in my life seen a river of such size. The Congo looked bottomless – it is one of the deepest rivers in the world – and at least several miles across. Beyond its girth, what also took my breath away was the knowledge that it had been here before any imagining and would still be here, shaping the whole future of the countries it passed through, more powerfully than explorers, historians, colonials, empires and politicians ever would.

The Congo is like an iceberg, hiding most of itself from view. But such is the power of its waters that every year it collects and then deposits 86 million tonnes of sediment during the course of its almost three thousand mile journey.

I sat on the bank for the next few hours, simply watching the waters roll past, alive to the strangeness and power that both scared and thrilled me. Here really was the Africa of my imagination, but an Africa I could never really know unless I'd been born and lived here, no matter how many books I read.

I remained watching the waters until it got dark; it felt like an act of respect.

***

Like most ports, the part of Lisala we saw from our camp, was a ramshackle place, with no discernible sense of history. I'm sure there was more to see and explore deeper into the city, but the latest delays with ferries had reinforced Terry's determination that we be in and out as quickly as possible. Indeed, the only reason he'd stopped in Lisala was because his original itinerary offered us a chance to disembark here and join the river boat plying its way between the capital of Kinshasa and Zaire's second city, Kisangani, where the trucks were heading next. It was a six-day journey: offering almost a week at a different pace, with different companions and a chance to really experience the Congo.

The snag to this plan was that the riverboat was already ten days late and was not expected for at least another six. Meaning that anyone wanting to join it from our trucks would then be playing catch up and certainly wouldn't make a rendezvous with us in Kisangani.

I was surprised to hear that in spite of this uncertainty a number of people were going to leave us and wait in Lisala to join the river boat. They were all Aussies and Kiwis and included my latest cooking partner, Lloyd, whose humour I'd miss, if not his – non-existent – cooking skills

***

As we said our farewells to this second breakaway group, two Europeans entered the melee, offering to sell us more Zaire notes at black market rates.

It bothered me that they did so openly, in full view of the crowds who'd made a temporary home around the port and campsite to wait for the boat's arrival.

Grubby notes were changing hands without any attempt to disguise what was going on. So it wasn't a surprise when, on the road out of the city, Wayne suddenly braked hard.

The back flap of G truck was tugged aside and we blinked out into the darkness, registering a couple of men shouting: "Police. Don't move. Stay where you are", as though we'd stumbled into an American cop movie.

My heart sank. We'd left the city behind, it was dark on this road and we were alone out here. The police could exact any justice they chose.

"What's going on. Someone knock for Heather," Kitty Chris shouted, but our courier was already at the back of the truck with the men.

"We see your currency papers. And your money. Get them out. Now," the two men demanded. But as they came closer we clocked that they were not wearing any kind of uniform.

"Where are your badges?" Heather demanded. "Show me *your* papers."

"Show me YOUR papers," one of the so-called policeman tried raising his voice louder than Heather's, hoping perhaps he could out-authority her. But she was having none of it.

"You're not police. Get lost." She turned her back on them, calling their bluff, while the rest of us waited, wondering what would happen next.

There was a pause, a brief standoff, before the two men turned tail and vanished as quickly as they had come. I was beginning to like Heather very much. She seemed to have the measure of all these difficult men and the confidence to stand up to them. Once again I thanked my lucky stars I'd ended up on G truck rather than as part of Terry's miserable crew on Q.

CHAPTER 25

Will preparing our supper at the Kisangani camp site, watched by Leader (Paul)

We were in Bumba, another port along the Congo, and I sat on the riverbank under a palm tree, journal in my lap, fat slices of juicy pineapple spread out on banana leaves at my side. Mark's razor-sharp diving knife lay beside them, sticky with the juice. Mark himself was in the river, along with some of the others, bilharzia warnings unheeded. I could see his sun-bleached head bobbing up and down in the thick soupy water, close enough to the bank not to be tugged into the current. Their idle chatter made a peaceful backdrop to my journaling.

I'd intended to write to my sister Shushie but instead found myself pouring out thoughts about the trip, the months we'd now spent on the road, and what it had shown me about myself and the future I might want.

I knew whatever work I returned to I needed to allow more time in the days for me. All the hours we had spent on board the truck keeping our own company. At first I'd resented the claustrophobia of it; but over the months I had come to make my peace with the long hours on board when all there was to do was read, talk, look, watch, think or daydream.

I had learned that time, lots of it, can be a gift and there is no need to fill every unforgiving minute. The more time I had, the more alive I somehow felt, as if I was seeing the world, my own life and the lives of others, in a way I never had when I was rushing between work, home, family and a hectic social life. A human doing.

Whatever I chose for myself back home I wanted more time to just be.

In order to come away for five months I'd had to give up my job and my London flat. I felt that I needed to draw on the same reservoir of courage – and trust – to reimagine my future, without it needing to look the same as it had; the same as most other people's, working to live, squeezing in all of the things that actually mattered rather than the other way around.

If Chad had taught me one thing it was what did matter. And none of it involved squeezing into a tube resembling a cattle truck to rush my way into a tiny office where I'd spend all day at a desk, scarcely pausing to talk to my colleagues or stop for a sandwich at lunchtime.

Something else I had learned too, was about how we are seen and see ourselves. The closeness which had sometimes suffocated me, the challenges we had faced individually and as a group, meant there had really been no place to hide. Though I haven't written much about it here – it wouldn't be fair on my companions whose own lives, I'm sure, have moved on dramatically in the 40 years since I knew them - we had seen the best and worst of each other: the snideness, the selfishness, the fear and suspicion; we'd also seen selflessness, generosity, empathy and courage. Perhaps after all it was ok for me to be me; to show up in life as myself, good and bad. And if that was true, then I need not worry if other people did not understand or disapproved of my choices when I got home.

Let's be real here, we had only been away three and a bit months and had spent much of that time with people from the same background, if not country. And yet I felt, deep in my core, that I was being changed by it and that life afterwards would never be quite the same again. Nor did I want it to be.

***

Terry intended to follow the Congo as far south as we could but in Bumba the couriers consulted with other European drivers who counselled against it.

They said the bridges and ferries further upstream were poor structures, unreliable, especially if the rains came early. They reported that just the previous week a lorry carrying not only its cargo but dozens of paying passengers had overturned on one of the rickety bridges: the vehicle and everyone on it were tipped down into the Congo. Several of the passengers drowned.

When Heather told us this story around the campfire that night I thought how uncanny it was that we seemed always to be skirting on the edge of disasters. Time after time we heard, on the campsite grapevines, horror stories that had happened to overland trucks a week or two ahead of us on the same route.

For instance there was the woman passenger riding on the tailgate who slipped and was mangled under the trailer; someone on the same trip who had developed dysentery and died on board.

We had been robbed and mugged often enough, but we heard about other overlanders who'd been beaten to within an inch of their lives. One local bus driver was even less fortunate – he was lynched by a mob after accidentally running over a small child.

Some of these stories may have been myths, or much embroidered over time: things that happened to someone once.

But a month or so after this campfire conversation, there was no disputing the newspaper reports of a whole group of overlanders poisoned by a faulty heating system as they slept - in the very same Tanzanian game lodge that some of our group had stayed in a week earlier.

Nor with Terry's own account of his last Long Haul trip, which reached Nairobi intact, only for two of the group to lose their lives in a bus crash a few days after the trip officially ended. On the whole we had little to complain about.

***

Our next goal, after we'd elected to take the safer but less interesting route from Bumba, was a place which had seen its share of death. In the 1960s, when Kisangani was still known by its colonial name of Stanleyville, hundreds of local people and white settlers were taken hostage, tortured and murdered during the Simba rebellion.

Outside the city we stopped to photograph the shell of a rusting Congolese air force DC3, stripped of its innards within hours of its crash landing in this inaccessible corner of jungle. The story we heard was that the crew survived the fall, perhaps cushioned by the tree canopy from a direct plunge to earth. However, they were shot by the local military and then eaten by local cannibals. I can find absolutely no evidence of this in the vast encylopaedia that is Google! However, less than 20 years later, the vegetation grew up around the faded metal like a soft grass skirt, while not a blade of grass nor a single creeper invaded the plane's interior.

It was the briefest of stops. Terry pushed us hard as he always did when he could scent the possibility of a cold beer and a break from his passengers.

Zaire's second city Kisangani promised both. So the only stops we made were to buy bananas to add to the breakfast rice pudding, and once to photograph a vast column of giant ants, an army on the move like a vast oil slick, spreading out along the red dust track. Those who got too close were rewarded with stinging bites.

It was midnight when we reached Kisangani, exhausted by an 18-hour drive, pulling into the grounds of the Olympic Hotel, where we were to camp.

The hotel looked small and, even in the blackout of an African night, I could see it was rundown. It lay at the end of a backstreet, and the grounds were just a scrubby backyard.

There was a brick toilet and shower block at one end and a few dilapidated garden tables and chairs at the other. A clump of trees gave a little shade from the heat of the day.

By daylight we could see we were not the only travellers: there were a couple of small tents whose occupants had no doubt been enjoying what space there was before our arrival. And there was another overland vehicle whose passengers turned out to be mainly German with a few Swedes and a lone Canadian.

I've already written about my embarrassment at staring out at Africa from our high-up perches within the trucks, but this one took grandstanding to a new level: inside was a single raised bank of seats perched high in the centre of the vehicle, offering a lofty view in each direction. I realise they, like us, had paid to see Africa, but I squirmed at the idea of travelling in a way that seemed to say Africa was a theatre and this the paying audience.

***

For those with cash in their pockets, however ill-gotten, Kisangani offered many temptations, not least Terry's longed-for bar and some tantalising smells of sizzling meat coming from the hotel restaurant. Beyond the hotel grounds the city had a bustling market, an artist's quarter, and more evidence of its' colonial past in the shape of two patisseries.

I, of course, had next to no cash: just the remains of Tom's original loan and I hesitated to ask for more. So I put out word that I was willing to do washing in return for a few Zaires, and very quickly accumulated piles of filthy tee-shirts, grubby underwear and grey sleeping bag inners, from Mark, Kitty Chris and a few others.

I genuinely didn't mind the work but taking Chris' soiled clothes off his hands stuck in my throat a little: we had never learned to like each other.

Still, it earned me enough Zaires for a few treats plus I had kitty money when my turn to cook came around again. I'd decided, after the loss of my third cooking partner, to go it alone, but knew I could count on Annie, Gai, Mark, Tom and sometimes Will – my closest friends on board – to muck in and help.

It was Annie who said she'd come with me to shop in the market: a chance for her to take photos while I haggled for whatever I could cook up for breakfast and dinner.

We entered the melee like kids in a toy store, spotting, for the first time, aubergines, spinach, leeks, even green beans – tastes we'd long since forgotten. There was plentiful bread too: tables piled high with fresh sausage-shaped loaves, and a whole line of stalls selling dried meats and fish.

Despite the fact that they'd been dried, the smell was overpowering: acrid and heavy, catching at the back of our throats.

Worse was to come when we reached the end of the aisle: creatures scorched and blackened, their limbs cruelly splayed, miniature fingers and toes curled in shock, faces frozen in macabre grins. They looked for all the world like human babies; I felt no less horrified when I realised they were baby monkeys, fur singed off in the same preservative fires that blurred their facial features and caused my mistake in the first place.

I couldn't get away fast enough, but just around the corner was another stomach-churning sight: a large enamel bowl full of writhing witchety grubs, fat as plums and yellow like catarrh, squirming against each other in their confusion. African shoppers were buying them by the handful, then spearing them onto wooden skewers and roasting them on an open fire.

The stallholder, enjoying our shocked expressions, assured us they tasted just as good raw, with the bonus that they tickled your throat as they slipped down.

With so much choice I couldn't fail at supper: I served sweet potato bubble and squeak with buttered corn on the cob, followed by bananas in hot fudge sauce. Even better, I finally found some edible eggs: most of those we'd been offered in Africa were either fertilised or completely rotten, having been kept for weeks to sell to passing travellers. I mixed the fresh eggs with milk and fried them in palm oil to serve up omelette sandwiches the next morning.

***

On our third and last night in Kisangani I was unable to sleep, perhaps unsettled by a night in the hotel bar when so much of the talk had been of people's plans for the end of the trip.

I had nothing much to say on that subject, and it bothered me to be asked to think more about the future when we still had four countries to visit and – for me – the section I'd been looking forward to most, East Africa's wildlife reserves. (To be clear, in the less-enlightened 1980s we were still calling them game parks as if they existed solely for the pleasure of inadequate white men with guns wanting to bag a prize).

As I lay in the tent trying to get to sleep there seemed to be a lot of comings and goings around the campsite, urgent whispers, the zipping and unzipping of tents, and sometimes torchlight flashing through the thin surface of the inner tent I was lying under. I recognised Tim's voice but not the others, and must eventually have drifted to sleep because in no time at all I heard Terry shouting that we needed an early start and should get up. Apparently we were not going to wait any longer for the boat party: he said in all likelihood they were still in Lisala, still waiting for the ferry, and would have to catch us up when they could.

"What was all the noise about last night?" I asked Will once we were all packed up and the trucks began their rumble through the city's outskirts.

"Haven't you heard? A group of them got offered some gold."

"Gold? What, from locals?"

"Yeah. These guys came into the bar on the first night and offered a 30 ounce ingot for $50."

"That's huge isn't it? Almost two pounds." My mind boggled.

"Well they said it was a good price because it was stolen. They needed to shift it quickly."

"Uh oh", I could guess what was coming.

"The guys never showed up when they said they would so our little gold-buying consortium was spitting and cursing that they'd found a better price somewhere else. Then the gold guys finally show up last night and the group's so relieved they can't wait to close the deal."

"I'm guessing it wasn't gold."

"It was dark to be fair," Will said. "Course as soon as the guys left everyone started getting antsy. So some bright spark suggested they should try and melt the ingot to check it's gold.

"Thing was Jane, the moment the heat is under it all of us could smell the paint. It was rubbing off on their fingers. Gold paint." Will shook his head sagely and I once again pondered quite who was getting the best of who during this crossing of the African continent.

CHAPTER 26

Another day, another ferry crossing in Zaire

Our experiments with the local weed got more adventurous as our time in Zaire drew to a close. One night Tim stole eggs and flour from the stores, mixed in the chopped bongo and fried up dozens of little pancakes which we ate with sugar to disguise the bitter taste.

We were soon lost in our own heads, stumbling to our sleeping bags and drifting off, a whole world away from each other and Terry's strange trip.

All that is except for Dave the guitarist who had always been one of the quietest on board. I'd never heard him raise his voice, much less express excitement.

"Heather, Heather, wake up; you've got to hear this." He sounded urgent.

"Umph. What is it?" Heather grumbled from under her covers.

"Listen. This is important. Heather!!!"

"What?"

"I'm going to fly home and marry my girlfriend. We broke up before I came to Africa. Heather? Are you listening to me?"

"Go to sleep."

"You don't understand. I know what I have to do to be happy. I'VE ACHIEVED ENLIGHTENMENT."

I must confess I envied Dave his moment of enlightenment. The bongo pancakes which we continued to munch at breakfast the next day, had the opposite effect on me, zoning me out entirely.

The rest of the time, the entire five months I was away, are etched on my memory as deeply as stone carvings that have survived the centuries. I can recall smells and sounds, and how I felt. But the day of the bongo breakfast is entirely blank – as it was for almost everyone else on board G truck.

Just one memory has survived, of Wayne stopping around the middle of the day, presumably for lunch, then, when no-one moved, coming down to the back of the truck and lifting the tarpaulin to peer inside and find out why.

"Jeez, what are you lot on?" he spluttered, before dropping the flap again and returning to the cab to drive on.

***

By the next day the effects had worn off and we were able to appreciate another change of scenery as we motored closer to the border with Rwanda via the Ruwenzori mountains. There were fewer huts now alongside the roads and in places the jungle fell away, allowing us to see further across the fields and forests of Zaire. The road began to climb and the air tasted fresher, cooler.

The style of people's homes changed too: some looked more like chalets than the simple huts we were used to, sturdy with steep rooves overhanging the structures below. In the far distance I could begin to make out hilltops, rising and curving, their outlines softened by an almost bluish haze.

The next morning, when we rose from our tents, the canvas was studded with crystal drops of dew, and breathing the air was like gulping ice cold water.

It was impossible not to feel excited at this change of scene, after weeks in which we'd been dwarfed by the jungle scenery, unable to see through it or beyond it.

Now we were flying, climbing up into the sky, with Africa spread out like a soft green blanket beneath us.

As we continued our transition from Africa's central heart into its eastern plains we began to encounter other overland trips.

And here I must digress to note an interesting facet of human nature: that no matter how ill-conceived and managed Terry's expedition was, confronted with other overlanders we somehow closed ranks and sought to convince ourselves of our own superiority to their trips.

First came an Exodus truck, journeying all the way from Johannesburg to London in 22 weeks – just two weeks more than our itinerary, but several thousand miles more.

Perhaps we were right to conclude we were better off: if our trip had largely involved driving, I cannot imagine the punishing drives this group must have been put through to meet such an ambitious timetable. Worse, in my view, they were travelling FROM Africa to Europe. The Puritan in me has always wanted to save the best for last, so it just felt wrong that they were moving from difference and drama to the familiar shapes of Europe and home.

The other notable overlanders we met were on a three-week tour of East Africa, they told us, a strange combination of elderly British men wearing Marks and Spencer's safari suits, and beautiful young Scandinavian women with glamorous hairstyles and miniscule shorts.

They'd been stuck at Gatwick for the first of their three weeks due to a strike.

"We're supposed to be doing Kampala to Kinshasa and back through the game parks," one of the men, the self-appointed spokesman, told us. "Bad luck of course. That's gone to pot."

Will, as always the politest of us, enquired: "What do you think of Africa so far?"

The old man pursed his lips. "Much as I expected. Nice scenery. Shame about the people. Should warn you by the way, watch out for the kids. Bloody terrors. Always after something. It's not safe to stand still."

He remembered his manners then: "How long's your trip?"

"Five months."

I watched his gaze settle on our grubby clothes, the wood piled under our feet, the red dust covering the tarpaulins. "I see. Shouldn't be teaching granny to suck eggs should I?" And then, as an afterthought, "I suppose it's hard to keep up standards in these primitive surroundings."

***

Goma is the border city, sitting alongside its Rwanda counterpart, Gisenyi, on the edge of a wide grey lake. The backdrop to both cities is the dramatic Virunga mountains – a chain of volcanoes straddling the borders of Zaire, Rwanda and Uganda.

Unfortunately the weather changed as we climbed up towards the border and by the time we reached our campsite alongside the lake we couldn't see the volcanoes, merely a place where the cloud and drizzle were a darker shade of grey in the distance. It was a strange experience, after weeks of heat, to touch my skin's dampness and feel droplets like a thin veil on my hair.

Most of the volcanoes are dormant but not all: every ten years or so these craggy beasts rumble a reminder of their looming presence over Goma and the surrounding towns and villages. As recently as the 1970s a vast tongue of lava had slithered down from the active Nyrigongo volcano towards Goma, swallowing up fields in its path, scarring everything it passed, pausing only when it reached the first buildings so that it now sits strangely on the outskirts, higher than anything around it, like an unfinished road.

It is sad to think that the people we met in 1985, living in the shadow of this natural threat, would less than a decade later face far worse as the Rwandan genocide spilled over into Goma.

More than one million sick, starving and persecuted refugees would make their home here. And later, that influx would spread its own tidal ripples into the country we had just been passing through, becoming a major factor in the first and second Congo wars.

Even if we had been told then how deep and dark the shadows would fall over these beautiful countries I don't think we would have believed it.

Zaire had been a breath of air, as Rwanda would soon be too: the friendliest people we would encounter throughout the whole five months, with a kind of innocence that enabled us to connect with them heart to heart rather than with any agenda. I wrote in my introduction how lucky I feel to have been able to visit these countries when I did, when the death and destruction had not yet wrought such an awful toll on people who opened their villages and their lives to us. Nowhere is that more true than of Goma and the Rwanda we were about to enter.

***

Only now as I write this do I realise I need to reconsider a small event that happened in Goma and which I have previously related as a funny anecdote.

I was guarding the trucks – of course; nothing had changed in that respect: it was always my turn whenever we pulled into a big town or city, especially one such as Goma where, it was rumoured, it was possible to buy cheese and MARS BARS!

A rather excited Will was first back to let me know the rumours were true. "Guess what though. I sold my Tuareg sword. Eighteen quid I got. Only paid five back in Agadez. Hit the jackpot there my love didn't I? You got anything to sell?"

"How come?" I asked, thinking of the little silver dagger I'd buried in the bottom of the locker after picking it up in Agadez market.

"I got talking to this chap in the street and he said he knew a guy who bought things. So he takes me there. It was a pretty smart place, official looking; maybe the town hall, who knows. They were all wearing shirts anyway."

"So what happened?"

"We go down a corridor and he knocks on this door and we're in an office with a man in a suit sitting at the desk. Big man. Serious looking. I show him the sword and his eyes light up like Blackpool and he offers me the price I said I wanted straight away. No haggling. Nothing."

"But what did he want it for?"

"That's the strange thing," Will said. "I'm still in the room and he opens this cupboard and it's stuffed, I mean floor to ceiling, with guns and swords and daggers. Gave me the creeps."

"What do you think? A private army? Is he planning to start a civil war?"

"No idea," Will shrugged. "When he saw my expression though he put his finger on his lips like he's saying it's our secret. Not that I'd dare say anything about someone who's got that much stuff in his cupboard…"

I thought for a moment. "Will you take me there? I could use some cash."

Reader, in my ignorance, I sold the dagger without regret at the time. Only now I wonder whether I should have done so and how it might later have been used. It is no consolation to tell you that though I blew some of the proceeds on cheese and chocolate they were both a big disappointment. Somehow our mainly vegetarian diet had changed my taste buds: these western tastes were altogether too rich for me in comparison – the cheese seemed glutinous and the chocolate merely sickly.

***

The dagger didn't raise enough to enable me to join a side trip Heather organised, up the volcano to peer into its crater. But I made the best of being one of the few left behind, camped beside the lake, enjoying the way the breeze ruffled its waters.

It felt good to be part of a smaller group, to be able to move around our camp without arguing, without the usual acrimony over that day's cooks ruining supper by inadvertently splashing diesel into the mix, or whose rubbish was lying around.

Instead, those of us who were left sat silently, comfortable with the only sounds being the suck and clink of soft waves on the lake's pebbled shore, the cloud slowly rising so that as dusk came we could see the shape of the volcano, a giant overshadowing everything around it.

I hoped the skies would remain clear for our companions' hike to the lip of the crater in the morning.

It turned out to be Tim's last night in the camp: he had had enough of Long Haul life and said since he'd already seen East Africa it was time to strike out with his next venture. Undeterred by the lack of success his rug and gold buying had had, his plan was to invest in an overland truck as a cover for smuggling goods from one country to another where they fetched a higher price.

I later heard that he went into partnership with another traveller in Uganda but before they even got their first paying customer Tim's partner vanished with the truck, and the remaining funds, as well as all the documents. It may or may not have happened: one thing about Tim was that he seemed to attract stories around him, the same way the rest of us attracted flies.

All of that lay ahead though when, the next morning, he made his low-key farewell, slinging his bag over his shoulder with a brief 'see you guys later'. I knew we'd all miss one of our biggest characters on board, not to mention his unshakeable ability to bounce back from bad luck.

There was another significant departure too: for some time we'd heard rumours that four people on Q truck were sick with hepatitis B – deadly if left untreated.

To be honest, there had been no real attempt at hygiene by any of us so it was very much the luck of the draw that Q was where disease broke out – in spite of the vaccinations we'd all had before we left home. Even after the unfortunate four travellers had departed for a flight home from Goma, we continued to pass water bottles and beer cans around the campfire, to share cutlery and fail to wash our hands before we started preparing or cooking food.

Worryingly, the group who we'd left in Lisala, planning to do the Congo boat trip, had been close friends of those who were now forced to fly home. We'd assumed they'd be trying to catch us up but it dawned on us it was likely sickness had broken out among them too. That would leave them truly stuck since we had all their travellers' cheques and currency declaration forms in the safes.

Later, back in the UK, I came across a guide to travellers' health in Africa, which mentioned not only the high incidence of hepatitis carriers in central Africa, but also singled out the swimming pool at the Chadian Hotel as an infamous breeding ground for that and many other nasties.

CHAPTER 27

Even though Goma lay so close to Rwanda, we had to wait for the volcano walkers to return and it was dark by the time we crossed the border.

Our first discovery was that there was absolutely nowhere to camp. Unlike Zaire, here every inch of land in Rwanda was cultivated: neat fields, plantations and homes crowded together.

We were lucky to be taken in by a French mission that offered us the floor of a church hall for the night. It had that comforting familiarity of junior school: child-size toilets, sparkling white sinks and the smell of disinfectant.

Initially, I loved the novelty of sleeping under a roof for the first time in months. But by morning I was very aware of how stale and bitter the air I was breathing was – people's night breath. I realised I had learned to prefer the smell and taste of outdoors.

Back in the trucks, leaning from the sides as we drove on, the impressions of a country bursting at the seams were confirmed.

As the road wound through a valley all I could see as far as the land stretched was a patchwork of fields with an occasional hut dotted among them. Even where the valley sides rose steeply towards a brilliant blue sky, everything had been claimed for farming.

We saw sweet potatoes and peanuts, maize and bananas. And we saw people out tending to the crops: rows of bent backs already at work despite the early hour.

It all looked busy and, to be honest, prosperous, compared to the countries we had driven through where so much of the land was sand or jungle or simply too harsh and desolate for any form of life. And yet our on-board copy of *Shoestring* warned that Rwanda is one of Africa's (and therefore the world's) poorest and most over-populated lands.

What we were seeing was not some peaceful rural idyll but a population that had outgrown its country and had to farm every last inch of earth in order to provide themselves with a subsistence diet.

Our goal was the Parc des Volcans, a vast reserve of wooded hills providing the last safe-ish haven for the world's remaining 200 mountain gorillas – and their champion, Dian Fossey, whose story is told in *Gorillas in the Mist*.

It was impossible not to be aware of the tensions between the communities: on the one hand the naturalist and her team of wardens, offering tourist treks to see the gorillas in order to raise funds to continue their work.

Ranged against them, poachers for whom the head of a gorilla was worth a fortune; if the wardens got in the way their lives were cheap too.

How to square the ethics of so much land dedicated to a handful of animals and the tourists who flocked to see them, with people starving at every edge of the park? True, the tourists brought foreign currency into the country but like most of Africa the dollars rarely ended up in the hands of those who most needed them.

I understood that giving up the national park in order that more people might eat would only ever provide a temporary solution, while condemning some of this planet's most gentle and fascinating creatures to extinction.

These days I would take an even harder line, believing as I do that the existence of planet earth depends on us recognising the equal rights of all life forms.

We have become so greedy, so certain that everything exists for our benefit, that we are willing to sacrifice our own planet. But the people of Rwanda and many other countries are as much victims of greed as the gorillas, forced by their leaders to grow cash crops for our consumption rather than their own need; squeezed into endless tight corners by our willingness to put up walls and tighten borders rather than share resources.

Africa had already shown me how fragile human life can be, and it was also teaching me that sometimes there are no easy answers no matter how long you think or argue about something.

What many of the communities we'd passed through seemed to have over us was an acceptance of how things sometimes are. As hunters they accepted their prey's right to kill them first if they were too slow. As farmers they accepted that the sun and rain could be kind or cruel and they were powerless to change that. Yet they also seemed to accept the smaller pleasures, of sitting around a fire with family and friends, dancing with strangers, taking their time.

I wanted the gorillas saved because they were part of the web of life, but then I had enough to eat. People were campaigning for the gorillas but who was campaigning for the Rwandans?

***

Back then, though, my thoughts were very much running on a track of regret, that with no funds I would not be joining the gorilla treks.

The upside was that we would be camping in the same spot for three or four days while smaller groups took turns following a guide up into the volcanoes park in the hope of glimpsing gorillas. I could imagine fewer places as beautiful in which to rest and regroup. On every side of our camp the hills rose, dark and wooded, soaring towards the distinct shape of ancient volcanoes, frosted each early morning in light mist.

Perhaps if I'd seen the gorillas with my own eyes I would have had my answers. My companions who went trekking returned with the air of those who have had a religious experience: full of awe and wonder to have got so close to a family of gorillas and watch them eating, grooming and at play.

Annie and Mark told me what surprised them was how affectionate the gorillas were towards each other. They were also well-used to small groups of silent trekkers hunkering down in the undergrowth to watch them at play; so much so that they sometimes stared back at the watchers.

Annie said she literally felt a connection, something moving between her and an old silverback who fastened his eyes on her own and held them there.

While I waited for my friends to return I spent a large part of each day half in and half out of the tent with my nose in a book. Or away in my own thoughts. Even though many of the trip's highlights were still ahead of us the departure of more people through sickness had given the trucks an end of term feel. I knew as soon as I returned to London, not just penniless but owing money to Tom and dad, the pressure would be on to dive straight back into work.

I went for long walks, but soon learned a single woman was too much of a curiosity to be left alone. Sometimes, as I walked between the fields, or stuck along the narrow national park tracks, people came up with their hands outstretched, asking frankly for money or 'cadeux'.

At other times they walked along behind me, a kind of chattering and giggling escort that froze, innocently smiling back at me, when I stopped and turned around, rather like a game of Peep Behind the Curtain.

One time when a teenager stepped in front of me I asked him why everyone was always asking me for something. "Because you are so rich," he replied simply in perfect English, his hand still outstretched.

***

Towards the end of our stay there was one more departure – Terry's.

It turned out that a major reason he'd always pushed our pace was because he had a pre-booked air ticket home. Terry was due to fly from Rwanda's capital Kigali, presumably to start arranging the next Long Haul expedition.

Just like Tim's, his departure early afternoon could hardly have been more low-key.

A few of us sought him out to say goodbye but he didn't make the rounds himself.

I suppose he had been mentally absent for so long, so clearly only in Africa on sufferance, we no longer paid much attention to him.

The past months had shown him he could trust Wayne and Heather too. Perhaps he would not need to accompany every trip he scheduled in future. He could sit at home and tell potential customers how wonderful Africa is, without actually having to go there.

When I saw him six months after the trip ended, at a reunion party in London, he surprised me with his warmth. Clearly distance was already working its magic for he spoke of our trip as one of the best he had done, as if the difficulties we'd come through had made it all that bit more special.

***

The gorillas had been the focus of our journey into Rwanda but we had one more stop before motoring onto neighbouring Tanzania: the country's capital, Kigali.

Kigali is set among hills and the drive up to it reminded me of Switzerland's alpine passes, chalet-like houses perched on wooded hills; the shadow of other hills and perhaps the volcanoes we had come from, etched misty-grey against the horizon.

There was nowhere to camp, either in Kigali or beyond, where the same intensive land-use extended right to the country's border. This meant we'd be forced to have another all-night drive. Before we did so, though, there was a capital city to explore, and marketing to be done since our next major stop – the Serengeti – would have no shops.

Exciting as it was to be in a capital city and discover tourist shops selling postcards, and cheap African artefacts that had probably been made in the Far East, for me nothing compared with the thrill of collecting seventeen letters at the post restante at Kigali's main post office.

I abandoned the shopping to take my haul back to the truck and dive back into the world I'd left behind: every inconsequential detail had new meaning because it described a familiar, privileged life that was waiting if I wanted it.

More than that, I felt emotional about the love and support implicit in these messages from miles away. I knew how lucky I was to have such friends and family, more precious than any other things in my life. A part of me couldn't wait to share with them the adventures we'd had.

Yet as I sat in the truck later that evening, replete after a café supper of beans and meat, I also knew how much I would miss this: sitting in the shadows with faces that had become so familiar to me, and with whom I really had shared the best of times and the worst of times.

I loved these new friends, even those I would never like such as Kitty Chris: it was the love that comes when you have shared something defining, something out of the ordinary.

Being in Africa had indeed been something extraordinary. What is it Karen Blixen says in her *Letters from Africa*? "Difficult times have helped me to understand better than before, how infinitely rich and beautiful life is in every way, and that so many things that one goes worrying about are of no importance whatsoever."

I had come away at a time when the ordinary problems of every life - heartbreak, loss, boredom, stress, busyness – had threatened to overwhelm me. I'd learned how a mind busy with thoughts of how hard life is dwells in a kind of prison. In Africa my mind had been allowed to take flight, and in doing so, had found more peace than I had ever known.

I could recall standing beyond the Hermitage, staring out in wonder at the battalions of Hoggar Mountains; the yellow emptiness of the endless Chad desert on Christmas morning; lying out under a mosquito net and staring up at the Zaire sky, humming with light and sound. As much as the people I'd met, it was these memories of soaring freedom that would be my companions when I returned home.

CHAPTER 28

Collecting water at Lake Victoria

After Rwanda's crammed countryside, the country's border with Tanzania felt like another world: there were no more buildings, no harvested fields; just a shabby hut serving as a customs post on the banks of a river.

The waters were swollen by the first rains of the season, thick as drinking chocolate oozing its way between the two countries.

On the far bank, Tanzania was familiar in a way I hadn't been prepared for. Suddenly we were entering a part of Africa that had been prized by generations of colonialists, including from the UK.

That recent heritage, shaped in the corridors of European bureaucracy, was starkly obvious: after all the ramshackle border points we'd crossed, Tanzania boasted a modern brick building.

We could see all the usual paraphernalia of office blocks through its shining windows. If there is one thing European involvement brought to its colonies it was a passion for paperwork and officialdom.

Oh, and signs. The one greeting us while we waited for Heather to complete customs formalities inside this important building read 'Tanzania welcomes careful drivers'.

Strangely, this sense of order, of reacquaintance with the familiar, helped shift the mood again. Every single country we had visited had its own vibe, its own character. Africa was no more one amorphous whole than the places that make up Europe are.

As we crossed into Tanzania I sensed a relaxation on board, as though everyone had taken a deep breath.

We were not only entering a country that had been run by Germans and then the British, a country that continued, since independence, as a member of the Commonwealth: we were also, finally, very much joining the tourist trail.

Who hasn't watched on TV the migration of tens of thousands of wildebeest across the Serengeti, or lions stalking their prey? Who hasn't gasped at pictures of Kilimanjaro's snow-capped summit surging through the clouds towards a cobalt sky?

And now we were here, no longer seeing this magnificent landscape on screen but actually entering it: stretching away from us in shallow green folds as far as the eye could see; mile upon mile, melting from green and gold into a lilac distance. This land was as expansive as Rwanda had been claustrophobic, a playground for nature's mysteries and miracles.

No doubt it was all those wildlife programmes that made Tanzania feel so familiar, so known. But a part of me wanted to believe that this familiarity and sense of homecoming I had came from some ancient ancestral memory. Africa, and specifically the Great Rift Valley we were now entering, were the birthplace of humankind: where creatures first stood upright and walked on two legs. I hoped that somewhere in my body's smallest cells lived the memory of those times three million years earlier; a time when these vast plains really had been home.

***

For two perfect days we sped unhindered across this huge canvas of throbbing life, the trucks somehow less substantial than the swaying grasses and impossibly large skies.

The landscape was inhabited by a wealth of rainbow species, from pink and purple lizards darting for cover, to the pride of lionesses who emerged from the grass to cross the road nonchalantly, aware they belonged and owned the landscape more than we ever would.

Some of the colours were so bright it seemed they must be artificial. I spotted a beetle in the undergrowth, its head iridescent green, its body a glittery purple, the colours separated with a collar of sparkling gold. There were birds whose breasts were the bright red of tomato soup, or like ripe lemons; and the splendid starling whose feathers flashed with the luminescence of deep sapphire. At night the entire scene turned into a glittering celebration of glow-worms, flashing their bright messages to each other.

The only unwelcome wildlife were the tsetse flies we knew could, on occasion, carry sleeping sickness. At the very least they were capable of delivering stinging red bites that itched raw.

They tended to arrive in noisy swarms and after several painful episodes - when our flapping arms proved useless in the face of their determination to feast on us - we discovered the way to deal with them was to smoke them out. The moment one appeared, packs of cigarettes were quickly passed around the truck and we all lit up and puffed away furiously, including non-smokers like me.

The second day in Tanzania it rained: not the hot rain of central Africa which had only added to the sense of suffocation, but a cleansing, refreshing rain, catching the airborne dust and settling it back to earth.

It was such a deluge that the track we were travelling dissolved. Instead of soaking away, the water gushed freely along its surface, carrying a top layer of soil so that the ground turned into a travellator, a moving layer of thick red mud.

At the foot of a shallow hill G truck bogged. It was strange hearing the tyres spinning helplessly again, as Wayne battled the gears. But we were still close enough to memories of Chad to know the drill. We jumped out and unhitched the sand mats ready to give the tyres some purchase to grip onto.

While we strained a local bus appeared at the top of the hill, heading our way. It was every bit a relic from the 1950s with a round bonnet and small windows like portholes down each side. Its driver seemed unaware that the rain had turned the hill to a massive water chute.

The sound of its roaring engine forced us all to look up from our matting. With open mouths we watched as the bus tipped beyond the lip of the hill and onto the mud slide, like a log going over a waterfall. Slipping and sliding it came, gaining speed, skidding from side to side - a missile heading implacably towards us.

At the very last minute we dropped the mats and hurled ourselves off the road into the grass, abandoning the truck to its fate. I clamped my hands over my ears and shut my eyes, imagining the head-on collision, praying Wayne had jumped clear.

And yet the next sound was not of metal crashing onto metal, two beasts fusing themselves together, but the screech of rope lashings being lifted and dropped again.

Somehow, at the very last moment, the bus driver had wrestled his vehicle a few inches away from our sitting duck truck and even now was hurtling through the quagmire hoping momentum would carry him up the other side – which it did.

That was another very, very near miss.

***

As far as I know, David Livingstone never visited Lake Victoria. Yet its name, its associations with an era when the continent was opening up to Europeans, meant that arriving on its shores was always going to be a significant moment.

So it proved as, towards the end of the second day, we rode up a track to the summit of a hillock where we caught our first glimpse of Africa's most evocative lake, spread out like a sheet of liquid silver.

It was actually the explorer Speke who, with Burton, was tracking the source of the Nile, who came to this vast body of water. It was known by local people as Lake Nyanza but - in true white man style - Speke renamed it for his queen.

Nyanza is Africa's largest lake by area, covering 23,000 square miles, so we had every right to be awed by its scale. That's three times the size of Wales.

Which meant in almost every direction all we could see was the shining water, as though we had actually reached the ocean.

We were at Victoria's southernmost tip where a ferry ride connects travellers with the regional capital, Mwanza, jumping-off point for the Serengeti.

Yet even though this is the narrowest part of the lake, still the water seemed to stretch away from us to infinity, peopled by long canoes, hollowed from trees, in which men sat with their nets, fishing to feed their families.

At the water's edge, others fished directly from the shore, hauling in nets and spearing their catch on sharpened sticks.

Close by sat a few women, ready to transfer the fish into enamel bowls. They put the bowls between their knees and used acacia branches to discourage flies, hypnotically waving these homemade switches back and forth. I assume their buyers were passengers coming on and off the Mwanza ferry.

Children played on the jetty where the ferry would arrive in the morning. They were more interested in their improvised toys than this adult business – or even in us. The whole scene, I guessed, was very much as it must have been a century before when white explorers first claimed to have 'discovered' the lake – news, I'm sure, to the Tanzanians.

But I was so glad we'd come too late to catch the ferry and would be camping beside the lake. I wanted to breath in as much of its magic and history as I could; to see it catch fire, turning from silver to red to gold as the sun set, to watch it soak up the light and return to darkness as the evening wore on; and to be there in the early morning when it woke; to watch the women arrive, huge aluminium buckets on their heads, to beat their clothes clean in its waters.

***

We reached Mwanza via the ferry at lunchtime on a Sunday, which was good news for everyone with money in their pockets. Among all the evidence of the city's colonial past, the large hotel advertising 'all you can eat Sunday lunch' was perhaps the most obvious.

Almost as surreal was an old red GPO phone box on the same main street. And a whole line of houses with wooden signs swinging in the breeze outside: guest house, vacancies

Annie and I chose the marketplace over a hotel lunch and not only to save money. I thought that there was a chance I might be able to sell a few more personal items to top up my almost non-existent funds – among them the handful of music cassettes I'd bought for the truck's player. They wouldn't be needed much longer.

We wandered backstreets, stopping to buy small handfuls of roasted nuts and a cup of coffee in one of the cafes.

It was Annie who spotted a small music store and who stood at my shoulder, giving me the courage to haggle with the shopkeeper who wanted to drive a hard bargain. He pointed out my four cassettes were very well used, their plastic cases scoured opaque by the dust and sand of our travels.

Still, it seemed western music was highly prized. After some half-hearted protesting the man gave me 100 shillings for each of them. At the time there was something like 20 shillings to the £ British - a fortune to me!

I hardly had time to pocket the crumpled notes and head onto the market square before the harsh tones of Jim Steinman came blasting out across the whole area: *that's no way to treat an expensive guitar.*

For the next hour, as we browsed market stalls laden with cork-soled platform shoes, flared jeans, and tank tops – clearly discarded and exported from Europe to Africa - our soundtrack was Meatloaf, the Moody Blues and Queen.

***

Tanzania was another country which required us to prove we'd exchanged a certain amount of currency – even though there was a tempting black market on which you could get almost ten times the value of your western currency in shillings.

We dutifully headed to the bank to get at least one official stamp on our declaration forms. It took an age, of course, as African bureaucracy must, and though we'd planned to move on after lunch it was late afternoon before we were ready to pack up the trucks.

Suddenly there was a cry: "Heather! Wayne! STOP!"

Hurtling towards us, red-faced and literally quivering with excitement, were three of the boat people we'd dropped off in Lisala. That was three fewer than had left the trucks, but still I could so easily identify with what they must be feeling: to have finally caught up not only with us but with much of their paperwork and most of their travellers' cheques, which we'd been carrying in the safes.

"Where you've been? Where are the others?" Heather was the first to speak.

"We could ask you the same question. Where were you?! We got to Kisangani and they said you'd left four days before. What happened to waiting for us?"

"Terry wouldn't let us," Gai said bluntly.

"We've been chasing you ever since. Nightmare. Thought we'd never catch you. As it is we had to leave the others behind at the border because they didn't have enough money to enter Tanzania. They think they're going to try going up through Uganda and catching us in Kenya. Gotta say that's Terry's fault. He knew you had all our money."

"Shit, that's tough," Will spoke. "So who's gone north to Uganda. All of them?"

"Not Lloyd," an English girl called Diane shook her head. He got ill. No idea what was wrong but he was exhausted. He had to fly home from Zaire."

The rest of us exchanged a knowing look. My cooking partner for a brief time, Lloyd, had been close to the gang who'd contracted hepatitis and been forced home for treatment. It was likely that's what he'd got too.

Bit by bit our numbers were dwindling. In my album I have a picture of our group taken in Algeria after we'd all scrubbed up, fifty fresh-faced newbies, still adjusting to life on the road, plus Terry, his two drivers and two couriers making up the numbers.

Then there are two photos taken as we crossed the Equator towards the end of our time in Zaire but before we lost the group with hepatitis, showing we were down to thirty-eight. A few weeks later sickness would make that thirty-four.

Perhaps attrition on this scale is standard for overland trips but it seemed careless to me. Especially as we were now about to get to one of the trip's highlights – the Serengeti. I could hardly wait.

CHAPTER 29

In the journals I kept during the expedition I've written that the days from 5-8 March were some of the happiest of my life.

"I think this must be one of the most beautiful places on earth," I wrote, as we arrived on the edge of the Ngorongoro Crater after two full days in the Serengeti.

What can I tell you that you that David Attenborough hasn't?

Perhaps that for the first time I really understood the expression 'teeming with life', for that's exactly what the Serengeti plains and crater offer: a vision of life before we stole the planet for ourselves, our homes and factories, our roads and flight paths.

Under a hot African sun the land stretched in every direction and on it thrived a myriad species of mammal, bird, reptile and insect life, still operating under ancient patterns, according to the habits and dependencies established over millennia. Killing only when they are hungry. Taking only what they need. A web that has always worked, until our greedy arrival.

We were greedy in the Serengeti too: to get close enough to the animals to film them. To make sure we could later tell people we had seen all of the Big Five. To get to the best watching spots ahead of the trail of other safari vehicles, ridiculously painted to mimic zebra, giraffe or leopards in order to please us rather than the animals we competed to see.

Yet I don't regret going because our entrance fees were also a part of the web, enabling the Tanzanian government to pay wardens to protect this precious Circle of Life.

***

On those wide open plains the air smelt warm, like freshly turned hay. We saw zebra, giraffe, wildebeest, hartebeest, gazelle, lions, hyenas, warthogs, topi, buffalo and hippopotami. We watched fish eagles and ostrich, the ungainly marabou stork – and yes, finally, the Bare-faced Go Away Bird. We glimpsed small monkeys and in the pools the silver fish they preyed on.

And we saw all of it as if for the first time. I realised that when you are used to seeing wildlife in zoos or picture books you are not prepared for the majestic reality of these creatures in their natural habitat. They no longer look curious or ungainly, out of place. Rather they seem to belong to the land: built for purpose.

The black and white lines of the zebras' coats were as distinct as if they'd been applied with paintbrushes that day. The giraffes, with spots of deep brown velvet, had nothing in common with their washed-out cousins in our safari parks. Free to stretch their powerful legs they looked worthy inhabitants of a landscape forged on the same larger-than-life scale as they themselves.

When we were lucky enough to see elephant I realised their skin can be as smooth as silk, not wrinkled and dusty. And that far from being a leftover relic from prehistoric times, they are perfectly adapted to life on the plains, hardly disturbing the grass with their gentle feet.

I learned that a lion's mane need not resemble a pantomime wig but can be as full and rich as corn stalks rippling in the wind.

Above all I saw that left to itself nature can achieve a balance more delicate and complex than anything we might artificially construct. The wildebeest need the lions to cull their numbers and prevent them over-grazing. The old and sick are picked off so they no longer hamper the herd's progress. Hyenas and jackal and vultures feed on what is left, cleaning the plains of decay and disease, and in their turn they become prey for others.

Zebra travel with the wildebeest for protection and graze the same grass, while giraffe are equipped to graze at a higher level. As the seasons change so the animals move, in a great tide from west to east and north to south. Find their tracks and you will discover not a handful of animals in isolation but a procession of God-like proportions, wave after wave of creatures caught up in a timeless story.

At one waterhole we came across a herd of elephants, a hundred or more, who quietly turned their backs and, pushing their calves into the middle of the throng, glided away, so well adapted they hardly made a whisper as they went.

I felt an overwhelming sense of gratitude, that such a place could still exist.

I think something of the same feeling settled on all of us for inside G truck there was mostly hush: a sense of wonder and shared respect. Even the cameras had been temporarily set down so that we might all sit with our backs to each other, looking out on so much space and beauty.

For a while I pondered whether things started to go wrong for our planet when humanity became too many to live on the plains; when we moved away, beginning the process of forgetting how it is to live in touch with the earth. I knew the truth was infinitely more complicated but the Serengeti was a powerful reminder that we too are part of nature.

As we drove deeper into the park I felt I knew how it was to be a blade of grass, tickled by the breeze, nuzzled by animals; or a ripple on the lake where hippos paused, sliding towards the shore; a point of light glittering in the night sky; a breath of air whispering through a thorn tree. And from this merging – if only in my imagination – came a deep, deep peace

***

The Serengeti melts into another national park, the Ngorongoro, whose heart is a vast ancient caldera, covering one hundred square miles and offering food and shelter to at least 25,000 animals.

Just beyond the gates of the Serengeti the road begins to wind slowly uphill, bringing the taste of cooler air, until it reaches the rim of what was a volcano two or more million years ago.

We reached it at dusk, as the sinking sun was turning the world pink. Above our heads small puffs of cloud looked like sugar-coated popcorn. Below us the same clouds were reflected on the still waters of a lake. The perfect symmetry of the scene struck us all: the whole scene, and us on the crater's edge, echoing with quiet.

Sadly that peace and beauty ended the very next morning when a series of scratchy rows exploded the calm of the previous three days.

Like so many of the rows we had, it was about something and nothing: who should travel in which Landrover down into the crater that day; whether the cooks had made enough breakfast; who'd moved someone's camera.

The whole melee reminded me of squabbling birds at the Serengeti waterhole, jostling each other from a need to assert ourselves as individuals within a single noisy crowd.

I could not wait for the Landrovers to leave and peace to return to the camp. I'd chosen to volunteer for guard duty rather than spend all day bumping in a Landrover. Mostly, I think, I wanted was just to stay with the feelings of peace and connection that I'd experienced since we entered this part of Tanzania.

And that couldn't happen if all around me was bickering and pettiness. Inside my head I could feel myself screaming 'shut up, shut up you stupid lot; get lost; get going!'

When the last Landrover departed, leaving me behind as solitary guard, I grabbed the book I was re-reading, Conrad's *Heart of Darkness*, and sat as close to the crater's edge as I could without neglecting my duties.

How lovely those hours of solitude on the edge of the crater were and how tough the shift to being a part of a big group once they all returned, flush from the adventure of exploring the crater, yet still arguing with each other.

Heather said we must race to the Ngorongoro exit or we'd be charged for another day, which meant suddenly we were rushing to pack up, moaning about the lateness of this decision, the peace shattered as dramatically as a tray of glasses exploding on the floor.

Glass is a good image for how I felt, as if my every nerve ending was exposed and the people around me a kind of sandpaper rubbing the nerves raw. It wasn't personal. But after four and a half months sitting cheek by jowl with these people I hated every one of them that afternoon.

***

Tanzania had one more wildlife park for us, the Manyara, which was home to many of the same creatures we'd already seen. Its main difference was it covered a smaller area. Which meant it was overrun by safari vehicles, their rooves open like sardine cans, occupants peering out like a crate-full of giraffes, wielding cameras with an air of desperation. So much to photograph: so little time.

Wayne pulled to a halt alongside a lake where hippopotami snoozed, only their hooded eyes and pink ears breaking the surface of the water

We jumped down with our cameras but then I spotted, in the far distance, a smudge of pink, too far to be distinct but undoubtedly a flock of flamingo, which get their pink colour from their diet and the water they roost and feed in.

Leaving the others to the hippos, I stepped further away for a better view. As I did so I must have crossed in front of one of the other safari groups. I turned at a movement to my side and saw a woman with sunglasses so huge she looked like a giant fly. She was actually 'shooing' me away.

In contrast to my t-shirt and shorts, faded and worn from so long on the road, she wore a beige safari shirt, pressed and spotless, and wielded a Pentax.

Sheer bloody mindedness rooted me to the spot. Perhaps I was taking out on her the anger I felt for my companions. In any case I stood my ground and stared back into the black abyss of her sunglasses, a snarl on my face.

Only when she turned away did I do the same, pleased to have won the staring battle. Still, I heard her words to her own fellow travellers: "Disgusting dropouts. Who the hell do they think they are?"

Someone replied: "I don't suppose they ever wash. Look at the state of them."

It was a shock to hear how we appeared to others and confirmed something Annie had reported after using the loos in the lodge at Ngorongoro. She'd overheard one of the other guests complaining that we smelt – unaware I suppose that she was in there.

For months now we'd lived in the same clothes and though we scrubbed them when there was a chance, the red dust of Africa was deeply ingrained in the fibres. Perhaps we did smell, but no longer noticed it on each other in the same way you can't detect your own home's distinctive odour as visitors immediately do.

I realised my irritation and impatience were signs the trip was drawing to a close for me. Would I, in a few weeks time, be like the woman with the big sunglasses, looking down my nose at strangers, seeing only difference? I hoped not.

Keen to put some distance between us and the press of the trucks Annie and I decided to scrub up and have supper in the tourist lodge that night, alongside bug-eyed woman and her ilk.

We hauled out the dresses we'd been saving to travel home in and dined together on wildebeest, which had been stewed to melting tenderness in a tomato and onion sauce. It tasted stronger than beef and was as lean as you'd expect from an animal surviving on the savannah.

Better yet, when we did return to camp it appeared we were the only ones with full stomachs: once again that night's cooks had wrecked camp supper by accidentally tipping tablespoons of salt into the vegetables. The stew they served up yasted as if it had been cooked in seawater: totally inedible.

CHAPTER 30

Pangani beach

We took another giant step back towards a world that was familiar when the trucks rolled into Arusha. This city of one million people was groaning with souvenir shops, tour agencies offering safaris, and treks up Mount Kilimanjaro. Its' cafes had names like 'The Hollywood' and 'Disneyland'. You could buy hamburgers in Arusha, and french fries and ice cream.

We'd hardly parked before the first thief dived into Wayne's cab and grabbed his bag. Luckily Wayne's reflexes were quick and he was able to grab the other handle, yelling at the thief who let go and vanished. It was a relief to hear we'd be camping outside of the centre, in the grounds of a school run by a Greek headmaster. It would be fractionally easier to keep ourselves safe from other opportunistic thieves, banking on our naivety to fill their own pockets. I imagined that the fact so many tourists would be arriving in Arusha fresh from the airport, their focus on the animals they'd see rather than their own potential as prey, encouraged such opportunism.

The school didn't allow campfires, but with black market currency helping us feel flush, our couriers Heather and Alison suggested we should have a group meal at one of Arusha's international hotels.

We duly smartened up and meandered, in groups, back into the town. I was with Annie, Tom, Mark and Sue from Reading.

We took one look inside the bland hotel restaurant, at the other courier, Alison, who seemed to have linked up with Kitty Chris, sitting together at a top table, muzak playing, people stuffing their faces from an all-you-can-eat buffet, the whole thing reminiscent of a 1970s wedding reception where no-one actually likes their relatives, and decided we weren't THAT ready to go home.

Down the road we found a small Indian café where the owners brought us plates of meatball curry, fried rice, salad, chapatis and beer, for a fraction of the price the others were spending.

Later, back at our school campsite, we learned its Greek headmaster kept goats and cows and would be delighted to sell us the cheese he made from their milk. For the two days we remained in Arusha we gorged on cheese on toast, cheese omelettes and macaroni cheese – forgotten tastes.

***

The next morning I asked Tom to accompany me up to Arusha's International conference centre, built by the government, and one of the city's great prides. In 1985 the outside of this modern glass and concrete building was decorated with a couple of banners, clearly directed at the middle-aged white men who attend conferences here from Western countries. One read 'Abolish capitalism, imperialism, racism and colonialism'.

Another read 'Famine is not God-willed but man-made', which I did not properly understand at the time. Only when I got home did I make it my business to learn as much as I could about the famine we'd travelled through and the role cash crops and climate change play in deforestation and drought.

On that day, however, my concerns were much more mundane.

With so little cash in my pockets I needed help with my flight home. So from a public call booth within the conference centre I connected to England, and to my dad who sounded as if he was in the next room. He'd got my begging letter and arranged for a flight voucher to be available for me to pick up from the Air Egypt office in Nairobi.

That was the first time, during the months away, and despite all I'd seen and failed to understand, that I cried, grateful for my family.

And perhaps there was another tear later that day when Will said he was leaving the trip. Without the funds to climb Kilimanjaro, he intended going straight to the Kenyan capital to look for work. Leader went with him.

Will and I exchanged addresses and promised to be in touch back home.

I want to say a little more about him because I was always fond of him, more so than he would have believed.

His life seemed dogged by bad luck but perhaps it was actually bad decisions.

Back in England Will came to London for a spell, trying to make a living as a salesman. He had the patter but not the conviction so the next big lead remained forever around the corner.

When he'd exhausted every last penny of credit, he spent some time on the south sea island of Vanuatu, but again, both his dreams of making money and his self-belief drained away.

Eventually he moved to Manchester, and when we last spoke on the phone he'd married and there was a child. Once upon a time he'd filled my head with his dreams for the future but none seem to have materialized. Drrp down I don't think he believed in himself. I doubt he ever realised how much the rest of us loved him.

***

Those of us who were left after this latest round of departures – Q truck also lost several people – drove due east from Arusha to Moshi which would be the jumping-off point for those committed to climbing Africa's most famous lookout – Kilimanjaro.

For the rest of us there would be a drive to the Indian Ocean to spend a few days chilling at the beach.

At first, Mount Kilimanjaro was only a faint shadow in the distance; it might have been a cloud, except for the distinctive dip in its profile – the scoop of the crater. Only as we got closer could we see the famous snows on its peak, dripping from the summit like icing from the top of a cake.

We made slow progress, stopping every few minutes to take photographs as the road offered a new angle and the climbing sun changed the scene's colours and shadows. Even though I hadn't the funds to climb, I found the sight of this massive volcano, rising from the savannah, almost as thrilling as Lake Victoria. It was another of those familiar symbols of Africa, a view everyone knows no matter where they live. A painting of it hangs on my wall to this day.

In the years since our visit, climbing Kili has become as familiar as trekking to Everest base camp, the sort of 'challenge' charities love to tempt supporter money with; more than a handful of celebrities have also had their attempts on the summit filmed.

It was perhaps a tad less commercial when we were there, though already aware of its ability to attract tourists in search of the next big thrill. All the budget overland trips, ours included, knew of a place where a couple of old Englishwomen ran their own unofficial Kilimanjaro operation. This meant the cost for tackling the five day climb there and back with tents, porters, food and park entrance fees was 3000 shillings – around £60 using black market rates; a fraction of the rate offered by hotels and tour agencies.

Tom and Annie were among those who fetched their luggage from the trailer and said they'd see us in six days' time. Kiwi Keith went with them, plus a further six climbers spread across the trucks. It was beginning to feel positively palatial on board.

***

Wayne drove all night, apart from a two-hour break when he and we fetched the sleeping bags and crept under the truck to escape the mosquitoes. This was one night drive that none of us minded, partly because with so much space on board we could spread out, but also because we could sense, even if we couldn't smell, the salt in the air: we were closing in on the Indian Ocean and with it the goal of having crossed this vast and brilliant continent. As the yellow light began to climb up from the horizon, so a breath of sea air filled the back of the trucks. On either side of the road were tall spindly palm trees. The countryside looked fertile, bright and vigorous, no longer starved of rain.

The palms were coconut, part of an agricultural system devised by government which designated each region responsible for growing a particular crop. It gave the coastal towns and villages the feel of a tropical paradise, a vision of tall waving fronds and, between them, a glimpse of opaline ocean.

We headed through the bustling town of Tanga to Pangani, something of a backwater, overshadowed by the popularity of Mombasa to the north and Zanzibar and Dar es Salaam, Tanzania's capital, due south.

No doubt it has changed in the decades since we were there but the Pangani we drove into was little more than a handful of houses set back from a white sand beach fringed by those coconut palms.

The trucks pulled in amongst the palms and we hurtled from the back, galloping along a narrow sand path which wound through the palms to reach the beach and the ocean beyond.

It was impossibly bright, incredibly beautiful: sand finer than salt, stretching in an arc to both horizons. It was covered in shells, sand dollars and pink-flushed coracle shapes, fluted razor shells, tiny cowries and craggy white shells whose insides were pearly sapphire.

The sand melted seamlessly into a flat Indian Ocean, almost as though it were a lagoon. The sea was unruffled, a pale turquoise, and transparent as far as we could walk in and still keep our heads above the water.

It was warm as a bath and we waded further out and swam in our clothes, a kind of baptism to represent the journey we had made to reach this coast.

Without my knowing it at the time, life was perhaps showing me the way forward. For a decade later I would be standing on the other side of the Indian Ocean, awestruck that the sand and shells, the colours and liberating sense of spacelessness, was the same when you looked out from Western Australia towards Africa as when I'd first, that day in Pangani, looked out in the opposite direction. More of that in the afterword…

***

Back on shore I simply flopped on the sand, waiting for the others to join me, knowing we had time to simply stop and stay still.

After all the months of activity we had four full days to just be here: a mini holiday. And since we agreed this was a holiday there'd be no cooking rota; we would look after ourselves.

The sand between my fingers was made of shells, millions of years of life ground to this white sand which squelched between my outstretched toes. I studied my body's outline too, beneath the soaked tee-shirt and shorts. There was still noticeably less of it than when I'd started out; the sharp lines, the muscles, the caramel colour of my skin: all of these things pleased me. It wasn't only that I wanted to live differently when I got home: I wanted people to be able to see the difference in me.

Further up the beach local children played games with the Aussie couple, Tony and Cookie. I was glad they were distracting them so I could be left alone.

After dark the beach and ocean took on a new character. There was no moon but when Mark switched on his torch we saw the whole beach was moving, alive with thousands of tiny crabs burrowing out from the sand to make their way, as one, back to the ocean.

We stripped and waded back into the sea, where the ocean had its own torch: a million diamond lights, minute sea creatures shining phosphorescence into the water.

It was like bathing in glitter, hypnotic and strange. I sank deeper into the water, then lay back allowing it to hold me while I studied the southern sky, as many lights from stars above our heads as there were lights in the dark water below. It was one of those moments when life becomes so intense, so magical, it feels almost as if you have slipped into a fourth dimension. I savoured every second and slept more deeply and for longer that night than at any point since London.

***

For the next three days we sunbathed and swam, rested and read. We made occasional forays into the village where there was a single café, a general store, and a laughing woman who turned the coconuts the children gathered into lush, creamy coconut ice. No day was complete without a trip to her front door where she sat on the step, a bowl of the sugary confection between her knees, doling it out into banana leaves for us to take away.

It didn't take long for the children to latch onto our appetites either and soon they were coming into camp with strange fish to sell us, or whole coconuts, and, inevitably, the local grass.

It was all good fun. The only stress I felt was when I wanted to bury my head in a book but one of the others came to hunt me out. I didn't want to be churlish – Mark, in particular, had become a good friend – but I craved as much of my own company as I could get.

When I found the others wouldn't leave me alone I retreated into the tent I no longer had to share and read or journaled or just day-dreamed. I'd learned how rare and precious stillness and my own company was to me and knew from here on I would have to keep claiming and reclaiming it for myself, for the rest of my life.

On our final night in the village we arranged to eat at the café. This required a huge amount of coming and going in advance as the nervous owner wanted absolute assurances about numbers, and our menu choices in advance. Very likely, we were the biggest crowd he'd ever catered for and he was scared to spend the money and time preparing food only to find he had an empty room.

"You come for sure?" The owner caught me as I passed by in search of a cold fizzy drink at the general store. "I do this but you must come. You sure you come?"

I reassured him as best I could but the strength of his reaction when we did arrive – 15 of us – showed he'd still harboured his doubts. His face almost split in half with pleasure as he pulled back chairs and ushered us to a long table he'd constructed from every stick of furniture he owned. We'd booked 12 places and now there were even more of us his delight was uncontained. A child was sent to fetch more chairs from neighbouring homes.

It was the same story with the utensils. Some of us had spoons, some forks. Presumably because there had never been a time when so many people sat down to eat together, he had not needed more cutlery.

But none of it mattered. Soon our noise and pleasure in the food and in the owner's delight lit up the café's interior, transforming its whitewashed walls and unshaded light bulb into the most intimate of settings. We just about squeezed in: luckily the café had no glass in its windows and cool air wafted in from the two black holes in the wall where the glass might have been.

Food appeared like magic and once it started there was no end to the relay of dishes and tastes and colours. Bowls of spicy fish in chilli sauce, fried potatoes, bread, rice, dough balls, fresh fruit salad, flat coke and sweet tea.

No feast in a Michelin-starred restaurant ever tasted as good as this home-cooking, flavoured by the exuberant look on our host's face when we rubbed our tummies, asked to shake his hand, and passed over a basketful of notes, more than he had quoted, by way of a thank you. He had triumphed and we shared in his success, knowing he'd earned enough in one day to keep his family going for weeks.

Because we were making so much noise we'd lost any awareness of what might be happening outside.

Only as we stood to go did we find that just through the doorway, and behind the black window holes, the rest of the village were having their own party, three or four deep, as they watched our strange meal together. Now, as we passed through them they burst into spontaneous applause, as though we had been providing a stage show all evening. They reached for our hands to shake them and wish us well.

When we left the next day, heels dragging, reluctant to leave this gorgeous ocean sanctuary, the whole village was there again, outside their homes and the café to wave us goodbye.

It was the second time in a week I had cried, only this time they were tears of gratitude and humility for the welcome the village had given us. Pangani was the first and only time we'd been able to leave the tents and trucks unguarded, knowing local people were looking out for us as we looked to them to provide us with a few comforts.

I prayed, as I waved furiously from the back of the truck, throwing kisses at those I'd met and talked to, that they never build a hotel in Pangani.

CHAPTER 31

Just outside of Nairobi, those of us left took a final group shot. Back row l to r: Kathy, Jacquie, Gail, Wayne and me. Front row: Sue Nobbs, Dave, Annie, Keith, Heather, Chris, Nuala, Tom, Jan (kneeling), Mark and Tony's back!

Much of our so-called expedition had been a lesson in carelessness and its consequences. The day and night we journeyed back to Moshi it was my turn to write a chapter in the book of all our mishaps.

I was cooking for no other reason than that, while the rota had been suspended, we'd all forgotten whose turn it was. Besides, I knew everyone would muck in to help since we weren't pitching tents but grabbing a few hours' sleep in the back of the truck again while Wayne drove through the night.

It was so hot. I had spent the previous day mostly on the beach and my skin tingled with the sort of heat that craves a cold shower or a dip in the ocean. But here we were, beside the road, with a huge fire heating water for vegetables, and the earth itself still sizzling from all the sunshine it had absorbed.

Heady with heat, I stripped to a vest and shorts, scraping my hair off my face into a band, keeping as far from the flames as I could while I stirred the cauldron's bubbling contents.

The sound of the fire crackling below, the boiling water, my companions around me setting out plates and bowls, completely drowned out the whine of clouds of mosquitoes homing in on *their* supper: that would be me.

Of course we had encountered mosquitoes before, and still took the daily and weekly anti-malarial tablets to guard against sickness. On this occasion I can only assume that we had unawares stopped beside a swamp or stagnant water.

Once supper was over, and it became quieter, it dawned on me that the whole sky was vibrating with the noise of innumerable mossies. Soon after that the first awful itching began.

It started with a small swelling on my leg, then moved up my thigh. My bottom began to itch then my back and neck and arms, then my face.

As the night wore on my entire skin became a mass of flaming red irritation: if I could have torn it from my body and flung it away I would have done so.

I literally didn't know what to do with myself; how to cope with the fury of my itching, inflamed body.

There was no sleep or any relief through the night. The itching just got worse, with new bites springing up.

After counting more than 200 I gave up; besides, there was now so much poison in my body that the swelling joined together under my skin, producing huge congealed boil-like masses covering both knees and elbows, and puffing up the rest of me like an overstretched balloon.

My knickers bit into the tops of my swollen thighs and as my body's defence system went into overdrive my limbs were so swollen with fluid they became too stiff to allow me to walk or use my arms.

My whole body was on fire and I had never, I was certain, felt so awful, not even during the time I had dysentery. Hot tears of self-pity and pain only aggravated the large red swellings under my eyes, running down hamster cheeks.

The others raided their own supplies of medicines and eventually drugged me into a kind of comatose oblivion. It was the only way to get through the agony without flaying myself.

To this day, the simplest of insect bites sends my body's immune system into overdrive, causing it to swell out of all proportion to the original bite.

I believe that as a result of this ,mossie attack I've also developed a potentially fatal reaction to wasp and bee stings. I'd had stings as a child with no consequences but one day, hanging out the washing in the garden, I must have pressed on a wasp. An hour later I looked like Frankenstein's monster, my swollen forehead overhanging my eyes, my clothes pinching everywhere, until the hospital pumped me full of anti-histamine and advised me to carry an adrenaline syringe from now on.

Such were the consequences of one evening's carelessness.

***

I remained comatose while we picked up the Kili climbers, and for another day after that. It was only later that I was conscious enough to talk to Tom and Annie and find out how their climb had been.

They made all the right noises but I got the impression being able to say they had stood on the roof of Africa, conquered their altitude sickness and seen a weak sunrise from Kili's snows, didn't quite make up for five days of pure slog.

For Annie, though, being a part of a smaller group had been fair compensation for the sickness and lack of sleep. "I hadn't realised how much it's been getting to me, being with the trucks all the time," she said when we at last sat down together to catch up. "I can't wait for Nairobi now. I shan't bother going to the coast with the trucks."

"What will you do then?"

"Head south as soon as I can. Go down to Botswana. I want to see the delta. Then maybe South Africa after."

"Sounds wonderful, and I know what you mean about being with the trucks. We had a great time at the coast with it being just a few of us. Not moving on every day we got to know some of the local people for a change."

"Did you?" Annie's tone bordered on disinterested and I realised that, having climbed to the heights, she had somehow already left the trip in all but name. We really were coming to a close, and with a whimper rather than a bang.

***

The trucks groaned with contraband, mostly hidden at the bottom of sleeping bags, as we crossed our final border from Tanzania into Kenya.

Our currency declaration forms claimed most of us had changed no more than £10 while we'd been in Tanzania for three weeks which would have made explaining all the souvenirs rather challenging.

As it was we weren't even stopped, much less searched; simply waved into a country whose recent past is so interwoven with British imperialism that the first sign to greet us was a 'Welcome to Kenya' in English rather than Swahili, and a billboard advertising Cadbury's Dairy Milk.

Much of the land we were now passing through, en route to Kenya's capital, Nairobi, is home to the Masai.

I'd seen pictures of them on postcards in Arusha: glamorous and severe, dressed in toffee-apple coloured robes, adorned with bead necklaces and heavy hooped earrings.

As we motored along we sometimes spotted groups of Masai, but they looked nothing like the pictures on the postcards. Their skins were not the polished mahogany of the cards but coated in white dust or clay for protection against the sun's relentless glare. Their clothes were thoroughly worn, their hair lank and unattended in thin plaits.

Nor did they pay any attention to us, moving across the Kenyan savannah as though their feet weren't in contact with the ground: *of* the earth but not *on* it.

They were not there for tourists but for themselves and the land, in a daily jostle with nature for the right to exist. And what they carried with them, in every fibre of their being, was separateness.

We stopped to pitch the tents a few hours out of Nairobi – it was never a good idea to drive into a new city at night, before we'd had time to acclimatise to its feel and mood.

Heather warned us that the Masai hated people camping on their land. She'd heard on the grapevine that two recent overland expeditions had been raided at spearpoint. Not only did the Masai strip the overlanders of clothes, money, water bottles and equipment, they even siphoned the diesel from the fuel tank.

Boldly however, once we were fed, knowing this would be our last group meal before many of us began to drift off, we chose not to keep a low profile.

Instead we sat late around the campfire, reading to each other from our journals, about our earliest impressions of each other, the disastrous meals, the mishaps, and all the ways in which Terry's tour not only failed to live up to his itinerary and promises, but at the same time had so far exceeded our expectations.

Looking from face to face that night I thanked God I had joined this group at this time to have the experience I'd had. I would miss times like this more than I could say, even as a part of me was already moving ahead, just like Annie, to my next chapter away from Long Haul.

I slept fitfully that night, imagining the wind crackling through the deep grasses was really Masai footsteps; but beneath my edginess was excitement about what the next day would bring.

CHAPTER 32

The last thing I expected from Nairobi was to be sitting in a rush hour traffic jam, inching forward beside cars crammed with smartly-dressed people, air thick with fumes as we toiled at traffic lights, hemmed in on either side by advertising hoardings and building sites. Nairobi was like nowhere else we had been – other than London perhaps.

It was the same story when we pulled into a car park at the end of one of the city's wide and wealthy avenues. The moment we left the trucks we were swept up in a tide of urgent bodies, heels clipping on the pavement, white shirts already wet with perspiration, heading for the high rises where hundreds of international companies had their African base.

I was reluctant to join the throng yet the moment I did so my legs began moving at the same speed as everyone else. I could feel my breath becoming more shallow, a knot in my stomach: old habits from my own years as a London office worker reasserting themselves.

Mark had volunteered to come with me to the post office and afterwards to get some breakfast together.

"Why am I hurrying? This is ridiculous. I don't have to get to a job," I wailed.

"D-doesn't take long does it?"

"They look like they're on automatic pilot."

"Yeah. It's a shock."

"I don't want to go back to this kind of life."

"What do you want then?"

I paused. "I don't know yet. But not this."

We collected our letters then took them into a nearby coffee shop.

Its glass shopfront and tables of polished metal delivered a kind of culture shock after the chai stalls and little Asian cafes we'd been used to. But I won't pretend the freshly brewed coffee and mammoth croissant spread with real butter didn't taste as I imagine heaven must. For a moment I was back in that Cameroonian hospital, tasting a boiled egg in the way I never had before. Perhaps it was almost worth going without in order to properly appreciate and be grateful for rediscovering familiar flavours, faces, experiences.

Only because I had the choice, of course.

As I would realise later that day in Nairobi, reminders of our world's inequalities are never far away. The city centre was stunning, the shops loaded with labels, buildings competing with each other for the highest views, the lushest restaurants.

Yet two streets away the majority of Nairobi's four million people lived in shanty towns – at least they did in 1984 – where rubbish piled up in the streets, maimed and desperate children begged for their next bite to eat, and we, as tourists, were no safer than the people forced to live there.

Heather had warned us that the backstreets were unsafe, a mugger's paradise where overlanders were easy prey for those who used knives to part them from anything they unwisely carried there. Camping in the city was likely to be a re-run of our time in Bangui when we had to be constantly on guard.

As I sat quietly opposite Mark, looking through my letters from home, I was suddenly tired of it all. Tired of the press of people on the truck, the noise and choking exhausts in Nairobi's streets, having to be careful where I went and what I carried. I was also very aware of the way my body was reacting to being thrust back into this fast-paced environment.

I hadn't really thought how long I would stay with the trucks, which were supposed to be going onto Mombasa after a few days in the capital - then motoring up the coast to the Arab island of Lamu and maybe to Mount Kenya, before returning to Mombasa's port and the long sea journey home.

"What will you do now?" I looked up at Mark.

"I want to visit the coast see. What about you?"

"I think I'm going to the station to catch a train down to Mombasa. A work colleague of mine has family there and gave me their number in case I want to stay with them."

And there it was. I hadn't known it until the words were out of my mouth but somehow I had decided this day in Nairobi would be my last with Long Haul.

***

Mark was a great sport about it, accompanying me to the Air Egypt offices to collect dad's flight voucher. I booked my flight home for Good Friday, which would give me almost two weeks recovery at the coast. It would also mean someone was available to meet me when I landed back at Heathrow.

Then we went to the station to buy me a ticket on the night service leaving at 7pm and arriving in Mombasa at breakfast time the next day.

"I guess I'll stick it out with Long Haul a bit longer. See it through," Mark said a little uncertainly. "But leave a message at post restante so I know where you're staying. It would be good to catch up in Mombasa."

"Of course."

Tom asked me to do the same thing when we arrived back at the trucks and offered to come with Mark to help carry my bags to the train later on.

Meanwhile, there was some exciting news for all of the men who remained on G truck: a chance to earn some money and enjoy 15 minutes of fame. There was a film crew in town and they were desperate to recruit Europeans for some crowd scenes. Not only were they paying extras £20 a day (remember this was 1984 and most of us had only bought £400 for the entire five months) but actors would get all meals on set – and a free haircut.

It was also a chance to rub shoulders with the film's stars: Meryl Streep and Robert Redford.

Now I've said that, of course, you will understand why *Out of Africa* has, since its release, been one of my favourite films.

It isn't only that the sweeping plains, the brilliant wildlife, the soaring music and the beauty of the African people, speak to me of my time in Africa. There is also a small illogical part of me that feels I have a stake in the film because a dozen or more of my travelling companions, Tom included, ended up as extras, waving their panama hats and shouting 'hurrah' as the First World War ended and Nairobi's colonial leaders paraded through the streets.

I gathered from Tom that the white-skinned extras were paid four times as much as their African counterparts. The Africans compensated in part by bringing empty sacks on set with them, and then loading up as much as they could carry from the buffet table. Their families dined well that week!

***

The only thing everyone was talking about when Mark and I got back to the trucks was the news that there would, despite Long Haul's promises, be no trip up the coast once the trucks reached Mombasa.

Half a world away, and out of reach of his paying passengers, Terry had quietly booked shipping for four days from now. That meant there would be no leisurely winding down at the Indian Ocean, but instead a scramble to get to Mombasa and prepare the trucks for the journey home. The drivers and couriers would fly home while the trucks took their time by sea.

While I reorganised my bags, reclaimed books from the battered library box and souvenirs from beneath the seats, others came and went discussing their plans. I had no regrets about my decision – only a little wariness at heading off alone. My previous forced excursion away from the trucks had not been without its challenges and I worried there would be more.

Yet it seemed others felt, as I did, that our time together was at an end. Annie came to find me and said she needed to find a dentist in Nairobi but wouldn't be returning to the truck after that. We hugged goodbye and with no fuss or fanfare my best friend on board was gone.

Perhaps that was how Tom felt as he and Mark loaded me onto the train at 7pm that evening. But I knew I would see them both again, possibly sooner rather than later, and was too enthralled by the station's colonial-era architecture to make much of our goodbyes. Everywhere I looked it seemed as if I had dropped through time to an age of elegance, beauty and wealth.

As I boarded the train through polished wooden doors I realised I was free and it felt good. Really good.

***

My carriage was as much a throwback to another age as the station buildings: upholstered in creaky leather, shining chrome, with seats so wide that when I leaned back my feet didn't touch the floor. Beyond the door of the compartment, which seated six second class passengers, the corridors were wide enough for white-jacketed waiters to rattle past, bringing cool drinks and white towels to those higher up the train in first class.

Before long I was no longer alone. Two smiling African women joined me, solid and middle-aged, laden with carrier bags and, in one case, two sacks of what I guessed to be seed or millet.

I was used to the train etiquette of Britain where you pretend you are alone in the carriage, no matter how many others push past you. It amused me to see the duo sit down in one corner together, so close they might almost have been on each other's laps. That left me marooned in the other corner and the rest of the compartment completely empty.

Not for the first time I pondered how very differently African and British people think about personal space. I actually felt a little foolish for my aloofness, even though the women smiled and nodded greetings at me and seemed unbothered that I had so much of the compartment to myself.

A part of me wanted to join their little huddle; but the other part of me was revelling in no longer being in a large group. I wanted nothing more than to sink deeper into my corner and gaze out of the window, or at the notes I'd made in five exercise books over the last 20 weeks.

Before long the women broke off from chatting to each other in Swahili and pointed at the light switch behind my head. Clearly it was time for us to sleep. The luggage rack above my head turned into a bunk and I climbed willingly up so they could have the bottom bunks. I covered myself with my trusty sarong and allowed the train's rhythm to lull me quickly to a deep sleep.

So deep that I was amazed to find I had slept through my companions rising, rearranging their side of the compartment, and settling in for another chat. Their faces were shiny like new pins from a morning wash and they looked delighted with themselves and life in general.

Looking out of the windows at a sparkling savannah, I knew exactly how they felt. The earth was once again fresh and new and the space stretched as far as the eye could see. It was a surprise to hear the train braking when there was nothing outside but more rolling countryside.

We pulled to a halt and still all I could see was the long grass and in the distance a few acacia trees. No hint of Mombasa. But now one of my companions was getting up and shaking my hand before opening the door and calling for a porter.

With the same ceremony as someone stepping onto a red carpet, my fellow traveller climbed from the train, the porter handing down her luggage and her two sacks of corn. Presumably someone would come to meet her and take her home to her village? I was impressed at her power to halt the train with no station in sight; but perhaps as Denis Finch-Hatton tells Karen Blixen in *Out of Africa*, it's considered rude not to stop.

Another hour passed and then the outskirts of Kenya's second city came into view, more spread out and rural than Nairobi had been, until we pulled into the station which was every bit as grandly Victorian as the one I'd departed from. Its platforms were bordered with flower beds, and there were separate exits for second and third class passengers.

I sailed through first class into a palatial booking office with a tiled floor and wood counters gleaming with polish. It was easy to imagine how this scene must have looked earlier in the century as the Happy Valley set came and went along with plantation owners and minor diplomats.

There had been bloody battles since, and the path to independence had been far harder on the Kenyan people than the colonialists they evicted. Yet Mombasa seemed to hold no grudges and I felt wholly at home in it from the moment I arrived.

***

I have travelled alone many times since that day in Mombasa and know that the best thing when you arrive somewhere new is to find a friendly café, talk to its staff, and take stock.

I had no choice about it in Mombasa because when I dialled the number for my colleague's family I was told they were actually in Nairobi, expected back later that day.

Dragging my bags with me, I found a lively café opposite the station and asked the owner for a recommendation: somewhere a single woman could stay that was safe.

I'm not sure the so-called 'People's Hotel' really met that simple brief. It may merit three stars on TripAdvisor these days but at the time it was little more than a grubby hostel where curious and not necessarily friendly eyes followed my movements and noted which room key I'd been given.

My room was cheap and at least had a shower even if the water coming out of it was ice cold. It felt good to use soap on my dust-caked body.

I shrugged on the only cleanish clothes I had, locked my door and uttered a short prayer that my things would be safe, before heading out to explore the old town.

Mombasa has a dark history as the port from which East Africa's slave trade operated. Between the 7th and 19th centuries more than four million people were captured by Arab and Swahili traders and sold as labour in households and plantations across the Middle East and Arab-controlled African states.

Fewer than one in five of the men, women and children forcibly captured inland survived the trek to the coast. For those that did, their fate makes grim reading.

I wandered through the old part of town, noticing Arabic influence everywhere in the whitewashed walls and architecture I'd last seen in Morocco and Algeria. Some of the doors had chains carved into them, bearing witness to a time when they had been home to the slave traders.

Beyond the houses stood the stark bulk of Fort Jesus, a statement of power built by the Portuguese who had three times invaded and razed the town. There was something about this past, the pain these buildings and the soil had seen, the sadness and despair, the fear, that sat heavy with me and my earlier mood of freedom. I was glad to escape back to the centre, where rows and rows of souvenir and craft shops showed me Mombasa's more recent face.

***

After lunch in another café I tried the phone number my friend Azmina had given me again. This time it rang only once.

"Riaz?" I asked doubtfully.

"Jane. They said you'd phoned. How are you? My goodness, so sorry we weren't here when you called first. Where are you calling from? Can we come and get you? Su and I didn't know when you might come. We had no news from England."

"No of course you didn't know when I was coming. I didn't know when I'd be here. I should have called from Nairobi but until the last minute I was unsure. Now I'm here but please don't rush. You've only just got back yourselves. I found a place to stay. We can meet up tomorrow."

Riaz's tone turned serious. "Where are you staying?"

"The People's Hotel. I checked in earlier so I could have a shower."

"You can't stay there. Meet us outside the hotel. We will be no more than 20 minutes."

He'd hung up before I could argue with him and to tell the truth I wasn't sorry. Clearly he and Azmina's sister Su knew Mombasa better than I did and were taking their responsibilities to me seriously.

Quite how seriously I only realised when they arrived and announced they'd booked some accommodation for me. Riaz's car headed out from the city northwards to an area of hotels and resorts looking out over a silver beach and the Indian Ocean. They deposited me in a wonderful self-catering apartment called Bamburi Villas, spirited away all my clothes for washing and loaned me some of Su's to be going on with. Then they promised to come back to the villa that evening to take me out for dinner.

Azmina and I may well have been friends back in London but this hospitality was beyond my wildest expectations. They even brought with them a cardboard box of groceries so I had food in for breakfast and lunch the next day.

"You can tell us all about the trip over dinner," Su said a little shyly, holding my hand in hers as she said goodbye. "I'm sure you've had many adventures. You look so thin and maybe not so well."

"Yes," I grinned. "We had a bit of trouble in Chad."

CHAPTER 33

Dining in a 'cave' with two more Good Samaritans: Su and Riaz

I had plenty of time at Bamburi Villas to look back on all we had done and seen. I spent the days putting my body back together, aided and abetted by Riaz and Su who came each evening to take me to Mombasa's best restaurants.

We dined in a cave whose ceiling was open to the sky, and at the end of a jetty from which we could look out at the twinkling lights of ships on the Indian Ocean.

Sitting beside the pool of the hotel the villas were attached to, my skin shed the layer of red dust and grime and soon shone with good health, toasty brown.

There was one remaining souvenir of my Long Haul days in the shape of a handful of tics, collected, I assume, in the field of long grass outside Nairobi.

They had burrowed their way into my buttocks so I did what I had seen the others do and bought a box of matches so I could touch their smouldering tips to the tics. The heat made them stick their heads out from the skin at which point I was able to use tweezers to yank them away. Each one I pulled out and flattened was fat with my blood.

Sometimes I took a towel onto the beach so I could enjoy the ridiculous sight of the hotel staff raking seaweed into piles then burying it under the sand in case it detracted from the view of hotel guests. After the close contact we'd had with so many Africans of different nations and tribes, after the generosity of our dear guardian angel Youssoufa, the warmth and welcome in Pangani, I cringed to see these Kenyan hosts treated with such disdain by the other hotel guests. On the hotel verandah British, German and other guests complained about the staff without bothering to lower their voices and snapped their fingers for attention.

I spoke to everyone who came past me on the beach, looking for a conversation, a sale, or more usually, an invite back to my bedroom. I didn't blame the men who tried it on: I imagine back then a single woman lying alone on the beach might be assumed to be looking for company.

One day one of them was more persistent than usual. "Jambo mama, jambo."

I buried my head deeper into the towel. "Jambo."

"I s-said jambo mama."

The way the man spoke made me look up. "Mark! How did you find me?"

"I asked in town. There's not that many women wandering around alone see."

"Sit down," I was surprised how glad I was to see him. Maybe the constant attention from men was getting to me. "Wait, a better idea. They serve coffee free to guests at the hotel. Let's go there."

By the time Mark left, a few hours later, I'd agreed to catch a bus up the coast to Malindi where he'd booked a hotel suite so he could go diving off the turquoise coast every day. There was plenty of room for me to join him there plus, I reasoned, it would give Su and Riaz a break from having to host me every night.

Malindi was, if possible, even more beautiful than Bamburi Villas and gave me a few wonderful days on which to end my time in Africa.

I saw Tom once more too, on my return to Mombasa to have a final supper with Su and Riaz before catching a taxi to Nairobi for my flight home.

We met in the same café where I'd first gone when I arrived in the city.

Tom seemed awkward and I sensed there was something he wanted to say about what had happened between us and his feelings for me. But his shyness enabled me to steer the conversation away from anything personal: I wasn't sure what I wanted from him; nor how I felt now that the trip was over. So I plied him with questions about the trip down to South Africa he planned to make with Leader, and the things he'd done since I left the trucks.

He asked if I'd mind if he wrote to me; I agreed.

My final brush with death in Africa was the matatu ride back to Nairobi, bounced along in the back of a minibus whose one-armed driver wanted to talk but couldn't do so without craning his head right around so he could meet my eyes, taking his functioning hand off the wheel to reinforce what he was saying with wild gesticulating. It didn't help that Kenya was right-hand drive and to change gears he had to cross the one working hand over his body to reach down to the gearstick.

Every so often, and for no reason I could fathom, he switched the vehicle headlights off completely.

We spent more time on the verge, or in the middle of the highway, than in our own lane, and just to add a little more danger to the drive he'd stamp on the accelerator and overtake a line of vehicles, forcing oncoming traffic off the road.

Not for nothing does Wikipedia note that these privately-owned minibuses are known for the criminality of their owners and reckless driving.

It was almost a relief to find, when we arrived at the airport, that the flight was delayed and I had time for a stiff drink to settle legs that would not stop shaking. It seemed there'd been a coup in Sudan which meant its airspace was closed and our flight home, via Cairo, was being diverted. For someone who'd spent the last five months being delayed by desert, breakdowns, incompetence and sickness, a few more hours was a doddle.

Ironically, the only other Brit in the lounge waiting to join our delayed flight was Kitty Chris, possibly the last person I'd have chosen to make this final stage of the journey home with. He must have felt the same about me because we pretended not to see each other.

The flight landed back in London at breakfast time on Good Friday and as I emerged through the arrivals gate there was my sister with flowers and a welcome home sign as well as a gigantic hug that lasted for minutes.

Dad and a new step-mother I scarcely knew stepped up next. "Had a good time dear?" dad enquired.

"Er, very good thank you," I flustered.

Outside the airport the sky was solid and dull, seeping drizzle onto closed houses and grey roads. Everything looked so washed out, as if someone had pulled a plug and all the colours of nature had drained away into the soil. Road noise drowned out any attempts at conversation and I was glad of it, already realising re-entry was going to be a challenge; my body, leaner, fitter, browner, was here in the car but my soul was somewhere else entirely.

I reached across the back seat for my sister's hand and felt her squeeze it reassuringly. Then I closed my eyes and the drabness was gone. There in its place were the purple and green of the hills, the golden savannah, the waves like sparkling opal as they washed the sand. There were the humming greens of the forest, the red soil and black night sky, a kaleidoscope dancing behind my eyelids: all the dazzling colours of Africa, with their promise of a fresh beginning.

AFTERWORD

First group photo in the Sahara: back row l to r: Mark, Lloyd, Tom, AJ, Keith, Will, Cockney Steve. Centre l to r: Wayne, Sue Nobbs, Dave, Mandy, Nuala, me, Gai, Kathy, Jan and Annie. Front l to r: Sue Cookie, Chris, Tim, Jenny, Jacquie and Leonie, with Leader lying on the ground.

So what happened next?

Let's talk about Terry the terrible first. After our trip he never did another major expedition through Africa, leaving it to his drivers and couriers.

Instead, Terry turned his attention to short haul summer trips through Northern Africa. It was during one of these that he suddenly collapsed. At first they thought it was a return of his malaria but it turned out to be a coronary and he died in the continent he'd loved and hated in equal measure for so long.

Heather and Wayne surprised us all by staying together and getting married. At first they lived in a mobile home near Oxford, which was easier to lock up so they could continue their travels, not only for Long Haul, but under their own steam. There are few corners of the globe they've not visited.

A few years ago they swapped the mobile home for bricks and mortar closer to Oxford's centre, and have hosted a few small reunions there for those of us who stayed in touch. Whatever we felt about Long Haul at the time has long since been overtaken by lifelong friendship. I love them both dearly and am proud Wayne agreed to be godfather to our son Paul.

Annie had a brilliant time journeying south with a series of other travellers she met en route and stayed longer than she'd expected in Botswana, getting a temporary barmaid's job in the Okavango Delta.

We met up once in her home town of Sheffield but, to the surprise of us both I think, our friendship fizzled out. When I googled her name a few years ago I learned she'd moved from Sheffield to the edge of the Lake District where she makes a living as a potter. Some of her most popular sculptures are the majestic African figures she carves.

Mark went back to his family's building business near Bracknell and rode several bank-breaking storms in the housing market before deciding to retire and spend his time waiting for the next diving holiday. I lodged with him for a while, when business was good and he'd achieved a lifetime dream of owning a jag. It was the late 80s and I'd just been given money to write a history book, which needed space and quiet. I found both in his home and he was always easy company. I am still grateful for his generosity at that time.

The last we heard of Kathy and Keith, he'd got work in a diamond mine in South Africa and she'd become warden at a nearby hostel. Everyone on the overland trail knew her for her iron rule and fiery temper. The world needs more larger-than-life characters like them.

Back home we finally met the girlfriend Cockney Steve had told us so much about. Their lovely Essex home also hosted plenty of reunions, especially after Steve returned briefly to Africa in order to take the photographs he'd missed when his Long Haul trip was cut short.

Steve never changed: his humour, goodness and raucous laugh transported all of us back to the dimly-lit interior of the truck and his endless joking. In 2007 Steve was thrown from his motorbike by a motorist not paying attention. His funeral was the reunion we'd never envisaged or wanted – even if it did end, in classic Steve-style, with the sound of *the Laughing Policeman* blasting out across the Essex countryside.

With us at the funeral was Sue, the girl from Reading whose company I'd enjoyed on board. 'Leader' was unable to get away from his work as a paramedic, mopping up the streets of south London. I guess it was our own version of the film *Four Weddings and a Funeral:* since our return in 1985 we've all got together for Sue's wedding to long-time boyfriend Paul, Leader's to Beth, Heather's to Wayne, and yes, mine to Tom.

You see reader, I did marry him.

At first Tom continued with his travels, heading off to work in the Egyptian desert, then to Turkey, following contracts. From there he went to America for a six-month road trip, then returned to do some backpacking through Europe. Every time he was in the UK we caught up, and every time we avoided talking about the feelings we'd had for each other in Africa and what had happened to them since.

Until 1989 when, bruised from several unsuccessful relationships, I proposed to Tom, certain that close loving friendship is a good basis for marriage.

We made it, in fits and starts, for ten years – enough time to have two beautiful and brilliant children who are *our* glue and have enabled us to hold our family together even though we've lived apart since 1999. I suppose we have realised that close and enduring friendship is where we fit together best.

As for me, after half-heartedly sending off a few job applications for professional work I instead became a waitress in an all-night café on the edge of Soho. The same vibrancy I'd loved in Africa used to turn up at Harry's Café in the early hours: drag queens, conjurers, strippers, dancers, actors and popstars. There was never a dull moment.

When lack of sleep finally kicked in after a year or so I took on a contract writing a history book, which led me, a little later, to journalism, and a chance to return to Africa.

My home town's mayor wanted to see how the funds his year of office was raising for Save the Children were being spent, and I sweet-talked the editor into paying for me to accompany him. We spent two eye-opening weeks in Uganda and Zimbabwe and, despite the poverty and hardships, I came home with a full heart once again and huge love and respect for people who seem able to remain hospitable and even joyful despite all life has thrown at them.

Marriage and parenthood reigned-in the travel more than I expected it would, and for rather too long I returned to the office and used my writing skills on the 'dark side' as a PR and marketeer.

Until the early 2000s when I returned to writing books and trained to lead workshops – both things aimed at helping others live the breadth of their lives as well as their length – and to heal from past trauma. This career is – as I am and always will be – a work in progress.

Of course there have been dark times - rather too many of them - since Africa. At such times one of the things that brings me back around to myself are the lessons I learned over the five months with Long Haul.

To live we need very little.

To be happy we only need to appreciate what we have, especially the love and support of loved-ones.

And to be truly alive, we need to remember to notice this amazing world we inhabit, to open ourselves every day to new experiences, sights, sounds, smells and tastes.

In 2011, when I finally turned my back on corporate life once and for all to be a freelance writer, coach and workshop leader, I came across the poet David Whyte and his poem *Sweet Darkness*.

"You must learn this one thing.
The world was made to be free in.
Give up all the other worlds
Except the one to which you belong…
Anything or anyone who does not bring you alive
Is too small for you."

ACKNOWLEDGEMENTS

In my notes at the beginning of this book I mentioned the affection I feel for my Long Haul companions. Like any group of people thrown together we were a real assortment. Yet each and every one added something to the mix and I thank them all for what they brought to those memorable times. Even Terry, RIP, for without him there would have been no Long Haul.

Among the 55 were a handful who have become lifelong friends, and have had a hand in reading this manuscript, correcting some of my mistakes, and reminding me of other incidents I had forgotten. Thank you especially to Tom, Heather and Wayne, but also to Will, Mark, Leader, Sue Nobbs, Nuala, Gai, Tony and Sue Cookie and Cockney Steve's partner Viv, for the precious gift of lifelong friendship – however far away from each other we live.

I've included a few photos in the book just to break up what is an awful lot of text! But it will be obvious to you at this point that my camera then was scarcely up to the job of capturing Africa's stunning and memorable landscapes. Tom and Heather also loaned pictures, but of course if you really want to see this amazing continent you need to visit yourself...

Thanks to my family for all the letters which made it to various post restantes and reminded me there was something important to come home to. To dad for his support, both financial and emotional. And especially my dear sister Shushie who travelled every mile with me in *her* imagination and continues to be my soulmate. She also agreed to draw a route map for me – the one that appears at the front – for those who've not been lucky enough to travel to Africa as I did.

Since Long Haul my family has grown, for which I must also thank Tom, a friend, partner and support for more than half my life now - and the father of our two amazing children, Amy and Paul, to whom I have dedicated this book.

Finally, my deep gratitude to Caroline Jarrett, who made it possible for me, during the long months of the pandemic lockdown, to spend time working on this book while she worked on her own. Ever since the African trip I'd hoped one day to be able to set my memories down for my children. Caroline's generosity in suggesting we work on our books alongside each other was what made this happen at last.

Printed in Great Britain
by Amazon